Frommer's®

PORTABLE
Rio de Janeiro

1st Edition

by Shawn Blore & Alexandra de Vries

WILEY
Wiley Publishing, Inc.

ABOUT THE AUTHORS

A native of California, **Shawn Blore** has lived and worked in a half-dozen countries and traveled in 40 more (but who's counting?). Now resident in Vancouver, Shawn is an award-winning magazine writer and the author of *Vancouver: Secrets of the City* and co-author of *Frommer's Vancouver & Victoria, Frommer's British Columbia & the Canadian Rockies, Frommer's Brazil,* and *Frommer's South America.*

Alexandra de Vries made her first journey to Brazil at the ripe old age of 1 month (alas, few of her food reviews from that trip survive). In the years since, Alexandra has returned many times to travel, explore, and live in this amazing country. Alexandra is co-author of *Frommer's Vancouver & Victoria, Frommer's Brazil,* and *Frommer's South America.*

Published by:

WILEY PUBLISHING, INC.

909 Third Avenue
New York, NY 10022
www.frommers.com

ISBN 0-7645-6482-X
ISSN 1536-9730

Editor: Myka Carroll
Production Editor: Donna Wright
Photo Editor: Richard Fox
Cartographer: Nick Trotter
Production by Wiley Indianapolis Composition Services

For information on our other products and services or to obtain technical support, please contact our Customer Care Department within the U.S. at 800-762-2974, outside the U.S. at 317-572-3993 or fax 317-572-4002.

Wiley also publishes its books in a variety of electronic formats. Some content that appears in print may not be available in electronic formats.

Manufactured in the United States of America

5 4 3 2

Contents

List of Maps

AN INVITATION TO THE READER

In researching this book, we discovered many wonderful places—hotels, restaurants, shops, and more. We're sure you'll find others. Please tell us about them, so we can share the information with your fellow travelers in upcoming editions. If you were disappointed with a recommendation, we'd love to know that, too. Please write to:

Frommer's Portable Rio de Janeiro, 1st Edition
Hungry Minds, Inc. • 909 Third Avenue • New York, NY 10022

AN ADDITIONAL NOTE

Please be advised that travel information is subject to change at any time—and this is especially true of prices. We therefore suggest that you write or call ahead for confirmation when making your travel plans. The authors, editors, and publisher cannot be held responsible for the experiences of readers while traveling. Your safety is important to us, however, so we encourage you to stay alert and be aware of your surroundings. Keep a close eye on cameras, purses, and wallets, all favorite targets of thieves and pickpockets.

WHAT THE SYMBOLS MEAN

The following abbreviations are used for credit cards:

AE	American Express	DISC	Discover	V	Visa
DC	Diners Club	MC	MasterCard		

FROMMERS.COM

Now that you have the guidebook to a great trip, visit our website at **www.frommers.com** for travel information on nearly 2,000 destinations. With features updated regularly, we give you instant access to the most current trip-planning information available. At Frommers.com, you'll also find the best prices on airfares, accommodations, and car rentals—and you can even book travel online through our travel booking partners. At Frommers.com, you'll also find the following:

- Daily Newsletter highlighting the best travel deals
- Hot Spot of the Month/Vacation Sweepstakes & Travel Photo Contest
- More than 200 Travel Message Boards
- Outspoken Newsletters and Feature Articles on travel bargains, vacation ideas, tips & resources, and more!

Here's what critics say about Frommer's:

"Amazingly easy to use. Very portable, very complete."

—*Booklist*

"The only mainstream guide to list specific prices. The Walter Cronkite of guidebooks—with all that implies."

—*Travel & Leisure*

"Complete, concise, and filled with useful information."

—*New York Daily News*

"Hotel information is close to encyclopedic."

—*Des Moines Sunday Register*

"Detailed, accurate, and easy-to-read information for all price ranges."

—*Glamour Magazine*

The Best of Rio de Janeiro

Few cities are as striking as Rio de Janeiro. The city folds itself into narrow bits of land between tropical beaches and mountains that leap to 2,500-foot heights. Rio offers much in the way of sightseeing, from nature to sunbathing to museums and historic neighborhoods. The culture, perhaps best expressed in its music and nightlife, is just as appealing. Samba is alive and well, augmented by many vibrant newer forms of distinctly Brazilian music. The event of the year is Carnaval, the biggest party in the world. And believe us when we say that Cariocas—as Rio residents are known—know how to throw a party. Following are our opinions of the best that Rio has to offer.

1 The Most Unforgettable Rio Experiences

- **Be the girl or boy from Ipanema:** Rio may have other beaches, but Ipanema is still the one with the best people-watching. Grab a spot, and food, drink, and eye candy will come to you. See "Beaches, Parks & Plazas" in chapter 6.
- **Explore Arco do Teles:** For a glimpse of old Rio, duck into the cobblestone alleys off Praça XV where you'll find perfectly preserved colonial buildings. Packed with restaurants, the area hums at night when office workers stop for a drink and a chat with friends. See "Architectural Highlights" in chapter 6.
- **Watch a soccer game at Maracanã stadium:** Nothing can prepare you for a game at the largest stadium in the world. Up to 100,000 fans sing, dance, and drum for hours in one of the biggest parties in town. See "Other Museums & Cultural Centers" in chapter 6.
- **Attend Carnaval in Rio:** The biggest party in the world! Whether you dance it on the streets, watch thousands participate in the samba parade with their elaborate costumes, or attend the fairy-tale Copacabana Palace ball, it's the one event not to miss. See "Everything You Need to Know About Carnaval" in chapter 8.

- **Stroll the streets of Ouro Prêto:** Ouro Prêto's cobblestone streets haven't changed much since the 18th century. Over a dozen baroque churches and beautifully preserved colonial architecture dot the hills of this charming town. See chapter 9.

2 The Best Hotels & Pousadas

- **The Copacabana Palace** (© **0800/21-1533** or 021/2548-7070): Fred and Ginger didn't dance just anywhere when they went "flying down to Rio." The Copacabana Palace is Brazil's most famous glamorous hotel, standing beautifully on the country's most famous beach. See p. 50.
- **Hotel Novo Mundo** (© **0800/25-3355** or 021/2557-6226): For that perfect postcard view of Rio's Aterro Park, the Glória Marina, and the Guanabara Bay against the backdrop of the Pão de Açúcar (Sugar Loaf Mountain), book the Suite Mar on the top floor of the Hotel Novo Mundo. See p. 60.
- **Hotel Sofitel** (© **0800/24-1232** or 021/2525-1232): Considered Rio's best hotel, the Sofitel combines old-world elegance and style with one of the city's best locations, across from the Copacabana Fort and steps from Ipanema. See p. 51.
- **Marina All Suites** (© **021/2540-4990**): The Marina All Suites is Rio's first designer hotel; all suites are luxuriously furnished. The two-bedroom oceanview Diamante suite is surely the city's most beautiful. See p. 47.
- **Marriott Rio de Janeiro** (© **800/228-9290** in the U.S. and Canada, or 021/2254-6500): The Marriott in Copacabana opened in May 2001 and has significantly raised the bar for hotels in Brazil. All rooms come with CD players and free mineral water. The staff wins high marks. See p. 52.
- **Sheraton Rio Hotel & Towers** (© **0800/11-1345** or 021/2274-1122): The Sheraton Rio is the only hotel that's really on the beach. No crossing the street; just walk down the steps and you're on the sand. See p. 57.
- **Colonna Park Hotel** (© **022/2623-2245**): On a hillside overlooking two beaches in Búzios, the Colonna has one of the best views in town. The elegantly furnished rooms are done in cool blue and white, and the best room in the house has a deck with views of both beaches. See p. 160.
- **Pousada Tankamana** (© **024/2222-2706**): Nestled in the hills above Petrópolis, Pousada Tankamana is a breath of fresh

air. The luxury chalets with Jacuzzi tubs and fireplaces are perfectly cozy on a cold winter day, just the kind of place to stay put and finish that book you've been trying to read. See p. 169.

3 The Best Dining & Nightlife Experiences

- **All beef, all the time!** Rodízio *churrascarias* are all-you-can-eat meat orgies. The best cuts of beef are served up one after another; try one or two or try them all. As long as you can take it, they dish it out. One of the country's most popular restaurants is the **Porcão,** a nationwide chain. Their flagship location is in Rio's Flamengo neighborhood ((C) **021/2544-7337** for reservations), with views of the bay and Sugar Loaf Mountain. See p. 73.

- **Arco do Teles:** Tucked away in an alley just off the Praça XV, the Arco do Teles reveals perfectly preserved colonial two-story walk-ups set on narrow cobblestone streets that are lined with restaurants and cafes. With over 15 *botequins* (bars), it doesn't matter which one you pick; walk around and see what's doing. If you get there after 10pm, you'll be lucky to find a seat at all. See "Bars & Pubs" in chapter 8.

- **The best *botequim* (bar):** Location, location, location. **Bar Amarelinho**'s large patio sits on Rio's most beautiful square, the Praça Floriano. Dwarfed by the National Library, the Museum of Fine Arts, and the National Theatre, this bar serves up excellent cold *chopp* (draft beer) and a host of Brazilian pub food: grilled beef, spicy sausage, cod-fish pastries, and manioc fries. Surely that's enough to munch on while you take in the views. See p. 67.

- **Carioca da Gema** ((C) **021/2221-0043**): One of the hottest nightlife spots in the city, Carioca da Gema offers some of the finest bossa nova and samba. Located just steps from the Lapa aqueduct, Carioca da Gema is one of the many small music venues in this funky bohemian neighborhood. The best night to come is Thursday. See p. 137.

- **Colonial Coffee:** For the most elegant coffee experience, visit **Confeitaria Colombo** ((C) **021/2221-0107**). This 19th-century Belle Epoque establishment is one of the most beautiful salons in all of Brazil. See p. 66.

- **Feijoada, the national dish:** It's impossible to single out one restaurant in all of Brazil for its *feijoada* (bean stew). Just try it . . . and try it right. Start with a *caipirinha* (that potent, delicious lime-and-sugarcane drink) and some *caldo* (soup), followed by steaming hot black beans with various meats. Side dishes include *farofa* (flour baked with oil), cabbage, orange slices, and white rice. Dab a bit of malagueta peppers on the beans for an extra kick. See chapter 5.

- **Rua das Pedras:** The hottest beach resort close to Rio, Búzios is the place if you're on a mission for a night out. Nightlife central is on the Rua das Pedras, where the pubs, bars, discos, and restaurants are open on weekends until 3 or 4 in the morning. One of the most popular spots is the Mexican bar and disco **Zapata,** which is very busy during vacations and weekends. See p. 163.
- **Street food:** Whether you want prawns, chicken, tapioca pancakes, coconut sweets, or corn on the cob, it can all be purchased on the street for next to nothing. Don't be afraid to try some of the best snacks that Brazil has to offer.

Planning Your Trip to Rio

This chapter helps you figure out how to prepare for your trip to Rio: where and when to go, how to get there, what precautions to take, and best of all, how to save money on your trip.

1 Visitor Information

Travelers planning their trip to Rio can browse the site of **Embratur,** the Brazilian national tourism agency, at **www.embratur.gov.br**. The Brazilian Embassy in the United Kingdom also has an outstanding website at **www.brazil.org.uk**. Travelers can also get in touch with Rio's tourist agency **Riotur** (© **212/375-0801** in the U.S., or 020/7431-0303 in the U.K.).

BRAZILIAN EMBASSIES

- **In the United States:** 3006 Massachusetts Ave. NW, Washington, DC 20008 (© **202/238-2700;** fax 202/238-2827; www.brasilemb.org).
- **In Canada:** 450 Wilbroad St., Ottawa, ON K1N 6M8 (© **613/237-1090;** fax 613/237-6144; www.brasemb ottawa.org).
- **In the United Kingdom:** 32 Green St., London W1K 7AT (© **020/7399-9000;** fax 020/7399-9100; www.brazil. org.uk).
- **In Australia:** 19 Forster Crescent, Yarralumla, ACT 2600 (© **02/6273-2372;** fax 02/6273-2375; www.brazil.org.au).
- **In New Zealand:** 10 Brandon St., Level 9, Wellington 6001 (© **04/473-3516;** fax 04/473-3517).

2 Entry Requirements

Nationals of the United States, Canada, Australia, and New Zealand require a visa to visit Brazil. British nationals (and holders of an EU passport) do not require a visa but do need a passport valid for at least 6 months and a return ticket. A number of visa types are available: cost, processing time and documentation requirements

---

Tips **Shameless Plug**

If you'd like to know more about traveling in Brazil, pick up a copy of *Frommer's Brazil* or *Frommer's South America*.

---

vary. U.S. citizens pay US$45 for a standard single-entry tourist visa that is valid for 90 days (add another US$10 for handling fees, passport photos, and courier costs if you don't live near a consulate). Count on at least 2 weeks of processing time. For Canadians, a similar visa costs US$40 (C$64) and takes about the same processing time. Visas for both New Zealanders and Australians cost US$35 (NZ$84 and A$69) plus local handling fees and again take about 2 weeks to process.

Upon arrival in Brazil, visitors will receive a 90-day entry stamp in their passport and a stamped entry card. Hang on to the card for dear life, as losing it will result in a possible fine and a certain major hassle when you leave. If necessary, the visa can be renewed once for another 90 days. Visa renewals are obtained through the local Policia Federal. This is best done in large cities where the staff has experience with tourists.

For more information regarding visas and to obtain application details, contact the Brazilian consulate in New York (© 917/777-7777; www.brazilny.org), in Los Angeles (© 213/651-2664; brconsular@earthlink.net), or in Miami (© 305/285-6200; www.brazilmiami.org). Canadians can apply through Toronto's Brazilian consulate, (© 416/922-2503; www.consbrastoronto.org). In the United Kingdom, more information is available at **www.brazil.org.uk**. Australians can log on to **www.brazil.org.au**, and in New Zealand, inquiries can be made in Wellington at © 04/473-3516 or via e-mail to brasemb@ihug.co.nz.

3 Customs

WHAT YOU CAN BRING IN

Upon arrival in Brazil, you will go through Customs, but as a visitor you are unlikely to be scrutinized very closely. Customs officers are too busy nabbing returning Brazilians loaded down with consumer goods far in excess of their duty-free limit. However, there are random checks and your luggage may be thoroughly inspected. Visitors are allowed to bring a reasonable amount of personal belongings, including electronics such as a camera or laptop.

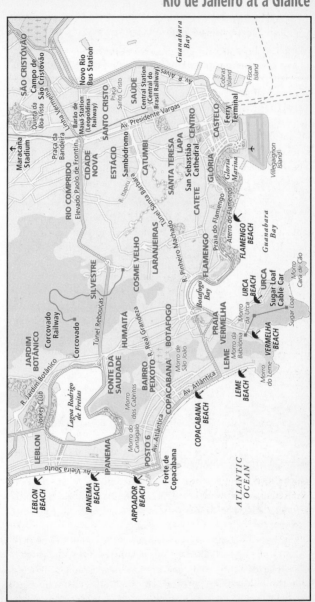

Tips   **Don't Leave Home Without a Picture ID**

Most hotels have in-room safes. Make use of them by keeping your passport, entry card, airline tickets, and other important documents in a safe place. We recommend bringing an alternative picture ID, like a driver's license or student ID, to use when you are out and about, instead of carrying your passport with you at all times. You are required to carry ID in Brazil, and it is sometimes requested when entering office buildings or even tourist sites.

WHAT YOU CAN TAKE HOME

Travelers returning to the **United States** are allowed to bring $400 worth of goods per person, and family members who live in the same home may combine their exemptions. Travelers who stay less than 48 hours outside the country or who have left the United States more than once in 30 days are given a $200 exemption only. You may include up to 1 liter of alcohol (provided you are over 21 years of age), 100 cigars, and 200 cigarettes; any more and you'll pay a duty. Keep your receipts handy. The legal limit for goods mailed home is no more than $20 per day for yourself; mark the package "FOR PERSONAL USE." You may mail one gift per day, worth no more than $100, marked "UNSOLICITED GIFT." Packages must clearly describe the contents on the exterior. You may not mail alcohol, perfume that contains alcohol, or tobacco products, but a legitimate company such as a wine dealer can ship alcohol to you in the United States (usually for a very steep shipping fee). Foodstuffs must be tinned or professionally sealed; you may not bring fresh foodstuffs into the United States.

Duty is a flat 10% tax on the first $1,000 worth of goods over $400. Anything over is subject to an item-by-item basis. For more information, contact the **U.S. Customs Service** at 1300 Pennsylvania Ave. NW (© **877/287-8667**) and request the free pamphlet *Know Before You Go*. It's also available online at **www. customs.gov**.

Citizens of **Canada** who've been out of the country for over 48 hours may bring back $200 Canadian worth of goods, and if you've been gone for 7 consecutive days or more, not counting your departure, the limit is $750 Canadian. The limit for alcohol is up to 1.5 liters of wine or 1.14 liters of liquor, or 24 12-ounce cans or bottles of beer; and up to 200 cigarettes, 50 cigars, or 200 grams of tobacco.

You may not ship tobacco or alcohol and you must be of legal age for your province to bring these items through Customs. For the helpful booklet *I Declare,* call the **Canada Customs and Review Agency** at © **800/461-9999** in Canada or 204/983-3500, or visit their website at www.ccra-adrc.gc.ca.

Returnees to the **United Kingdom** may bring back up to 200 cigarettes, 50 cigars, or 250 grams of tobacco; 2 liters of still table wine; 1 liter of distilled spirits over 22% volume or 2 liters sparkling wine, fortified wine, or other liqueurs; 60cc/ml perfume; 250cc/ml toilet water; and £145 worth of all other gifts and souvenirs. Travelers must be over 17 to bring back tobacco and alcohol. For more information, call the **HM Customs & Excise** at © **0845/ 010-9000,** or log on to www.hmce.gov.uk.

The duty-free allowance in **Australia** is A$400 or, for those under 18, A$200. Citizens can bring in 250 cigarettes or 250 grams of loose tobacco, and 1,125 milliliters of alcohol. If you're returning with valuables you already own, such as foreign-made cameras, you should file form B263. A helpful brochure available from Australian consulates or Customs offices is *Know Before You Go.* For more information, call the **Australian Customs Service** at © **1300/ 363-263,** or log on to www.customs.gov.au.

The duty-free allowance for citizens of **New Zealand** is NZ$700. Citizens over 17 can bring in 200 cigarettes, 50 cigars, or 250 grams of tobacco (or a mixture of all three if their combined weight doesn't

---

Tips **Begin Your Trip with Duty-Free Shopping**

Other countries normally force you to do your duty-free shopping before arrival, and they only allow you to bring in a single measly bottle of liquor, a box of cigarettes, and a few bottles of perfume. In Brazil you're allowed to spend up to $500 in the duty-free shop *upon arrival,* and it's completely up to you whether you blow the money on cases of Johnny Walker, gallons of aftershave, or chocolates enough to feed an army of kindergarteners. In the airport, just follow the signs after immigration and *before* going through Customs. Prices in these duty-free shops are pretty good on an international scale and much cheaper than you'll find in Brazil itself. Note that the generous import allowance only counts for goods purchased in the Brazilian duty-free shop upon arrival. Yes, they want your dollars. . . .

exceed 250g); plus 4.5 liters of wine and beer, or 1.125 liters of liquor. New Zealand currency does not carry import or export restrictions. Fill out a certificate of export, listing the valuables you are taking out of the country; that way, you can bring them back without paying duty. Most questions are answered in a free pamphlet available at New Zealand consulates and Customs offices: *New Zealand Customs Guide for Travellers, Notice no. 4.* For more information, contact **New Zealand Customs,** The Customhouse, 17–21 Whitmore St., Box 2218, Wellington (© **0800/42-8786** or 04/473-6099; www.customs.govt.nz).

4 Money

The Brazilian unit of currency is the *real* (R$), pronounced "hey-*al*" (plural *reais,* pronounced "hey-*eyes*") and made up of 100 centavos. The real comes in bills of 1, 5, 10, 50, and 100, and coins of R$1, 50, 25, 10, 5, and 1 centavos. In an attempt to rein in inflation, the Brazilian government introduced the real in 1994. It was stable for a number of years, then devalued by almost 50% in 1999, after which it remained stable for most of 2000 before embarking yet again on a slower but steady decline, losing over 20% in value against the U.S. dollar over the course of 2001. Throughout this guide we give the prices in reais and U.S. dollars; as of press time, the exchange rate was R$2 to US$1.

After years of experience with unstable local currencies, Brazilians learned to use the U.S. dollar as the unofficial yardstick for their economy and are consequently accustomed to keeping track of prices in dollars. Many tourism companies will quote prices directly in dollars. Sometimes websites or brochures list prices in U.S. dollars only. When in doubt, ask. And though it's a bad idea to carry large wads of cash, it can be helpful to bring a small amount of U.S. cash (10s or 20s only) as an emergency supply in case an ATM is broken or your credit card isn't working.

TRAVELER'S CHECKS Traveler's checks don't work well in Brazil. Most shops won't accept them, hotels give a miserable exchange rate, and many banks won't cash your traveler's checks unless you have an account at that branch of that bank. Others, such as Bank Boston, will only cash a minimum of $500. The Banco do Brasil is the only bank that will cash them with a minimum of hassle (expect to spend at least 20–30 min.) but charges a flat rate of $20 for the pleasure. Only American Express will cash their own checks for free.

Tips **Hoard Your Small Bills**

There seems to be a chronic lack of small bills in Brazil, particularly in the northeast. Try paying for a R$4 item with a R$10
bill and you may have to wait half an hour while the vendor
moans about the horror of making change, then runs around
begging his friends and neighbors and other shopkeepers to
please help him break a 10. Or he may simply refuse to sell
anything to you and tell you to come back when you've got
smaller bills. Buses, street vendors, and taxi drivers also usually
carry little or no change, so hoard those ones and fives!

ATMs Brazil's financial infrastructure is very sophisticated and
ATMs are everywhere in Rio. The only trick is finding one that
works with your card. ATMs are linked to a network that most
likely includes your bank at home. **Cirrus** (📞 800/424-7787;
www.mastercard.com) and **Plus** (📞 800/843-7587; www.visa.com)
are the two most popular networks; call or check online for ATM
locations in Rio. Be sure you know your PIN access number and
your daily withdrawal limit before you leave home. The vast majority of travelers find they are able to use the Banco do Brasil ATMs
bearing the Plus/Visa and Cirrus/MasterCard logos. Bradesco and
Citibank ATMs are both compatible with Cirrus/MasterCard.
However, it's not a bad idea to bring two different cards to increase
your access options with other banks. When in doubt, check with
your bank to find out which Brazilian bank networks are compatible with your card. Finally, make sure that during New Year's and
Carnaval you get enough cash ahead of time as machines often run
out of money by the end of the holidays.

CREDIT CARDS The best exchange rates can be obtained
through credit cards, which are accepted at most shops, hotels, and
restaurants. Just keep in mind that you are sometimes able to negotiate a better discount on a room or in a store if you pay cash. The
most commonly accepted cards are Visa and MasterCard. American
Express and Diners Club are also frequently accepted. It's a good
idea to have at least two cards as some stores and restaurants only
accept one card (usually Visa).

If you need to report a lost or stolen credit card or have any
questions, you can contact the agencies at the following numbers:
American Express, 📞 0800/78-5050; **MasterCard** and **Visa,**
📞 0800/78-4456; and **Diners Club,** 📞 0800/78-4444.

5 When to Go

High season in Brazil lasts from the week before Christmas until Carnaval (which falls sometime in February or early March, depending on the year). Flights and accommodations are more expensive and more likely to be full during this period. Book well ahead of time for accommodations during New Year's and Carnaval. This is the most fun time to travel—towns and resorts are bustling as many Brazilians take their summer vacations, the weather's warm, and New Year's and Carnaval are fabulously entertaining. If you want to spend New Year's in Brazil, it's best to arrive after Christmas. December 25 is really a family affair and most restaurants and shops will be closed.

Other busy times of year include Easter week and the month of July, when schools and universities take their winter breaks. This is probably the worst time of year to travel; prices go up significantly and the weather can be iffy. (One year in Rio, we suffered through 4 straight weeks of rain.) If you want to take advantage of the best deals and still have good weather, consider visiting Brazil in September or October. The spring weather means warm days in Rio, and you'll be able to attend some of the samba school rehearsals as they get ready for Carnaval. Another good period for a visit is after Carnaval (early to mid-March, depending on the dates) through May, when you can take advantage of low season prices, particularly in hotels, while still enjoying good weather.

WEATHER

Since Brazil lies in the Southern Hemisphere, its seasons are the exact opposite of what Northern Hemisphere residents are used to: summer is from December through March and winter from June through September. Rio has very hot and humid summers—100°F (38°C) temperatures and 98% humidity are not uncommon. Rio winters are quite mild, with nighttime temperatures dropping as low as 66°F (15°C), and daytime temperatures climbing to a pleasant and sunny 82°F (28°C). Cariocas themselves find this lack of heat appalling, and will often throw on a coat or heavy sweater when the temperature drops below 68°F (20°C). In the mountain resort of Petrópolis, it often gets cold enough to see your breath in the fall and winter.

HOLIDAYS

The following holidays are observed in Brazil: New Year's Day (Jan 1); Carnaval (Feb 1–4, 2003 and Feb 21–24, 2004); Good

Friday (Apr 20, 2003); Tiradentes Day (Apr 21); Labor Day (May 1); Corpus Christi (June 19, 2003); Independence Day (Sept 7); Our Lady of Apparition (Oct 12); All Souls' Day (Nov 2); Proclamation of the Republic (Nov 15); Christmas Day (Dec 25). On these days, banks, schools, and government institutions are closed, and some stores may be closed as well. Sometimes the holiday will be taken on the Monday closest to the actual date.

RIO DE JANEIRO CALENDAR OF EVENTS

January

Saint Sebastian Day. The patron saint of Rio de Janeiro is honored on this regional holiday. The highlight is a procession to the city's modern cathedral. January 20.

February

Celebration of Yemanjá. Devotees offer flowers, perfumes, and jewelry to the goddess of the sea. Celebrations take place on the beach with music and food. February 2.

Carnaval. The biggest party in the world. Whether you dance it out on the streets, watch the thousands of participants in their elaborate costumes in the samba parade, or attend the fairy-tale Copacabana Palace ball, this is one event not to miss! February 1 to 4, 2003, and February 21 to 24, 2004. For details, contact **Riotur** (© **021/2217-7575;** www.riodejaneiro-turismo.com.br) or **Alô Rio** (© **021/2542-8080**). See "Everything You Need to Know About Carnaval" in chapter 8.

June

Festas Juninas. This folklore event honors saints Anthony, John, and Peter. Celebrated throughout Brazil, this harvest festival offers country music, bonfires, hot-air balloons, and fun fairs. Contact **Riotur** (© **021/2217-7575;** www.riodejaneiro-turismo.com.br) or **Alô Rio** (© **021/2542-8080**). June 13 and 14.

September

Independence Day. This national holiday is celebrated all across Brazil. In Rio de Janeiro, the event is quite impressive and takes place around Avenida Rio Branco; it's worth seeing if you happen to be in town. September 7.

Film Festival Rio. Rio's film festival showcases Brazilian and international films. Subtitles are in Portuguese but there is usually a good selection of international movies. Contact **Riotur** (© **021/ 2217-7575;** www.riodejaneiro-turismo.com.br) or **Alô Rio** (© **021/2542-8080**). Late September to the first week of October.

October

Free Jazz Festival. A 3-day jazz festival with national and international acts. Contact **Riotur** (© **021/2217-7575;** www. riodejaneiro-turismo.com.br) or **Alô Rio** (© **021/2542-8080**). Mid- to late October.

December

Christmas Eve. One of the most important Catholic family events, when Brazilians go to midnight Mass to celebrate Christmas. Mass is usually followed by a late-night supper with family. December 24.

Reveillon (New Year's Eve). Copacabana beach is ground zero for the event that attracts over two million people. The 6 miles of sand are jam-packed with New Year's revelers and the entertainment never stops, with concerts and performances all evening long leading up to the best fireworks display in the world. The evening is also an important one in the African Candomblé religion; it's the night to make an offer to the sea goddess Yemanjá. December 31.

6 Health, Travel Insurance & Safety

HEALTH

Standards for hygiene and public health in Brazil are generally high. Before leaving, however, please check with your doctor or with the **Centers for Disease Control and Prevention** (**www.cdc.gov**) for specific advisories, as information is constantly updated.

VACCINATIONS It's always a good idea before going on a trip to check your vaccinations and get booster shots for tetanus and polio if necessary. Children aged 3 months to 6 years may be required to show proof of polio vaccination. The one vaccination that is definitely required for Brazil is **yellow fever.** If you're traveling to the Amazon, the Pantanal, Brasília, or even Minas Gerais, you may come in contact with it. Get an international certificate of vaccination as Brazilian authorities sometimes require proof of vaccination for people going to or coming from an affected area. Travelers who have been to Colombia, Bolivia, Ecuador, French Guyana, Peru, or Venezuela within 90 days prior to their arrival in Brazil are also required to show proof of yellow fever vaccination. Please keep in mind that the vaccine takes 10 days to take effect.

HEALTH PRECAUTIONS The **tap water** in Brazil is becoming increasingly safe to drink. However, as a result of the treatment process, it still doesn't taste that great and may leave your stomach

upset. To be on the safe side, drink bo̶
Brazilians do). However, you can certa̶
or rinse an apple with the water.

If you do wind up with traveler's tummy o̶
Brazilian **pharmacies** are a wonder. Each has a lice̶
who is trained to deal with small medical emergencies a̶
yet—fully authorized to give prescriptions. The service is fre̶
medication is fairly inexpensive. If you're taking medication tha̶
may need replacement while in Brazil, ask your doctor to write out
the generic name, as many drugs are sold under different brand
names in Brazil. Many drugs available by prescription-only in the
United States and Canada are available over the counter in Brazil.

According to recent U.N. statistics, Brazil ranks third in the
world for the total number of people with **HIV infections.** Be
careful and be safe—always insist on using a condom. Though
condoms are readily available in Brazilian pharmacies, it's best to
bring your own as North American and European brands are more
reliable. To purchase condoms in Brazil ask for *camisinha* (literally
"small shirt").

WHAT TO DO IF YOU GET SICK AWAY FROM HOME

It can be hard to find a doctor you can trust when you're in an unfamiliar place. Try to take proper precautions the week before you
depart to avoid falling ill while you're away from home. Amid the
last-minute frenzy that often precedes a vacation, make an extra
effort to eat and sleep well.

If you worry about getting sick away from home, you may want
to consider **medical travel insurance** (see "Travel Insurance,"
below). In most cases, however, your existing health plan will provide all the coverage you need; check you're your insurer to make
sure you're covered while you're on your trip. Be sure to carry your
identification card in your wallet.

If you suffer from a chronic illness, consult your doctor before
your departure. For conditions like epilepsy, diabetes, or heart prob-
lems, wear a **Medic Alert Identification Tag** (© **800/825-3785;**
www.medicalert.org), which will immediately alert doctors to your
condition and give them access to your records through Medic
Alert's 24-hour hot line. The first year of membership costs $35.

Pack prescription medications in their original labeled containers
in your carry-on luggage. Also bring along copies of your prescriptions in case you lose your pills or run out. Carry written prescriptions

form, in case a local pharmacist is unfamiliar with the
ame. If you wear contact lenses, pack an extra pair.

ntact the **International Association for Medical Assistance**
Travellers (IAMAT) (© 716/754-4883; www.sentex.net/
amat). This organization offers tips on travel and health concerns
n the countries you'll be visiting, and lists many local English-
speaking doctors. The United States **Centers for Disease Control
and Prevention** (© 800/311-3435; www.cdc.gov) provides up-to-
date information on necessary vaccines and health hazards by region
or country (by mail, their booklet is $25; on the Internet, it's free).
When you're abroad, any local consulate can provide a list of area
doctors who speak English. If you do get sick, you may want to ask
the concierge at your hotel to recommend a local doctor—even his
or her own. If you can't find a doctor who can help you right away,
try the emergency room at the local hospital. Many emergency
rooms have walk-in clinics for emergency cases that are not life-
threatening. You may not get immediate attention, but you won't
pay the high price of an emergency room visit (usually a minimum
of $300 just for signing your name).

TRAVEL INSURANCE

Check your existing insurance policies before you buy travel
insurance to cover trip cancellation, lost luggage, medical expenses,
or car-rental insurance. You're likely to have partial or complete
coverage. But if you need some, ask your travel agent about a
comprehensive package. The cost of travel insurance varies widely,
depending on the cost and length of your trip, your age and overall
health, and the type of trip you're taking. Insurance for extreme
sports or adventure travel, for example, will cost more than coverage
for a cruise. Some insurers provide packages for specialty vacations,
such as skiing or backpacking. More dangerous activities may be
excluded from basic policies.

For information, contact one of the following popular insurers:

- **Access America** (© 800/284-8300; www.accessamerica.com/)
- **Travel Guard International** (© 800/826-1300; www.travel
  guard.com)
- **Travel Insured International** (© 800/243-3174; www.travel
  insured.com)
- **Travelex Insurance Services** (© 800/228-9792; www.travelex-
  insurance.com)

TRIP-CANCELLATION INSURANCE (TCI)

There are three major types of trip-cancellation insurance: one, in the event that you prepay a cruise or tour that gets cancelled, and you can't get your money back; a second when you or someone in your family gets sick or dies, and you can't travel (but be aware that you may not be covered for a preexisting condition); and a third, when bad weather makes travel impossible. Some insurers provide coverage for events like jury duty; natural disasters close to home, like floods or fire; or even the loss of a job. A few have added provisions for cancellations due to terrorist activities. Always check the fine print before signing on, and don't buy trip-cancellation insurance from the tour operator that may be responsible for the cancellation; buy it only from a reputable travel insurance agency. Don't overbuy—you won't be reimbursed for more than the cost of your trip.

MEDICAL INSURANCE

With the exception of certain HMOs and Medicare/Medicaid, your medical insurance should cover medical treatment—even hospital care—overseas. However, most make you pay the bills up front at the time of care, and you'll get a refund after you've returned and filed all the paperwork. Members of **Blue Cross/Blue Shield** can now use their cards at select hospitals in most major cities worldwide (© **800/810-BLUE** or www.bluecares.com for a list of hospitals).

If you do require additional insurance, try one of the following companies:

- **MEDEX International** (© **888/MEDEX-00** or 410/453-6300; www.medexassist.com)
- **Travel Assistance International** (© **800/777-8710** for general information or 800/821-2828; www.travelassistance.com)

Tips Read the Fine Print

If you're investing in a travel insurance policy, check the fine print for restrictions before you sign up. Many policies do not cover extreme-sports activities, nor will they cover drink- and drug-related accidents. And look out for your valuables: Reimbursement is not guaranteed if you've been shown to be careless in protecting your possessions.

- **Divers Alert Network** (DAN) (*©* **800/446-2671** or 919/ 684-8181; www.diversalertnetwork.org) ensures divers.

The cost of travel medical insurance varies widely, so check your existing policies before you buy additional coverage. Also, check to see if your medical insurance covers you for emergency medical evacuation: If you have to buy a one-way same-day ticket home and forfeit your nonrefundable round-trip ticket, you may be out of big bucks.

SAFETY

In the 1980s, Brazil developed a reputation for violence and crime. Rio especially was seen as the sort of place where walking down the street was openly asking for a mugging. Some of this was pure sensationalism, but there was a good measure of truth as well. Brazil at the time was massively in debt to first-world banks and the combination of crippling interest payments and International Monetary Fund austerity measures left governments at all levels with no money for basics such as street lighting and police, much less schools and hospitals.

Fortunately in the early 1990s, things began to turn around. Governments began pouring money back into basic services, starting with policing. Cops were stationed on city streets, on public beaches, and anywhere else there seemed to be a problem. Very quickly the crime rate began to fall. Nowadays, though still not perfect by any means, Rio and Brazil's other big cities have bounced back to the point where they're as safe as other large international cities such as Paris or New York. Statistically, of course, Rio still has unfortunately high crime rates; most of that crime, however, takes place in the *favelas* (shantytowns) of the far-off industrial outskirts. Avoid wandering in or near the hillside favelas, and in the evening stick to well-lit and well-traveled streets. Take the usual common-sense precautions you would in any major city to protect yourself.

Before you depart for Brazil, you can check for travel advisories from the **U.S. State Department** (www.travel.state.gov), the **Canadian Department of Foreign Affairs** (http://voyage. dfait-maeci.gc.ca), the **U.K. Foreign & Commonwealth Office** (www.fco.gov.uk/travel), and the **Australian Department of Foreign Affairs** (www.dfat.gov.au/consular/advice).

7 Tips for Travelers with Special Needs

FOR TRAVELERS WITH DISABILITIES

Travelers with disabilities will find Brazil challenging. In fact, those who use a wheelchair to get around will find that very few places are accessible. In Rio, an increasing number of hotels, restaurants, and attractions are making themselves accessible. The trick lies in getting to them. Many sidewalks are uneven, ramps are usually absent, and buses and taxis are not adapted to handle wheelchairs.

For some additional resources on traveling with a disability, contact the **Society for Accessible Travel & Hospitality** (SATH) (② 212/447-7284; www.sath.org). The website has an extensive list of travel tips as well as resources on specific travel destinations. Another great source of information is **Access-Able,** P.O. Box 1796, Wheat Ridge, CO 80034 (② 303/232-2979; www.access-able. com). Their website has links to country-specific resources such as accessible hotels, tour operators, and other useful information. **Flying Wheels Travel** (② 800/535-6790; www.flyingwheels travel.com) offers escorted tours and cruises that emphasize sports and private tours in minivans with lifts.

FOR GAY & LESBIAN TRAVELERS

Gay and lesbian travelers will find a small but vibrant gay community in Rio, more often geared towards men than women. However, public displays of affection are not common amongst gays and lesbians even in the cities, and in small towns and communities, the level of acceptance is significantly lower—rude remarks and jokes are almost guaranteed, though physical violence is thankfully rare.

One Brazilian travel agency that specializes in tours for gay and lesbian travelers is **Alibi Turismo,** Rua Bahia 941, São Paulo (② 11/ 3663-0075; www.alibi.com.br). Trips include special New Year's and Carnaval events, as well as packages to some of the popular beach destinations in the northeast. Other travel agencies include **Above and Beyond Tours** (② 800/397-2681; www.abovebeyond tours.com), which offers gay and lesbian tours worldwide and is the exclusive gay and lesbian tour operator for United Airlines; and **Now, Voyager** (② 800/255-6951; www.nowvoyager.com), a San Francisco–based gay-owned and -operated travel service. For other operators and gay-friendly hotels, check with the **International Gay & Lesbian Travel Association** (IGLTA) (② 800/448-8550 or 954/776-2626; www.iglta.org).

FOR SENIORS

Brazil treats its elderly well. Seniors often live with their family and are treated with respect and affection. Senior travelers may try to ask for discounts, though these are reserved for those over 60 or 65 years of age who can show Brazilian ID. Still, it's always worth asking at tourist attractions if there's a discount. The phrase to use is *"Tem disconto para idosos?"* (Teng dees-*kon*-toh para ee-*doh*-sos?)

The Elderhostel organization runs a number of trips to Brazil for travelers 55 and over. Structured with their trademark educational focus, the itineraries include lectures and interesting excursions. Contact **Elderhostel** at 75 Federal St., Boston, MA 02110-1941 (© 877/426-8056; www.elderhostel.org). **Interhostel** (© 800/733-9753; www.learn.unh.edu/interhostel), organized by the University of New Hampshire, also offers educational travel for senior citizens. On these escorted tours, the days are packed with seminars, lectures, and field trips, with sightseeing led by academic experts. Interhostel takes travelers 50 and over (with companions over 40), and offers 1- and 2-week trips, mostly international. **Grand Circle Travel** (© 800/221-2610 or 617/350-7500; www.gct.com) offers package deals for the 50-plus market, mostly of the tour-bus variety, with free trips thrown in for those who organize groups of 10 or more.

FOR FAMILIES

Brazilians love kids. They will go out of their way to please children—yours and everyone else's. In fact, you will see children out and about a lot more than in the United States or Canada, even at restaurants, bars, or late-night events. Perhaps because Brazilian children are used to going out a lot more, they seem to always behave very well in public, playing with other kids or amusing themselves, with few of the hissy fits that sometimes accompany evenings out with North American youngsters. Traveling with children is a wonderful way to meet Brazilians, as people will be receptive and inquisitive. Hotels are very accommodating but do usually charge 10% to 25% extra for children over a certain age (usually 6 or 12) who stay in the same room as a parent or guardian. In most hotels, the age limit and extra charges can be flexible and are certainly worth bargaining over. **Travel with Your Children** (www.travelwithyourkids.com) is a comprehensive website offering sound advice for traveling with children. **Family Travel Network** (www.familytravelnetwork.com) offers travel tips and reviews of family-friendly destinations, vacation deals, and thoughtful features.

STUDENT TRAVEL

The best resource for students is the **Council on International Educational Exchange**, or CIEE (**www.ciee.org**). They can set you up with an ID card (see below), and their travel branch, **Council Travel Service** (© **800/226-8624;** www.counciltravel.com), is the biggest student-travel-agency operation in the world. It can get you discounts on plane tickets, rail passes, and the like. **STA Travel** (© **800/781-4040;** www.statravel.com) is another travel agency catering especially to young travelers, although their bargain-basement prices are available to people of all ages.

From CIEE you can obtain the student traveler's best friend, the $22 **International Student Identity Card** (ISIC). It's the only officially acceptable form of student identification, good for cut rates on rail passes, plane tickets, and other discounts. It also provides you with basic health and life insurance and a 24-hour help line. If you're no longer a student but are still under 26, you can get a **GO 25** card from the same people, which will get you the insurance and some of the discounts (but not student admission prices in museums).

In Canada, **Travel CUTS** (© **800/667-2887** or 416/614-2887; www.travelcuts.com) offers similar services. In London, **Campus Travel** (© **0171/730-3402;** www.campustravel.co.uk), opposite Victoria Station, is Britain's leading specialist in student and youth travel.

FOR WOMEN

Machismo is alive and well in Brazil, but it's a kinder, gentler machismo than in other parts of Latin America. Single women—even a few women traveling together—will undoubtedly attract masculine attention. It's usually fairly harmless and can sometimes lead to some fun conversations. Brazilian men, it seems, have an insurmountable urge to flirt. Perhaps because flirting is such a way of life, they take rejection well. Indeed, the object of the exercise lies mostly in the act of flirtation itself—actually making a conquest appears to be not terribly important. Wearing a wedding ring (fake or real) will throw up only the flimsiest of barriers; it will be either completely ignored or solicit questions such as "How married are you?" or "What kind of husband would let you out of his sight?"

However, if you are not interested, just say so or walk away, if necessary, and that is usually enough.

The downside to this attention is that it's difficult for a woman to go out for a drink by herself without being bothered. If you're not comfortable with this, you may want to form a mixed group with other travelers or stick to higher-end restaurants or hotel bars. Use common sense to avoid situations where you may find yourself alone with someone giving you unwanted attention. At night, taking taxis is safer than walking by yourself.

TRAVELERS WITH FOOD ALLERGIES

If you are allergic to nuts, you should be extra careful around certain dishes. Many stews from the northeast, such as *moqueca, vatapá,* and *bobó,* may have ground-up peanuts or cashews in the sauce. Desserts often have nuts in them, so always ask before digging in. Peanuts are called *amendoim* (ah-man-doo-*een*), cashews in Portuguese are *castanha de caju* or *caju* (ka-*stan*-ya de *ka*-zhoo) for short, and Brazil nuts are known as *castanha do Pará* (ka-*stan*-ya doh pa-*rah*). The general word for nuts is *nozes* (no-*zhes*), and you can let people know that you have an allergy by saying *"Tenho alergia de amendoim"* (*Ten*-yo ah-lehr-*gee*-ah de ah-man-doo-*een*).

8 Getting There

BY PLANE

Most major airlines fly to Rio de Janeiro, sometimes with a stop or connection in São Paulo. Carriers departing from the United States and Canada include **United** (© 800/241-6522; www.ual.com), **American** (© 800/433-7300; www.aa.com), **Continental** (© 800/231-0856; www.continental.com), and **Delta** (© 800/241-4141; www.delta.com). From Canada, **Air Canada** (© 888/247-2262; www.aircanada.ca) and its partner **Varig** (© 800/468-2744; www.varig.com.br) provide daily flights. European carriers include **Air France** (© 800/237-2747; www.airfrance.com), **Lufthansa** (© 800/645-3880; www.lufthansa.com), and **British Airways** (© 0845/702-0212; www.britishairways.com). The Brazilian airlines Varig and **TAM** (© 888/2FLY-TAM; www.tam.com.br) also offer regular service from within South America, North America, and Europe.

BY PACKAGE TOUR

Many travel agencies offer package tours to Brazil but few have the knowledge to effectively customize your trip or make interesting recommendations. To book a package with Brazil travel experts, contact **Brazil Nuts,** 1854 Trade Center Way, Suite 101A, Naples, FL 34109 (© **800/553-9959** or 914/593-0266; www.brazilnuts. com). The owners and staff are indeed nuts about Brazil and possess a vast amount of knowledge about the country and its attractions. Depending on your needs, you can book just a flight and hotel or you can add one or more group excursions in more inaccessible places such as the Amazon. Their website is a wealth of information, and the staff can answer any questions you may have about Brazil.

Newer on the scene but still good is the Internet-based company **4StarBrazil,** 322 SE Park Hill, Chehalis, WA 98532 (© **866/ 464-7827;** http://4starbrazil.com). Similar to Brazil Nuts, 4StarBrazil offers packages customizable to whatever level you're comfortable with. A number of interesting add-ons are available.

FLYING FOR LESS: TIPS FOR GETTING THE BEST AIRFARES

Passengers within the same airplane cabin are rarely paying the same fare for their seats. Business travelers who need to purchase tickets at the last minute, change their itinerary at a moment's notice, or get home before the weekend pay the full fare. Passengers who can book their tickets well in advance, who don't mind staying over Saturday night, or who are willing to travel on a Tuesday, Wednesday, or Thursday after 7pm, will pay a fraction of the full fare. Here are a few other easy ways to save:

- Airlines periodically lower prices on their most popular routes. Check the travel section of your newspaper for advertised discounts or call the airlines directly and ask if any **promotional rates** or special fares are available. You'll almost never see a sale during the peak summer vacation months of July and August, or during the Thanksgiving or Christmas seasons; but in periods of low-volume travel, you should pay as little as $400 for a flight from the United States to South America. If your schedule is flexible, ask if you can secure a cheaper fare by staying an extra day or by flying midweek. If you already hold a ticket when a sale breaks, it may even pay to exchange your ticket, which usually incurs a $100 to $150 charge.

  Note, however, that the lowest-priced fares are often nonrefundable, require advance purchase of 1 to 3 weeks and a certain length of stay, and carry penalties for changing dates of travel.

- **Consolidators,** also known as bucket shops, are a good place to find low fares. Consolidators buy seats in bulk from the airlines and then sell them back to the public at prices below even the airlines' discounted rates. Their small ads usually run in the Sunday travel section of the newspaper at the bottom of the page. Before you pay, however, ask for a confirmation number from the consolidator and then call the airline to confirm your seat. Be aware that bucket shop tickets are usually nonrefundable or rigged with stiff cancellation penalties, often as high as 50% to 75% of the ticket price. Protect yourself by paying with a credit card rather than cash. Keep in mind that if there's an airline sale going on or if it's high season, you can often get the same or better rates by contacting the airline directly, so do some comparison shopping before you buy.

    Council Travel (© 800/226-8624; www.counciltravel. com) and **STA Travel** (© 800/781-4040; www.statravel.com) cater especially to young travelers, but their bargain-basement prices are available to people of all ages. Other reliable consolidators include **1-800-FLY-CHEAP** (**www.1800flycheap. com**); **TFI Tours International** (© 800/745-8000 or 212/736-1140), which serves as a clearinghouse for unused seats; or "rebators" such as **Travel Avenue** (© 800/333-3335; www.travelavenue.com) and the **Smart Traveller** (© 800/ 448-3338 or 305/448-3338), which rebate part of their commissions to you.

- Search the **Internet** for cheap fares—see section 9, "Planning Your Trip Online," below, for more information.

- Book a seat on a **charter flight.** Discounted fares have pared the number available, but they can still be found. Most charter operators advertise and sell their seats through travel agents, thus making these local professionals your best source of information for available flights. Before deciding to take a charter flight, however, check the restrictions on the ticket: You may be asked to purchase a tour package, to pay in advance, to be amenable if the day of departure is changed, to pay a service charge, to fly on an airline you're not familiar with (this usually is not the case), and/or to pay harsh penalties if you cancel— but be understanding if the charter doesn't fill up and is canceled up to 10 days before departure. Summer charters fill up more quickly than others and are almost sure to fly, but if you decide on a charter flight, seriously consider buying cancellation and baggage insurance. Also be prepared for late departure hours and long airport delays, as charters usually do not have priority.

- Look into **courier flights.** Companies that hire couriers use your luggage allowance for their business baggage; in return, you get a deeply discounted ticket. Flights are often offered at the last minute, and you may have to arrange a pretrip interview to make sure you're right for the job. **Now Voyager** (☎ 212/431-1616), flies from New York. Now Voyager also offers noncourier discounted fares, so call the company even if you don't want to fly as a courier.

- Join a travel club such as **Moment's Notice** (☎ 718/234-6295; www.moments-notice.com) or **Sears Discount Travel Club** (☎ 800/433-9383, or 800/255-1487 to join; www.travelersadvantage.com), which supply unsold tickets at discounted prices. You pay an annual membership fee to get the club's hot line number. Of course, you're limited to what's available, so you have to be flexible.

9 Planning Your Trip Online

The benefits of researching and booking your trip online can be well worth the effort in terms of savings and choice. These days, Internet users can tap into the same travel-planning databases that were once accessible only to travel agents—and do it at lightning speed. Sites such as **Travelocity, Expedia,** and **Orbitz** allow consumers to quickly comparison-shop for airfares, access special bargains, book flights, and reserve hotel rooms and rental cars.

But don't fire your travel agent just yet. Although online booking sites offer tips and hard data to help you bargain-shop, they cannot endow you with the hard-earned experience that makes a seasoned, reliable travel agent an invaluable resource, even in the Internet age. And for consumers with a complex itinerary, a trusty travel agent is still the best way to arrange the most direct flights to and from the best airports.

Still, there's no denying the Internet's emergence as a powerful tool in researching and plotting travel time. The benefits of researching your trip online can really pay off:

- **Last-minute specials,** known as "E-savers," such as weekend deals or Internet-only fares, are offered by airlines to fill empty seats. Most of these are announced on Tuesday or Wednesday and must be purchased online. Some are only valid for travel that weekend, but some can be booked weeks or months in

Frommers.com: The Complete Travel Resource

For an excellent travel-planning resource, we highly recommend **Frommers.com** (www.frommers.com). We're a little biased, of course, but we guarantee that you'll find the travel tips, reviews, monthly vacation giveaways, and online-booking capabilities thoroughly indispensable. Among the special features are our popular **Message Boards**, where Frommer's readers post queries and share advice (sometimes even our authors show up to answer questions); **Frommers.com Newsletter**, for the latest travel bargains and inside travel secrets; and Frommer's **Destinations Section**, where you'll get expert travel tips, hotel and dining recommendations, and advice on the sights to see for more than 2,500 destinations around the globe. When your research is done, the **Online Reservation System** (www.frommers.com/booktravelnow) takes you to Frommer's favorite sites for booking your vacation at affordable prices.

advance. Sign up for weekly e-mail alerts at airline websites (see below) or check mega-sites that compile comprehensive lists of E-savers, such as **Smarter Living** (smarterliving.com) or **WebFlyer** (www.webflyer.com).

- Some sites will send you **e-mail notification** when a cheap fare becomes available to your favorite destination. Some will also tell you when fares to a particular destination are lowest.
- The best of the travel planning sites are now **highly personalized;** they track your frequent-flier miles, and store your seating and meal preferences, tentative itineraries, and credit-card information, letting you plan trips or check agendas quickly.
- All major airlines offer **incentives**—bonus frequent-flier miles, Internet-only discounts, sometimes even free cell-phone rentals—when you purchase online or buy an e-ticket.
- Advances in mobile technology provide business travelers and other frequent travelers with **the ability to check flight status, change plans, or get specific directions** from hand-held computing devices, mobile phones, and pagers. Some sites will e-mail or page a passenger if a flight is delayed.

TRAVEL PLANNING & BOOKING

The best travel planning and booking sites
domestic and international flights, hotel an
plus news, destination information, and
vacation packages. Keep in mind that free (one
often required for booking. Because several ai̇   no longer
willing to pay commissions on tickets sold by online travel agencies,
be aware that these online agencies will either charge a $10 sur-
charge if you book a ticket on that carrier or neglect to offer those
air carriers' services.

The sites in this section are not intended to be a comprehensive
list but rather a discriminating selection to get you started.
Recognition is given to sites based on their content value and ease
of use and is not paid for—unlike some website rankings, which are
based on payment. *Remember:* This is a press-time snapshot of
leading websites—some undoubtedly will have evolved or moved by
the time you read this.

- **Travelocity** (**www.travelocity.com** or www.frommers.
  travelocity.com) and **Expedia** (**www.expedia.com**) are the
  most longstanding and reputable sites, each offering excellent
  selections and searches for complete vacation packages.
  Travelers search by destination and dates coupled with how
  much they are willing to spend.
- **Orbitz** (**www.orbitz.com**) is a popular site launched by
  United, Delta, Northwest, American, and Continental airlines.
  It shows all possible fares for your desired trip, offering fares
  lower than those available through travel agents.
- **Qixo** (**www.qixo.com**) is another powerful search engine that
  allows you to search for flights and accommodations from
  some 20 airline and travel planning sites (such as Travelocity)
  at once. Qixo sorts results by price, after which you can book
  your travel directly through the site.

SMART E-SHOPPING
The savvy traveler is one armed with good information. Here are a
few tips to help you navigate the Internet successfully and safely:

- **Know when sales start.** Last-minute deals may vanish in
  minutes. If you have a favorite booking site or airline, find out
  when last-minute deals are released to the public. (For example, Southwest's specials are posted every Tuesday at 12:01am
  central time.)

Tips Staying Connected: Internet Cafes in Rio

- **Wollner Outdoor/Geographic Café,** Rua Visconde de Pirajá 511, Ipanema, offers Internet access with prepaid cards starting at R$3 ($1.50) for 15 minutes and R$5 ($2.50) for 30 minutes. Cards are reusable. Awesome cappuccinos in the cafe! Open Monday through Friday from 9am to 8pm and Saturday from 9am to 4pm. Bus: 415.
- **Acesse Aqui Cyber Cafe,** Rua Francisco Otaviano 67, loja K, Arpoador between Ipanema and Copacabana (✆ 021/247-8189), has one of the fastest connections in town and the prices are also reasonable. Each 15 minutes in cyberspace will set you back R$2.50 ($1.25). Open daily from 9am to 9pm. Bus: 415.
- **Telenet,** Rua Domingos Ferreira 59, loja B, Copacabana (✆ 021/2547-4946), has the best hours and lowest rates for some late-night surfing, charging R$2 ($1) for the first 15 minutes (minimum amount) and then R$0.08 per additional minute. Open Monday through Saturday from 9am to midnight and Sunday from 3 to 9pm. Metrô: Arcoverde.
- **Telerede,** Av. N.S. de Copacabana 209, loja A (✆ 021/3687-5200), has so many terminals that you will never have to wait in line. Internet access costs R$2 ($1) per 15 minutes. Open daily from 8am to 11pm. Metrô: Arcoverde.

- **Shop around.** Compare results from different sites and airlines—and against a travel agent's best fare, if you can. If possible, try a range of times and alternate airports before you make a purchase.
- **Follow the rules of the trade.** Book in advance, and choose an off-peak time and date if possible. Some sites will tell you when fares to a particular destination tend to be cheapest.
- **Stay secure.** Book only through secure sites (some airline sites are not secure). Look for a key icon (Netscape) or a padlock (Internet Explorer) at the bottom of your web browser before you enter credit-card information or other personal data.
- **Maintain a paper trail.** If you book an e-ticket, print out a confirmation, or write down your confirmation number, and keep it safe and accessible—or your trip could be a virtual one!

ONLINE TRAVELER'S TOOLBOX

Veteran travelers usually carry some essential ite
easier. Following is a selection of online tools to

- **Foreign Languages for Travelers (www.tra**
  basic terms in more than 70 languages and c⟋   under-
  lined phrase to hear what it sounds like. *Note:* Speakers and
  free audio software are required.
- **Intellicast (www.intellicast.com)**. Weather forecasts for all 50
  states and cities around the world.
- **Cybercafes.com (www.cybercafes.com)** or **Internet Café
  Guide (www.netcafeguide.com/mapindex.htm)**. Locate
  Internet cafes at hundreds of locations around the globe.
- **Universal Currency Converter (www.xe.net/currency)**. See
  what your dollar or pound is worth in more than 100 other
  countries.

Getting to Know Rio

Rio is a city whose reputation precedes it. Ask someone to picture Albuquerque or Tampa and odds are nothing much will come to mind. Say "Rio" and mental images explode: the statue of Christ, arms outspread on the mountaintop; the beaches at Ipanema and Copacabana, crowded with women in the most miniscule of bikinis; the rocky height of the Sugar Loaf; the persistent rhythm of samba; the glittering skimpy costumes of Carnaval. With some cities, the image is all there is. Fortunately in Rio, there's much more beyond the glittering mental images: historic neighborhoods and compelling architecture; dining fine and not so fine, nightspots, bookshops, cafes, museums; and enclaves of rich and poor. In Rio, the more you explore, the more there is.

1 Orientation

ARRIVING
BY PLANE

ANTONIO CARLOS JOBIM AIRPORT Rio de Janeiro's Antonio Carlos Jobim Airport (© **0800/99-9099**) is where all international flights and most national flights arrive. Located 12 miles (20km) from downtown, this airport was recently renamed after the legendary bossa nova composer who wrote "The Girl from Ipanema," but most locals still refer to it as **Galeão Airport.** Terminal 2 has just been inaugurated, connected to Terminal 1 by a walkway.

You will find the Banco do Brasil office and ATMs on the third floor in Terminal 1. These ATMs are compatible with the Visa/Plus system. To exchange money, you can use the Banco do Brasil, open daily from 8am to 10pm, or the American Express office, located in the arrival hall of Terminal 2, open daily from 6:30am to 10:30pm.

There are several types of taxis at the airport. The most comfortable ones are the radio taxis, usually with air-conditioning, that allow you to prepay the fee to your destination. That way it doesn't matter whether the driver takes the long route or you get stuck in

---

> **(Tips** **Do Your Duty-Free Shopping Upon Arrival**
>
> Unlike airports in Europe and North America, the interna-
> tional airport in Rio de Janeiro has a duty-free shop upon
> arrival **before clearing customs,** where you can purchase up
> to $500 of goods.

---

traffic. They are usually a little bit more expensive but give you
peace of mind. Buy prepaid vouchers at the **Transcoopass** desk in
the arrival hall (© **021/2560-4888**). Rates vary from R$38 to R$43
($19–$21.50) to Centro and Flamengo and R$58 to R$65
($29–$32.50) to the beach hotels of Copacabana and Ipanema.
Regular taxis can be hailed from outside the terminal. Meters start
at R$2.30 ($1.15) and a ride to Copacabana should cost about
R$45 ($23) in average traffic conditions, less in light traffic, and
much more if there's a traffic jam.

　　Realtur/Reitur Turismo (© **0800/24-0850** or 021/2560-7041)
runs an airport bus service to the major tourist areas along the
beaches of Flamengo, Botafogo, Copacabana, Ipanema, Leblon, and
Barra da Tijuca. From 5:30am to 11pm, a bus departs every half
hour and takes approximately 1 hour to make the full trip from the
airport to Barra; the fare is R$4 ($2) per person. Please note that it
only stops along the beach avenue. Please check with your hotel to
see if it is located within walking distance of the bus stop and
whether it is advisable to do so.

SANTOS DUMONT AIRPORT　Rio's second airport, Santos
Dumont, Praça Senador Salgado Filho (© **0800/24-4646**), is
located downtown. Surrounded on three sides by the Baia de
Guanabara (Guanabara Bay) and a hop and a skip from Sugar Loaf
Mountain and the Flamengo and Botafogo beaches, this small and
scenic airport is used by the TAM, VASP, and Varig, as well as by
some flights to Brasilia, Belo Horizonte, and a few other national
destinations. The airport is within walking distance of downtown,
but do not attempt this with your luggage as it involves crossing a
number of major streets with hectic traffic, both car and pedestrian.
The Realtur bus from the Galeão picks up travelers on its way to
Barra as well as on its way to the airport. From Santos Dumont to
Copacabana takes approximately 30 minutes. Regular taxis are
available in front of the airport; a ride to Ipanema will cost about
R$20 ($10), or a prepaid voucher can be purchased at the taxi

counter in the arrivals hall. A Banco do Brasil ATM is located on the mezzanine level, up the spiral staircase.

BY BUS

All long-distance buses arrive at the **Novo Rio Rodoviaria,** Av. Francisco Bicalho 1, Santo Cristo (℃ **021/2291-5151**), just 5 minutes from downtown in the old port section of the city. The most convenient way to get from there to your destination in Rio is by taxi. Despite its closeness to downtown, it's not a good idea to walk with all your belongings. Prepaid taxi vouchers are available at the booth next to the taxi stand. A ride from the bus station to Ipanema will cost about R$28 ($14) prepaid.

BY CRUISE SHIP

Arrivals by water will dock in the cruise ship terminal almost opposite the Praça Mauá. From there, the entire downtown is within walking distance and public transit is close by. Please note that the area around Praça Mauá, a business district during the day, turns into a red-light district in the evenings.

VISITOR INFORMATION

Riotur (℃ **021/2217-7575;** www.riodejaneiro-turismo.com.br) provides information on the city of Rio de Janeiro and operates a number of offices and kiosks around town. At Rio's international airport, you will find a booth in the international arrivals hall of Terminal 1, open daily from 6am to noon, and one in the international arrivals hall of Terminal 2, open daily from 6am to noon and 5 to 11pm. There's also a booth in the domestic arrivals hall, open from 6am to noon and 5 to 11pm. People arriving at Rio's main bus station, Rodoviaria Novo Rio, can pick up information in the arrivals area from 8am to 8pm. The main **Riotur information center** (℃ **021/2541-7522**) is located on Av. Princesa Isabel 183, Copacabana. Open Monday through Friday from 9am to 6pm, this office has the largest selection of brochures and information. This office also operates an information phone line, **Alô Rio** (℃ **021/ 2542-8080**), with English-speaking staff. They can be reached Monday through Friday from 9am to 6pm.

A must-have is Riotur's *Rio Incomparavel* booklet, published quarterly. This guide in both English and Portuguese lists all tourist attractions, events, festivals, and many useful phone numbers. In addition to this booklet, Riotur also publishes a number of brochures specifically on outdoor sports, museums, and Carnaval. The office in Copacabana is most likely to stock all these publications.

The state of Rio de Janeiro offers tourist information for destinations outside of the city. The **TurisRio** office, Rua da Ajuda 5, 6th and 12th floors, Centro (© **021/2544-7992;** www.turisrio.rj.gov.br), is open Monday through Friday from 9am to 6pm.

Embratur, the national tourism association, has an office in downtown Rio at Rua Uruguaiana 174, 8th floor, Centro (© **021/2509-6017;** www.embratur.gov.br). Unfortunately, this office seems to be perpetually out of brochures and folders.

CITY LAYOUT

Geography has had a huge influence on Rio, with the city squeezing itself into whatever space was available between mountain and ocean. Rio is normally divided into three zones: *Zona Norte* (north), *Centro* (central), and *Zona Sul* (south).

THE NEIGHBORHOODS IN BRIEF

Zona Norte   Largest and least interesting from a visitor's perspective, the Zona Norte stretches from a few blocks north of Avenida Presidente Vargas all the way to the city limits. With only a few bright exceptions—the Maracanã stadium, the Quinta da Boa Vista gardens, and Galeão Airport—the region is a dull swath of port, industrial suburb, and *favelas* (shantytowns). After dark, it is not the sort of place one should wander unaccompanied.

Centro   The oldest part of the city, Rio's Centro neighborhood contains most of the city's notable churches, squares, monuments, and museums, as well as the modern office towers where Rio's white-collar elite earn their daily bread. Roughly speaking, Centro stretches from the São Bento Monastery in the north to the seaside Monument to the Dead of World War II in the south, and from Praça XV on the waterfront east to the Sambodromo (near Praça XI).

South of Centro   Just to the south of Centro lies the fun and slightly bohemian hilltop neighborhood of **Santa Teresa,** and then one after the other the neighborhoods of **Glória, Catete,** and **Flamengo.** These last three were the fashionable sections of the city around the start of the 20th century, located as they were on flat ground by the edge of Guanabara Bay. Other neighborhoods in this section of the city include **Botafogo** and **Urca** (nestled beneath the Sugar Loaf), and in the narrow valley behind Flamengo, the two residential neighborhoods of **Laranjeiras** and **Cosme Velho.** Though not actually in downtown, all of these neighborhoods fall within the broader category of Centro. Today they're all still pleasant and walkable, but their fortunes all faded in the 1920s when engineers finally succeeded in cutting a tunnel through the mountainside to Copacabana.

Zona Sul & the Beaches   Then, as now, the big attraction was the ocean. Where Centro and Flamengo sit on Guanabara Bay, Zona Sul neighborhoods such as **Copacabana, Ipanema, São Conrado,** and **Barra de Tijuca** face the open Atlantic. The waves are bigger, the water cleaner, and the beaches more inviting. First to be developed, Copacabana officially covers only the lower two-thirds of the beach. The northernmost third (the bit closest to Urca, furthest from Ipanema) is known as **Leme.** That said, it's impossible to tell where Leme ends and Copa begins. Taking a 90° turn around a low headland, one comes to Ipanema. Like Copacabana, Ipanema is a very modern neighborhood, consisting almost exclusively of high-rise apartments from the 1960s and '70s. Here, too, the same stretch of beach is considered to be two neighborhoods: Ipanema sits next to Copacabana, while the area at the far end of the beach is known as **Leblon.** Again, aside from there being possibly a few more restaurants in Leblon, the two ends of the beach are nearly indistinguishable. Behind Ipanema, in place of a mountain there's a lagoon, the Lagoa Rodrigo de Freitas. Known universally and without exception simply as **Lagoa,** this body of water is circled by a pleasant 5¼-mile (8km) walking/cycling trail. At its north end, farthest from the beach, stand the two quiet residential neighborhoods of **Lagoa** and **Jardim Botânico,** the latter named for the extensive botanical gardens around which the area grew up.

At the far end of Ipanema stands a tall, sheer, double-pointed rock called the *Pedra Dois Irmãos* (Two Brothers Rock). The road carries on, winding around the cliff face to reach the tiny enclave of **São Conrado.** One of the better surfing beaches, this is also where the hang gliders like to land after swooping down from the 830-meter Pedra de Gâvea. Beyond São Conrado, the road goes up on stilts to sneak beneath the cliffs until reaching Barra de Tijuca. More like Miami Beach than Rio, Barra—as it's usually called—is a land of big streets, big malls, big cars, and little intrinsic interest.

Backstopping all of these Zona Sul neighborhoods is the massive **Tijuca National Park.** Mostly mountainous, the 3,300-hectare forest was begun in the 1800s as a personal project of the Emperor Dom Pedro II. It's invariably shown on maps as one big swatch of green, but, in fact, any number of favelas have taken over parkland, usually in areas adjacent to official city neighborhoods. The park that's left—and there's lots of it—is cut through with excellent walking and hiking trails, many leading to peaks with fabulous views. Climb to the top of the Pico de Tijuca (1,022m) on a sunny day and beneath your feet you'll have a view of every neighborhood in Rio.

2 Getting Around

BY PUBLIC TRANSPORTATION

Rio may seem like a large and sprawling city, but the neighborhoods in which visitors spend most of their time are very easy to get around in. From Centro south to São Conrado, the neighborhoods hang like beads on a string on the narrow strip of land between the ocean and the mountains. Most neighborhoods are thin and narrow; Copacabana is in some sections only 5 blocks deep. You can almost always see the mountains or the ocean or both. With landmarks like that, it's pretty hard to stray too far from where you want to go.

BY SUBWAY

By far the easiest way to get around is by subway. Rio's subway network is not extensive compared to London or New York but in Centro and the Zona Sul, it covers almost all the major areas of interest. (The exception is Ipanema/Leblon, which isn't slated to get subway service for another 4 or 5 years.) There are only two lines: Line 1 goes northwards from downtown. It's useful for going to the Maracanã and the Quinta da Boa Vista. Line 2 starts at the Central Station and goes south, covering most of Centro, then swinging thorough Glória, Catete, Flamengo, and Botafogo before ducking through the mountain to its final destination in Copacabana. Extremely quick, the ride takes about 20 minutes to move you from Centro to Copacabana (as compared to a 40- to 60-min. bus ride in rush hour). The system is very safe and efficient. You purchase tickets at the station entrances, either from a machine or from a ticket booth. A single ride costs R$1.30 (65¢) and a double ride R$2.60 ($1.30); the only advantage of the double ticket is that you don't have to line up twice. There are no day passes but if you plan to use the subway a lot, you can purchase a 10-ride card for R$12 ($6).

BY BUS

Buses in Rio are a revelation. Where North American city buses seem to meander along from point A to point B via all other stops in the alphabet, Rio's buses follow direct, logical pathways, sticking to the main streets along much the same route you'd take if you were

---

> (*Tips* **Know the Subway Hours**
>
> The subway operates Monday through Saturday from 6am to
> 11pm. The subway does not operate on Sunday and statutory
> holidays, except for New Year's and Carnaval, when there are
> special schedules.

---

driving. What's more, they're fast. Indeed, once inside it's a good
idea to hang on or wedge yourself in your seat; Rio drivers like to
lean into the turns.

Some of the more important routes are listed with hotel or attraction listings, but you'll likely find many more that suit your needs.
From Centro to Copacabana alone there are more than 30 different
buses. Figuring out which to take is quite straightforward. The route
number and final destination are displayed in big letters on the front
of the bus. Smaller signs displayed inside the front window (usually
below and to the left of the driver) and posted on the side of the bus
list the intermediate stops. Armed with that information and a map,
it's fairly straightforward to figure out which route the bus will take
and how close you will get to your destination. A bus going from
Praça XV in Centro out to Copacabana, for example, would show
Copacabana as the final destination, and on the smaller sign list
intermediate destinations such as Cinelândia, Glória, Largo do
Machado (in Catete), and Rio Sul (the big mall in Botafogo). *Tip:*
If you're going from Ipanema or Copacabana all the way to Centro
(or vice versa), look for a bus that says VIA ATERRO in its smaller win-
dow sign. These buses get on the big waterfront boulevard in
Botafogo and don't stop again until they reach downtown.

Buses only stop if someone wants to board. If you see your bus
coming, wave your hand up and down at the driver. Buses are
boarded from the rear and exited from the front. Have your bus
money ready—R$1 to R$1.50 (50¢–75¢)—as you will go through
a turnstile right away. You pay for each ride; there are no transfers.
Buses are quite safe during the day, just watch for pickpockets when
it gets very busy. Later in the evening (say after 11pm), particularly
on weeknights when there are fewer passengers, it may be better to
take a taxi.

BY TAXI

Taxis are plentiful and relatively inexpensive. They're the perfect way
to reach out-of-the-way places and the best way to get around late

at night. Regular taxis can be hailed anywhere on the street. You will also find taxi stands throughout the city. A ride from Copacabana to Praça XV in Centro will cost about R$16 ($8), a ride from the main bus station to Leblon R$20 ($10) in traffic. Radio taxis are about 20% more expensive and can be contacted by phone. Try **Coopertramo** (© 021/2560-2022) or **Transcoopass** (© 021/2560-4888). Most hotels work with radio taxis, so if you don't want to pay extra, just walk to the corner and hail your own. The advantage of radio taxis is that they have air-conditioning and are supposedly more reliable, but we've never had a problem with any of the regular taxis.

BY FERRY

Rio has a number of ferries operated by **Barcas SA** (© 021/2533-6661), departing from Praça XV downtown. The busiest ferry route is the one connecting downtown Rio with the city of Niterói across the bay. The service to Niterói runs 24 hours a day, with hourly service between midnight and 5am. The cheapest ferry is the regular one, taking about 25 minutes to cross; it costs R$1 (50¢). The catamaran and *aerobarco,* a hydrofoil, cross the same route in less than 5 minutes and cost R$4.50 ($2.25). A popular ferry for tourists as well as Cariocas on the weekend is the route to Paquetá, a large car-free island in Guanabara Bay. The ferries to Paquetá depart Rio at 5:15am, 7:10am, 10:30am, 1:30pm, 4pm, 5:45pm, and 7pm, and the ride costs R$4.50 ($2.25).

BY CAR

A car is not really required for exploring Rio, as a combination of public transit in the daytime and evening with taxis late at night gets you pretty much anywhere in the city for very little money. But for information about renting a car, see the entry for "Car Rentals" under "Fast Facts: Rio de Janeiro," below.

The truth is that driving in Rio is not for the meek of soul or weak of heart. Traffic is hectic, street patterns confusing, and drivers just a few shades shy of courteous. Better to get used to the city traffic as a pedestrian for a few days and rent a car only if you are going out to destinations such as Petrópolis and the historic towns of Minas Gerais. Roads are usually good, but things get a little hectic later at night when drivers start to look on red lights as merely optional. Be careful when approaching intersections.

SPECIAL DRIVING RULES   The special rules are that there are no rules. OK, that may be a bit exaggerated. Traffic has actually improved by huge amounts in the last 6 years since new transit laws came into effect and police began relying heavily on photo-radar (a tragedy for all the would-be Ayrton Sennas who had to begin paying attention to the speed limit). People now wear seat belts and stop at red lights during the day. However, they still have a very aggressive style of driving. Lane dividers are often absent and when present are used as a suggestion only.

 FAST FACTS: Rio de Janeiro

American Express There's an office at Av. Atlântica 1702, loja 1, Copacabana (© **021/2548-2148**), open Monday through Friday from 9am to 4pm. There's also an office in the Galeão Airport arrivals hall of Terminal 2 (© **021/3398-4251**); it's open daily from 6:30am to 10:30pm.

Area Codes   Rio de Janeiro 021, Petrópolis 024, Búzios 022.

Babysitters Contact the hotel concierge regarding babysitting services. Often the housekeeping staff will provide babysitting services.

Business Hours Stores are usually open weekdays from 9am to 7pm, and Saturdays from 9am to 2pm. Shopping centers are open Monday through Saturday from 10am to 8pm and Sunday from 2 to 8pm. Banks are open Monday through Friday either from 10am to 4pm or from 9am to 3pm.

Camera Repair **Foto Cantarino,** Largo de São Francisco de Paulo 23, first floor (© **021/2221-4918;** Metrô: Uruguaiana), is one of the best repair shops in town. It's open Monday through Friday from 9am to 4:30pm.

Car Rentals **Hertz** has offices at both of Rio's airports, and at Av. Princesa Isabel 334, Copacabana (© **021/2275-7440**). Other car companies include **Interlocadora,** Galeão Airport (© **021/2398-3181**) and Santos Dumont Airport (© **021/2240-0754**); **Localiza Rent a Car,** Av. Princesa Isabel 214, Copacabana (© **021/2275-3340**); and **Unidas,** Galeão Airport (© **021/3398-3452**) and Santos Dumont airport (© **021/2240-6715**). Rates start at R$100 ($50) per day for a compact car with air-conditioning. Insurance adds another R$30 ($15) per day.

Cellphone Rentals Cariocas are certainly cellphone happy, and if you're an avid cellphone user, you can expect to develop a serious case of cellphone envy (see "Telephone," below). Fortunately, it's not too late to rent one. **PressCell** (✆ **021/3322-2692** or 021/9617-2000; www.presscell.com) will deliver right to your hotel. Call for a free estimate.

Consulates **Australia,** Av. Presidente Wilson 231, Suite 23, Centro (✆ **021/3824-4624**). **Canada,** Rua Lauro Muller 116, Suite 2707, Centro (✆ **021/2543-3004**). **United States,** Av. Presidente Wilson 147, Centro (✆ **021/2292-7117**). **Great Britain,** Praia do Flamengo 284, Flamengo (✆ **021/2553-3223**).

Currency Exchange **Banco do Brasil** has branches at Rua do Acre, Centro (✆ 021/2223-2537); and Av. N.S. de Copacabana 594, Copacabana (✆ 021/2548-8992); and Galeão Airport Terminal 1, third floor (✆ 021/3398-3652).

Other places to exchange money include **BankBoston,** Av. Rio Branco 110, Centro (✆ 021/2508-2700); **Citibank** at Rua da Assambleia 100, Centro (✆ 021/2291-1232); and **Imatur,** Rua Visconde de Pirajá 281, loja A, Ipanema (✆ 021/2219-4205).

Dentists/Doctors For medical attention, contact **Galdino Campos Cardio Copa,** Av. N.S. de Copacabana 492, Copacabana (✆ **021/2548-9966**), or **Medtur,** Avenida N.S. de Copacabana, Copacabana (✆ **021/2235-3339**).

Ask at your hotel for further recommendations, as they may have an arrangement with a doctor nearby.

Electricity Generally Rio's voltage is 110V. Some hotels have plugs for both 110 and 220 volts.

Emergencies Police ✆ **190**; Fire and Ambulance ✆ **193**; Tourist Police, Av. Afranio de Melo Franco 159, Leblon (24-hr. contact line ✆ **021/3399-7170**).

Hospitals Emergency rooms can be found at **Miguel Couto,** Rua Bartolemeu Mitre 1108, Leblon (✆ **021/2274-6050**), and **Rocha Maia,** Rua General Severiano 91, Botafogo (✆ **021/ 2295-2121**).

Language The language of Brazil is Portuguese. If you speak Spanish, you will certainly have an easier time picking up words and understanding Portuguese. If you are picking up language books or tapes, make sure they are Brazilian Portuguese and not Portuguese from Portugal—big difference!

Laundry/Dry Cleaning **Lavanderia Ipanema,** Rua Farme de Amoedo 55, Ipanema (✆ **021/2267-2377**), is open Monday through Saturday from 7:30am to 9pm. For a medium load, washing and drying will cost R$11 ($5.50). For an extra R$3.50

($1.75), the attendant will look after everything and you just return to pick up your laundry nicely folded and packed. **Lavakilo,** Rua Almirante Gonçalves 50, loja A, Copacabana (✆ 021/2521-5089), is open Monday through Friday from 7:30am to 7:30pm and Saturday from 8am to 5pm. Charged by the kilo, a 1-kilo load will set you back R$5 ($2.50) for washing and drying and an extra R$5 ($2.50) for ironing everything. Dry cleaning starts at R$6.50 ($3.25) per item.

Liquor Laws Officially, Brazil's drinking laws only allow those over 18 years to drink alcohol. Beer, wine, and liquor can be bought any day of the week from supermarkets, grocery stores, and delis.

Mail Mail from Brazil is quick and efficient. You will find post offices all over town—look for the yellow-and-blue sign saying "CORREIOS." The downtown branch is at Rua Primeira de Março 64, Centro (✆ 021/2503-8331). A postcard or letter to Europe or North America costs R$1.20 (60¢). Parcels can be sent through FedEx or regular mail (express or common; a small parcel costs about R$30 ($15) by common mail and takes about a week).

Maps Alas, it is tough to find good maps in Rio, or in Brazil for that matter. Riotur (✆ 021/2217/-7575; www.riodejaneiro-turismo.com.br) has some helpful small maps of the main tourist areas. A good map book for sale at newsstands is the *Guia Quatro Rodas—Mapas das Capitais.* This pocket-sized booklet comes with maps of all the state capitals of Brazil with street indices.

Newspapers *O Globo* and *O Jornal do Brasil* are the two best-selling daily newspapers in Rio. Newspapers and magazines are sold through *bancas de jornais* (newsstands). Your best bet for international papers are the stands along Visconde de Pirajá in Ipanema and the bookstore **Letras e Expressões,** Visconde de Pirajá 276, Ipanema (✆ 021/2521-6110).

Pharmacies In Ipanema, **City Farma,** Rua Gomes Carneiro 144 A (✆ 021/2247-3000 or 021/2523-2020; www.farma24h. com.br), is open 24 hours and delivers any time of the day as well. All credit cards accepted. Also open 24 hours is **Drogaria Pacheco,** Av. N.S. de Copacabana 115, Copacabana (✆ 021/2295-7555).

Restrooms Public washrooms are scarce, except in parks or attractions where you often have to pay a small amount, usually R$0.25 to R$1 (13¢–50¢). Your best bet is to try a hotel or restaurant. *Mulher* (or "M") is for women; *Homem* (or "H") is for men.

Taxes The city of Rio charges a 5% accommodations tax, collected by the hotel operators. This amount will be added to your bill. There are no other taxes on retail items or goods.

Telephone International cellphones usually don't work in Brazil. Public phones can be found everywhere and are called *orelhões* (big ears), as the cover is shaped like a giant ear. To use these phones, you need a phone card, for sale at all newsstands. Ask for a *"cartão telefonico."* The dialing is where it gets interesting. You will often see numbers listed, for example, as 0-XX-21-3199-0449. Since the deregulation of phone companies, there are now a variety of *prestadora* (service providers); the two digits that fill in the XX are the appropriate service provider. The only provider that works in all of Brazil is Embratel and its code is 21 (which also happens to be the area code of Rio). Whenever you see the "XX" in a phone number and you are dialing long distance, you need to insert the "21." To phone internationally, dial 0+21+ the country code + area code + phone number. International collect calls can be requested by dialing **000-111,** or dialing directly 90+21+ country code + area code + phone number.

Time Zone Rio de Janeiro is 3 hours behind Greenwich mean time; this means that it is 2 hours later than it is in New York and 5 hours later than Los Angeles. During daylight saving time, Rio's time difference changes to 2 hours behind GMT, making it 3 hours later than in New York and 6 hours later than in Los Angeles.

Tipping A 10% service charge is automatically included on most restaurant and hotel bills, and you are not expected to tip on top of this amount. Taxi drivers do not get tipped; just round up the amount to facilitate change. Hairdressers and beauticians usually receive a 10% tip. Bellboys get tipped R$1 (50¢) per bag. Room service usually includes the 10% service charge on the bill.

Vaccinations Should you require any further vaccinations, contact the **Health Office** at Rua Mexico 128, Centro (© **021/ 2240-3568**). Vaccinations are given Monday through Friday from 10am to 11am and 2 to 3pm.

Visa Renewal Your visa is valid for 90 days from the day of arrival. If you are staying longer than 90 days, you need to extend your visa at the **Policia Federal,** Av. Venezuela 2, Centro, just behind the Praça Mauá (© **021/2291-2142**). It's open Monday through Friday from 10am to 5pm. The fee is R$60 ($30), and you may need to show evidence of sufficient funds to cover the remainder of your stay as well as a return ticket.

4

Where to Stay

Though Rio boasts a huge number of hotels, there's surprisingly little variety: no pleasant *pousadas* (small inn or B&B), not even many heritage buildings. The vast majority of hotels are in modern high-rises, many built in the 1960s and '70s, most with a similar layout and design. The difference between hotels thus lies in the location, the room size, the amenities, and of course, the view.

The best-known hotel area is Copacabana, with easy access via metrô back to the city core, and a good selection of inexpensive hotels close to the beach.

One beach over from Copacabana, Ipanema and Leblon have become increasingly popular over the past decade and now boast better nightlife and trendier shopping than Copa. The only real disadvantage to staying here is the lack of a subway line, but there are lots and lots of buses.

Back towards downtown you'll find the lively and more historic neighborhoods Glória, Catete, and Flamengo. Located only a 10- to 15-minute subway ride from both downtown and Copacabana, they offer a good range of hotels, with some excellent budget options as well as luxury accommodations that rival the Copacabana Palace but at a much better price.

Hotel rates in Rio are often all over the map. In the lobby, hotels always list the rack rates on a sign behind the desk, but you can usually expect to pay 50% to 80% of this amount, depending on the season, the staff member you're dealing with, and your bargaining skills. As prices really are quite flexible, always negotiate. It can make a big difference to ask for a better price (*preço melhor,* pronounced *pray*-so *may*-yore). Sometimes just paying with cash instead of a credit card can result in a 10% to 15% discount. Make sure to ask about taxes that will be added to your bill. Most hotels charge a 10% service tax, a 5% city tax, and, if they are a member of the Rio Convention and Visitor's bureau, a tourist tax of R$2 to R$6 ($1–$3) per day.

Tips **Where *Not* to Stay in Rio**

The only neighborhood to avoid hotel-wise is downtown Rio. The hotels around the Praça Mauá may look like a bargain, but that's because this area transforms into a red-light district at night when the office workers have gone home.

Breakfast (*café de manha*) at Brazilian hotels is almost always included and at most places includes a nice buffet-style spread including bread, assorted meats, cheeses and fruits, eggs (sometimes), and *café com leite,* strong coffee served with hot milk. In recent years a few of the more expensive hotels have taken to charging for *café de manha;* if this is the case, we've noted it in the review.

The only time of year for which it's difficult to get good deals is during high season—from the week before Christmas until Carnaval in February. The city is literally swamped, not only with visitors from overseas but also with tourists from Argentina and Brazilians taking their summer holidays. New Year's and Carnaval are the cash cows for the tourism industry and hotels milk them for all they're worth. None of the rates listed here apply during those periods. The majority of hotels only accept reservations for set package deals—usually a 2- or 3-night minimum stay for New Year's and a 5-night minimum stay for Carnaval—at highly inflated prices. Shop around ahead of time if you're going to be in Rio during these events, as packages (especially the less expensive ones) sell out by October or November. Most hotels now have websites and will provide quick information upon request.

1 Ipanema & Leblon

The beach neighborhoods of Ipanema and Leblon are a popular destination for many visitors. There are a number of affordable hotel options as well as some outstanding luxury accommodations. The neighborhood itself is very safe and clean, with many upscale apartment buildings and some of the best shopping, dining, and nightlife in Rio. The only drawback is that it's a bit far from downtown and as yet lacks a subway connection. The bus ride into Centro is normally about 40 minutes, but during weekday rush hours, it can be up to an hour.

Where to Stay in Ipanema, Leblon & Copacabana

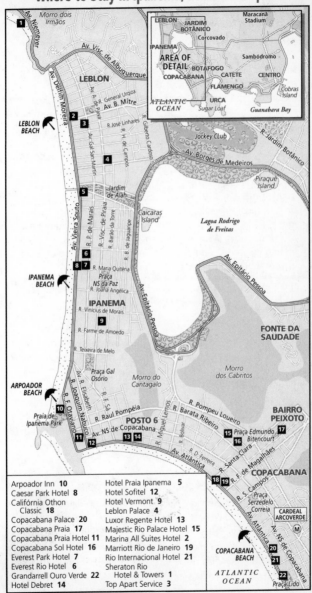

Arpoador Inn **10**
Caesar Park Hotel **8**
Califórnia Othon
    Classic **18**
Copacabana Palace **20**
Copacabana Praia **17**
Copacabana Praia Hotel **11**
Copacabana Sol Hotel **16**
Everest Park Hotel **7**
Everest Rio Hotel **6**
Grandarrell Ouro Verde **22**
Hotel Debret **14**

Hotel Praia Ipanema **5**
Hotel Sofitel **12**
Hotel Vermont **9**
Leblon Palace **4**
Luxor Regente Hotel **13**
Majestic Rio Palace Hotel **15**
Marina All Suites Hotel **2**
Marriott Rio de Janeiro **19**
Rio Internacional Hotel **21**
Sheraton Rio
    Hotel & Towers **1**
Top Apart Service **3**

Tips The No-Tell Motel

A motel in Brazil is a very different thing from a motel in America. Brazilian motel rentals are strictly short-term, and strictly for sex. They're used by young couples looking to escape from parents and in-laws, older couples looking to escape from kids, and cheating couples looking to escape from spouses. Despite the carnal focus, there's really nothing sleazy about them. Most Brazilians live at home until they get married and though moral standards have changed, premarital sex is still somewhat taboo. Once married, couples often live with in-laws or other relatives, making it difficult to find privacy. Motels provide a perfect escape, with affordable hourly rates and 4- to 6-hour specials. Though none are listed below, they're certainly worth trying out, even if you're just looking for a bit of short-term luxury. Some motels have luxurious suites with Jacuzzis or hot tubs, saunas, or even swimming pools, and many offer free lunch or dinner to attract couples during off-peak hours.

VERY EXPENSIVE

Caesar Park Hotel ★★★   One of Rio's most luxurious hotels, the Caesar Park is very popular with visiting Americans, both tourists and business travelers alike. The location is fabulous, directly facing the most famous stretch of Ipanema beach, and close to the neighborhood's swanky shops, excellent restaurants, and bars. The hotel has just undergone major renovations and is in tip-top shape. All 220 rooms received new furniture, mattresses, carpets, and soundproof windows, and the bathrooms were completely redone with granite counters and tile. The rooms are all spacious—even the standard rooms—and each comes with a bathtub, suit rack, large luggage rack, and a well-lit work space. The usual "view hierarchy" applies. The standard rooms are those from the 5th to 10th floors, looking out over the side street. Superior rooms face the same way as standard rooms but are located from the 11th floor up. The deluxe rooms provide an ocean view. Unfortunately, the building has alcoves around the windows that restrict views to the side. For the ultimate in luxury reserve the junior suite. The elegantly furnished sitting room offers front and side views towards Copacabana or Leblon.

Av. Vieira Souto 460, Ipanema, Rio de Janeiro, RJ 22420-000. ✆ 021/2525-2525. Fax 021/2521-6000. www.caesar-park.com. 220 units. R$600 ($300) standard;

R$680 ($340) superior; R$736 ($368) oceanview deluxe; R$1,016 ($508) junior suite. Higher rates during New Year's and Carnaval. Extra person R$60 ($30). Children 12 and under stay free in parents' room. AE, DC, MC, V. Free valet parking. Bus: 415. **Amenities:** Restaurant, bar; rooftop pool; excellent health club; sauna; concierge; tour desk; car-rental desk; business center; shopping arcade; 24-hr. room service; massage; babysitting; laundry service; dry cleaning; nonsmoking rooms; executive-level rooms. *In room:* A/C, TV, dataport, minibar, fridge, hair dryer, safe.

Everest Rio Hotel 🐒🐒

Unassuming from the outside, this elegant hotel provides surprisingly luxurious accommodations on the inside. All rooms are very bright and beautifully appointed thanks to a recent and complete renovation. Large closets, a good-size desk, and separate table add to the spacious feel of the rooms. And though the hotel is a block off the beach, views from the higher floors are none too shabby, looking either towards the lagoon and the mountains or out to the ocean. Unlike other hotels, there are no extra charges for a room with a view, so remember to book up when reserving. Well worth the splurge are the junior or executive suites, which feature sitting rooms and wonderfully large bedrooms elegantly decorated in pale colors. Breakfast in the Grill 360 Degrees on the 23rd floor features outstanding views of Ipanema and Lagoa.

Rua Prudente de Morais 1117, Ipanema, Rio de Janeiro, RJ 22420-041. (℃) 021/2523-2282. www.everest.com.br. R$300 ($150) standard double; R$360 ($180) deluxe double; R$594 ($297) suite. Children under 8 stay free in parents' room, 8 over 25% extra. AE, DC, MC, V. Parking R$15 ($7.50) per day. Bus: 474. **Amenities:** 2 restaurants, bar; rooftop pool; business center; 24-hr. room service; babysitting; laundry service. *In room:* A/C, TV, dataport, minibar, fridge, safe.

Marina All Suites Hotel 🐒🐒🐒 *Finds*

The Marina All Suites is the brainchild of a consortium of local architects and decorators who bought, gutted, replanned, and redecorated all the rooms, in the process reducing the original layout of six rooms per floor to a very spacious three. What must surely be the most beautiful suite in Rio is the two-bedroom Suite Diamante. Looking out the large windows, it seems like the room adjoins the ocean, the white tones of the room merging with Ipanema's white sands and the blue ocean beyond. All suites feature an American kitchen (microwave, fridge, and wet bar), ample desk space and sitting areas, spacious bathrooms, and large bedrooms, making this truly one of Rio's most outstanding hotels. On the top floor, there's a business center and reading lounge. For those rare rainy days, pretend you're a celebrity in your own DVD movie theater; just pick a movie and get comfortable in one of the eight leather chairs.

Av. Delfim Moreira 696, Leblon, Rio de Janeiro, RJ 22441-000. (℃) 021/2540-4990. Fax 021/2294-1644. www.marinaallsuites.com.br. 38 units (some with shower only). R$360–R$420 ($180–$210) deluxe; R$440–R$600 ($220–$300) master and junior suites; R$840 ($420) Suite Diamante. AE, DC, MC, V. Free parking. Bus: 474. **Amenities:** Restaurant; pool; excellent gym; sauna; game room; concierge; business center; 24-hr. room service; massage; babysitting; laundry service. *In room:* A/C, TV, dataport, kitchen, minibar, fridge, coffeemaker, hair dryer, safe.

EXPENSIVE

Everest Park Hotel 🎎🎎

Less luxurious than its sister hotel the Everest Rio, the Everest Park is also cheaper, making it a reasonable option for travelers looking to economize. All 25 units have Internet access and dataports and large workspaces upon which to spread out papers. The rooms themselves are also spacious, with a small hallway area at the entrance opening up to two twin beds. (Reserve a double bed when booking and the staff will join the twins together to make a comfortable double.) Recent renovations have added new carpets, and the bathrooms have also been redone and now feature bathtubs, large bright mirrors, and hair dryers.

Rua Maria Quiteria 19, Ipanema, Rio de Janeiro, RJ 22410-040. © 0800/24-4485 or 021/2525-2200. www.everest.com.br. 25 units. R$250 ($125) double. Up to 25% discount in low season and weekends. No discount for children. AE, DC, MC, V. No parking. Bus: 474. **Amenities:** Limited room service; laundry service. *In room:* A/C, TV, dataport, minibar, fridge, safe.

Hotel Praia Ipanema 🎎🎎🎎

Straddling the border between Ipanema and Leblon, the Praia Ipanema offers luxury beachside accommodations at a less-than-luxury price. All of the 101 units offer ocean views, a full one in the case of the 55 deluxe rooms and a partial (from the side) view for the 46 standard rooms. The best rooms begin at the 10th floor and carry upwards, as the views of strand and sea get ever more spectacular. All rooms are very large, elegantly furnished, and each has a balcony. The hotel also offers a number of excellent amenities. The business center with its friendly staff has some of the best Internet rates of all luxury hotels: R$6 ($3) for 30 minutes or R$12 ($6) for 1 hour. The outstanding breakfast buffet is served in the elegant La Mouette restaurant overlooking Ipanema beach.

Av. Vieira Souto 706, Ipanema, Rio de Janeiro, RJ 22420-000. © 021/2540-4949. Fax 021/2239-6889. www.praiaipanema.com. 101 units. R$290 ($145) standard double; R$360 ($180) deluxe-view double. AE, DC, MC, V. No parking. Bus: 474 or 404. **Amenities:** Restaurant, 2 bars; rooftop outdoor pool; beach service; small gym; tour desk; business center; 24-hr. room service; laundry service; dry cleaning. *In room:* A/C, TV/VCR, dataport, minibar, fridge, hair dryer, safe.

MODERATE

Arpoador Inn 🎎 *Value*

The only budget-priced oceanfront hotel in Ipanema, the Arpoador Inn is located on a quiet stretch of beach popular with the surf crowd, just off the Garota de Ipanema park and just a hop and a skip from Copacabana. The five-story building is in the process of being renovated, so with some luck and persistence you can get an even better bang for your buck by booking one of the refurnished rooms. The deluxe rooms all face the ocean and are bright and spacious (those ending in "04" have already been renovated). Obtaining these does require booking ahead. If they're full, the superior rooms, which look out over the street behind the beach, make a fine alternative. Indeed, the only rooms to avoid are the standard ones, which are very small, dark, a tad beat up, and look into an interior wall.

Rua Francisco Otaviano 177, Ipanema, Rio de Janeiro, RJ 22080-040. ℂ 021/ 2523-0060. Fax 021/2511-5094. http://ipanema.com/hotel/arpoador_inn.htm. 50 units (shower only). R$90 ($45) standard; R$120 ($60) street-view superior; R$180 ($90) deluxe oceanview. Extra person R$25–R$40 ($12.50–$20). Children 6 and under stay free in parents' room. AE, DC, MC, V. No parking. Bus: 474. **Amenities:** Restaurant; limited room service; laundry service. *In room:* A/C, TV, minibar, fridge, safe.

Hotel Vermont 𝒜

The Vermont sits smack in the middle of Ipanema's swankiest shopping district. Be aware, however, that though Visconde de Pirajá quiets down nicely at night, during the daylight hours it's a very busy street with intense traffic. Rooms at the Vermont come standard or special. Standard rooms face out the back and are simply furnished with two twins or a double bed, a small dresser, and a desk. The very spacious special rooms are a much better deal and well worth the R$25 ($12.50) premium. In addition to bed(s), desk, and dresser, they come with a pleasant sitting area equipped with a sofa bed, convenient for those traveling with children. Some rooms also have a bathtub, but the majority have showers only.

Rua Visconde de Pirajá 254, Ipanema, Rio de Janeiro, RJ 22410-000. ℂ 021/ 2522-0057. Fax 021/2267-7046. 85 units (most with shower only). R$100–R$125 ($50–$62.50) double. Extra person R$20 ($10). Children 2 and under stay free in parents' room. AE, DC, MC, V. No parking. Bus: 474. **Amenities:** Tour desk; laundry service. *In room:* A/C, TV, minibar, fridge, safe.

Leblon Palace

Located on Leblon's main shopping strip, the Leblon Palace offers pleasant accommodations within walking distance of the beach. Deluxe rooms are of a good size and pleasantly furnished with tile floors instead of carpet and sturdy soundproofing that effectively keeps out the traffic and street noise. Suites are nearly identical to deluxe rooms, except for the addition of a small and very sparsely furnished anteroom. Given the price jump, they're probably not worth it.

Av. Ataulfo de Paiva 204, Leblon, Rio de Janeiro, RJ 22440-030. ℂ 021/ 2512-8000. www.leblonpalace.com.br. 94 units (shower only). R$176 ($88) double; R$250 ($125) suite. Extra person R$45 ($22.50). AE, DC, MC, V. No parking. Bus: 474. **Amenities:** Restaurant; pool; salon; 24-hr. room service; laundry service. *In room:* AC, TV, minibar, fridge, safe.

Top Apart Service 𝒜𝒜 (Kids)   The biggest advantage of staying at an apart-hotel is the space: You get a one- or two-bedroom suite, fully furnished with a completely equipped kitchen. Top Apart is run by the Accor group, which also manages a number of excellent apart-hotels in São Paulo. The most recently renovated suites have tile floors for a pleasant, clean look, modern furniture, and granite countertops in the kitchen and bathroom. Other suites feel a little dated but are still spacious and comfortable and very well maintained. All suites have a small balcony and a sofa bed in the living room. Unlike some apart-hotels, Top Apart Service doesn't skimp on amenities, providing free parking, an outdoor pool, sauna, and gym, and all this only 2 blocks from the beach.

Rua João Lira 95, Leblon, Rio de Janeiro, RJ 22430-210. ℂ 021/2511-2442. www.accorhotels.com.br. 120 units (shower only). R$160 ($80) 1-bedroom suite; R$220 ($110) 2-bedroom suite. Extra person 25%. Up to 20% discount during low season. AE, DC, MC, V. Free parking. Bus: 474. **Amenities:** Restaurant; outdoor rooftop pool; small gym; sauna; limited room service; laundry service; dry cleaning. *In room:* A/C, TV, kitchen, minibar, fridge, hair dryer.

2 Copacabana

The best beach neighborhood in the world from the 1940s to the '60s, Copacabana went into a bit of a downward spiral in the '80s. Young people moved over to Ipanema and with them went the trendy cafes and restaurants. By the late '80s, Copacabana had became a pale and slightly seedy shadow of its former elegant self. Only recently has it begun to rise up again. Many of the Zona Sul's budget hotels are found around the busy Nossa Senhora de Copacabana Avenue and its side streets. There are a few good bargains to be had, but expect high-rise buildings with fairly basic amenities and higher prices than in Catete or Flamengo.

VERY EXPENSIVE

The Copacabana Palace 𝒜𝒜   The spot where beachfront luxury in Rio all began, The Copacabana Palace is the place to splurge. True, the surrounding neighborhood may have lost some of its appeal in the 8 decades since this opulent vision first appeared on a lonely stretch of sand, but the Palace itself maintains all its Jazz Age charm. Taking advantage of that charm, however, requires approaching things with Gatsbyesque confidence. Take, for example, the superior rooms and Avenida suites. Or rather, don't take them. Though cheaper, they offer not a drop of ocean view, so really what's the point? Deluxe rooms do offer a partial ocean view, but for the price you can do better elsewhere. If you're going to get value for money at the Palace, it's really a case of go big or go home, and there's nothing bigger than the penthouse suites. Elegant and tastefully decorated, these spacious one-bedroom suites have their own private verandas overlooking Copacabana beach. Now that is the kind of life we were intended to live. Of course, this kind of lifestyle comes with a hefty price tag, but how often do you fly down to Rio?

Av. Atlântica 1702, Copacabana, Rio de Janeiro, RJ 22021-001. ℭ **0800/21-1533** or 021/2548-7070. Fax 021/2235-7330. www.copacabanapalace.orient-express. com. 226 units. R$730 ($365) superior; R$850 ($425) deluxe; R$990 ($495) junior suite; R$2,500 ($1,250) penthouse suite. Seasonal discounts may be available, particularly June–Aug. Extra person about 25%. Children 10 and under stay free in parents' room. AE, DC, MC, V. Free parking. Metrô: Arcoverde. **Amenities:** 2 restaurants (see Cipriani on p. 76), bar; large outdoor pool; rooftop tennis courts; health club; Jacuzzi; sauna; concierge; tour desk; car-rental desk; business center; salon; 24-hr. room service; massage; babysitting; laundry service; dry cleaning; executive-level rooms. *In room:* A/C, TV, dataport, kitchen, minibar, hair dryer, safe.

Hotel Sofitel ⭐⭐⭐   One of Rio's most elegant hotels, the Sofitel is also one of the most cleverly designed: The U-shaped structure guarantees all 388 rooms either a full or partial view of the beautiful shimmering ocean. Located on the edge of Copacabana directly opposite the Copacabana Fort, this flagship of the French Sofitel chain also offers superb and sophisticated service and—thanks to a US$25 million renovation—a clean, modern look to match. The majority of the rooms in the Sofitel are classified as superior and have been elegantly decorated with brand-new furnishings and fixtures. All rooms have balconies, soundproof windows, and electronic safes, each big enough to hold a laptop. The deluxe rooms differ only in location and offer a guaranteed full ocean view. For sunbathing, there are a variety of choices: Copacabana beach itself, with complimentary hotel beach service, or a choice of two swimming pools—one designed to take advantage of the morning sun and the other to catch the softer rays of afternoon.

Av. Atlântica 4240, Copacabana, Rio de Janeiro, RJ 22070-002. ℭ **0800/24-1232** or 021/2525-1232. Fax 021/2525-1200. www.sofitel-brasil.com.br. 388 units. R$390

> **Fun Fact   Flying Down to Rio**
>
> The Copacabana Palace has a glamorous pedigree that goes
> way back. In 1933, to celebrate the inauguration of regular
> Clipper air service to Rio, RKO Pictures released *Flying Down
> to Rio*, a light and fluffy musical set largely in and around the
> then 11-year-old Copacabana Palace hotel. Highlights of the
> flick include an intricate aerial ballet with lots of beautiful
> women capering about on the wings of sleek '30s aircraft,
> and a very young Fred Astaire and younger Ginger Rogers
> gliding around the Copa's ballroom in their first-ever dance
> number together.

($195) superior; R$440 ($220) superior Imperial Club; R$440 ($220) deluxe; R$520
($260) deluxe Imperial Club; R$770–R$990 ($385–$495) junior or executive suite.
Children 12 and under stay free in parents' room. AE, DC, MC, V. Free parking. Bus:
474. **Amenities:** 2 restaurants (see Le Pré-Catalan on p. 76), bar; 2 pools; health
club; sauna; concierge; tour desk; car-rental desk; business center; shopping arcade;
24-hr. room service; massage; babysitting; laundry service; dry cleaning; nonsmoking rooms or floors; executive-level rooms. *In room:* A/C, TV, dataport, minibar,
fridge, hair dryer, safe.

Marriott Rio de Janeiro ✧✧✧   Open since May 2001, the
brand-new Marriott's unique glass design stands out amongst the
1950s- and '60s-style buildings that line Copa's long beach boulevard. Inside, the expansive lobby and soaring multistory atrium give
the hotel an incredibly light and airy feel. The architectural price for
using up so much space on empty atrium, unfortunately, is that the
rooms themselves are a bit on the small side, though brand-new and
well laid out to maximize the space. For an oceanview room, book
early and pay the R$100 ($50) premium—you won't regret it. In
addition to location and architecture, the Marriott also offers an
outstanding level of friendly and efficient service combined with
excellent amenities. It's the only hotel we've found in Brazil that provides every room with a free newspaper, complimentary mineral
water, coffeemaker, iron and ironing board, and CD player. The
hotel also provides beach service—drinks, towels, chairs, and
umbrellas, and—another rarity in Brazil—is fully accessible for
travelers with disabilities. Breakfast costs R$20 ($10).

Av. Atlântica 2600, Copacabana, Rio de Janeiro, RJ 22041-001. © 800/228-9290
in the U.S. and Canada, 021/2254-6500, or 011/3069-2807. Fax 011/2545-6589.
www.marriott.com. 245 units. R$440 ($220) interior view; R$540–R$580
($270–$290) ocean view. Children 11 and under stay free in parents' room. AE, DC,

MC, V. Parking R$10 ($5) per day. Metrô: Arcoverde. **Amenities:** Restaurant, bar; rooftop pool; state-of-the-art health club; concierge; tour desk; car-rental desk; business center; 24-hr. room service; massage; babysitting; laundry service; dry cleaning; nonsmoking rooms; executive-level rooms. *In room:* A/C, TV, dataport, high-speed Internet, fridge, coffeemaker, hair dryer, iron, safe.

Rio Internacional Hotel ⭑⭑ The Rio Internacional fills a particular niche in Copacabana. Though by no means cheap, it's cheaper than the Copacabana Palace and other top full-service business hotels like the Marriott. Superior rooms in this 10-year-old building get the side view. Each comes with a king-size bed, very modern furnishings, a work desk with two telephone jacks, and a balcony. Deluxe rooms have similar furnishings but because they're located on the building's corner, they get two-directional views from the wraparound floor-to-ceiling windows. The 13 suites each feature a long narrow bedroom (with either a king-size or two double beds) separated by Japanese sliding doors from a sitting area and balcony. Breakfast costs R$21 ($10.50). Note that the prices given below are *not* the rack rates but the 40% business discount rates, which are offered to registered businesses and anyone else who can flash a business card. They're in effect year-round, except during holidays like Carnaval.

Av. Atlântica 1500, Copacabana, Rio de Janeiro, RJ 22021-000. ℂ **800/344-1212** in the U.S., or 021/2546-8010. Fax 021/2542-5443. www.riointernacional.com.br. 117 units. R$311–R$401 ($156–$200) double; R$590 ($295) suite. Extra person 25%. 1 child 7 or under stays free in parents' room. AE, DC, MC, V. Valet parking R$5 ($2.50) per day. Bus: 415. **Amenities:** Restaurant, small coffee shop, bar; small rooftop pool; small weight room; sauna; concierge; business center; 24-hr. room service; laundry service; dry cleaning; 3 nonsmoking floors. *In room:* A/C, TV, dataport, minibar, fridge, hair dryer, safe.

EXPENSIVE

Califórnia Othon Classic ⭑ To get a taste of Copacabana's elegant history without breaking the bank, check into the Califórnia Othon Classic, located right on the lovely Avenida Atlântica. This graceful 1950s apartment building was constructed in the days before space came at a premium. That said, be aware that the rooms are a bit of a hodgepodge of different sizes and amenities. The deluxe units look out over the ocean, while the standard rooms offer a "nonview" of surrounding apartment buildings and back lots. Some standard and deluxe rooms have spacious bathrooms with tubs whereas others provide really tiny showers. If at all possible, it's worth having a look at a few rooms before deciding. The ocean views are magnificent and certainly worth the money. Breakfast is not included.

Av. Atlântica 2616, Copacabana, Rio de Janeiro, RJ 22041-001. ℂ and fax **021/2257-1900.** www.hoteis-othon.com.br. 112 units. R$180–R$230 ($90–$115) standard; R$210–R$280 ($105–$140) luxo. Extra person 20%. Children 12 and under stay free in parents' room. AE, DC, MC, V. Very limited street parking. Metrô: Arcoverde. **Amenities:** Restaurant, bar; concierge; tour desk; car-rental desk; business center; limited room service; laundry service; dry cleaning. *In room:* A/C, TV, dataport, minibar, fridge, safe.

Grandarrell Ouro Verde Hotel 🎔🎔

Not the place if you like things brand-spanking-new, but if spacious and gracious and a little dated are your cup of chai, the Grandarrell Ouro Verde might appeal. Erected on the Copacabana beachfront just in time for the 1950 World Cup, the Ouro Verde has a Mediterranean feel, the abundant blue tile in stairways and corridors illuminated by natural light filtered in via a large central light well. Standard rooms are very spacious and come equipped with well-preserved 1950s beds, desks, and chairs (only the TVs are modern). The nearly identical Standard Extra rooms cost R$30 ($15) more but come with a good-size balcony. The top-floor Deluxe Extra rooms come with monster-size balconies and a great view of the ocean. Note that a recent change in ownership resulted in a slight revision of the hotel's name, but when we visited 8 months into the new regime, the old name—Grandville Ouro Verde—was still the one on display out front. This being Brazil, it probably still is. Breakfast costs R$15 ($7.50).

Av. Atlântica 1456, Copacabana, Rio de Janeiro, RJ 22021-000. ℭ 0800/31-1188 or 021/2543-4123. Fax 021/2543-3503. www.grandarrell.com.br. 63 units (shower only). R$200–R$320 ($100–$160) double. Extra person R$20 ($10). Children 7 and under stay free in parents' room. AE, DC, MC, V. No parking. Bus: 415. **Amenities:** Restaurant, bar; concierge; business center with Internet access; 24-hr. room service; laundry service; dry cleaning. *In room:* A/C, TV, minibar, fridge, safe.

Luxor Regente Hotel 🎔🎔

Don't let the somewhat dark glass exterior of the lobby put you off. Once inside, the Luxor Regente Hotel is surprisingly modern and bright. Fresh from major renovations, it is impossible to tell that this one has been around for 40 years. Everything from the elevators to the fitness center and the lobby has been redone and all the rooms have had a major overhaul as well. The 240 rooms are quite spacious and nicely furnished. The best rooms in the house are the deluxe ones offering a full ocean view of Copacabana beach. The standard rooms have no view and the superior ones just a partial ocean view that gets better the higher up you go. Breakfast is not included but the hotel runs regular specials (particularly in the Brazilian winter—June–Sept) and good deals can be had, such as a 2-night stay in an oceanview room, including breakfast, for a total of R$340 ($170) per room. Check their website for more details.

Av. Atlântica 3716, Copacabana, Rio de Janeiro, RJ 22070-001. ✆ **0800/16-5322** or 021/2525-2070. Fax 021/2267-7693. www.luxor-hotels.com. 240 units (most units with shower only). R$250–R$315 ($125–$157.50) standard; R$270–R$360 ($135–$180) superior; R$350–R$440 ($175–$220) luxo. Children 12 and under stay free in parents' room. AE, DC, MC, V. Parking R$11 ($5.50) per day. Bus: 128, 474. **Amenities:** Restaurant, bar; rooftop pool; exercise room; sauna; concierge; tour desk; car-rental desk; business center; 24-hr. room service; babysitting; laundry service; nonsmoking rooms or floors. *In room:* A/C, TV, dataport, minibar, fridge, hair dryer, safe.

MODERATE

Copacabana Praia Hotel 🅐 One of the smaller hotels in this area, the 65-unit Copacabana Praia Hotel stands in the shade of the luxury Sofitel Hotel, just a few blocks from the beach and Arpoador park. Each room is comfortably furnished with a spacious closet, a desk, and a double bed or twin beds. All rooms have small verandas and from the higher floors limited ocean views can be had. Unusual for a budget hotel, all bathrooms come with bathtubs and a second phone, and the hotel has a rooftop swimming pool and sauna.

Rua Francisco Otaviano 30, Copacabana, Rio de Janeiro, RJ 22080-040. ✆ **021/ 2522-5646.** Fax 021/2287-3344. www.copacabanapraiahotel.com.br. 65 units. R$150 ($75) double. Extra person R$30 ($15). Children 5 and under stay free in parents' room. AE, DC, MC, V. Limited free parking. Bus: 128, 474. **Amenities:** Pool; sauna; tour desk; laundry service. *In room:* A/C, TV, minibar, fridge, safe.

Copacabana Sol Hotel 🅐🅐 *Finds* From the outside this hotel looks just like any other high-rise, but the Sol has recently undergone some renovations and offers good value and pleasant accommodations only 4 blocks from Copacabana beach. Much of the money obviously went into the lobby—with its colorful furniture and modern art it almost borders on funky. Rooms were not neglected, however, and the suites in particular are a great deal. Spacious and cool with granite floors, each suite has a comfortable sitting room and gorgeous bathroom with Jacuzzi tub and separate shower. The superior and standard rooms have very small bathrooms with showers only but are spotless and well maintained. Superior rooms overlook the street and have balconies and small sitting areas. As the Rua Santa Clara is not too noisy—especially at night—these rooms are preferable to the standard rooms that look out the back of the building and lack balconies.

Rua Santa Clara 141, Copacabana, Rio de Janeiro, RJ 22041-010. ✆ **0800/ 25-4477** or 021/2549-4577. Fax 021/2255-0744. www.copacabanasolhotel. com.br. 70 units. R$130–R$175 ($65–$87.50) standard and superior; R$200–R$265 ($100–$132.50) suite. Extra person R$40 ($20). Children 5 and under stay free in parents' room. AE, DC, MC, V. Free parking. Bus: 128, 474. **Amenities:** Restaurant;

concierge; tour desk; business center; 24-hr. room service; laundry service. *In room:* A/C, TV, dataport, minibar, fridge, safe.

Hotel Debret Probably the reason so many tourists end up at Debret is because it is one of the more affordable beachfront hotels in Copacabana. That's fine if you can book yourself into one of the oceanview deluxe rooms or suites (especially one of three renovated ones), and a disaster if you get put in one of the 39 standard rooms. Small, murky, and with a view of nothing but the maze of adjacent buildings, these units are thoroughly unpleasant unless you're a vampire or a sucker for the '70s brown furniture. The superior rooms are slightly better as they look out over the side street and provide partial ocean views.

Av. Atlântica 3564, Copacabana, Rio de Janeiro, RJ 22060-040. © 021/ 2522-0132. Fax 021/2521-0899. www.debret.com. 110 units (shower only). R$120–R$235 ($60–$117.50) standard or superior; R$165–R$275 ($82.50–$137.50) luxo; R$190–R$315 ($95–$157.50) suite. Extra person R$40 ($20). Children 8 and under stay free in parents' room. AE, DC, MC, V. Limited street parking. Bus: 128, 474. **Amenities:** Restaurant, bar; tour desk; business center; limited room service; laundry service. *In room:* A/C, TV, minibar, fridge, safe.

Majestic Rio Palace Hotel ⭐ *(Finds)* Set back about 5 blocks from the beach on a quiet street with a view of the hills between Copacabana and Botafogo, the 8-year-old Majestic Hotel offers a number of amenities and extras that make it well worth seeking out. Unusual for a hotel in this price category, it offers a rooftop pool and sauna as well as free parking. As usual with Rio hotels, the rooms come in standard and deluxe, but in this case there is more of a difference than just the view. The deluxe rooms are not only larger but also have bathtub-and-Jacuzzi combinations. From higher floors you will also get a nice view of the hills. In recent renovations, the second- and third-floor rooms had tile floors put in; all others still have carpet. For a special occasion or a fun splurge, the Majestic offers two suites on the 15th floor. Each has a large sitting room and a huge bathroom with Jacuzzi; one suite also has a private sauna.

Rua Cinco de Julho 195, Copacabana, Rio de Janeiro, RJ 22051-030. © 021/ 2548-2030. Fax 021/2255-1692. www.majestichotel.com.br. 108 units (standard units with shower only). R$135–R$195 ($67.50–$97.50) double; R$150–R$220 ($75–$110) luxo double; R$240–R$325 ($120–$162.50) suite. Extra person R$40 ($20). Children 5 and under stay free in parents' room. AE, DC, MC, V. Free parking. Metrô: Arcoverde. **Amenities:** Restaurant, bar; pool; sauna; concierge; tour desk; business center; 24-hr. room service; laundry service. *In room:* A/C, TV, minibar, fridge, safe.

INEXPENSIVE

Copacabana Praia 🐾 *Value* *Kids*   Not to be confused with the Copacabana Praia Hotel (see p. 55), this hotel offers excellent inexpensive spacious suites in a former residential building. The catch? Location. The hotel is a good 15- to 20-minute walk from the beach and situated away from Copacabana's restaurant and nightlife scene. But for budget-minded travelers who don't mind a short walk or cab ride, it offers spacious lodgings for up to six people with a full kitchen and sitting room at just R$50 ($25) a night. The nicest apartments are the ones overlooking the pleasant neighborhood park out front.

Rua Tenente Marones de Gusmão 85, Copacabana, Rio de Janeiro, RJ 22041-060. ✆ 021/2547-5422. Fax 021/2235-3817. www.copacabanapraiahotel.com.br. 56 units (shower only). R$50–R$70 ($25–$35) double. Extra person R$20 ($10). Children under 2 stay free, ages 2–12 R$10 ($5) extra. No credit cards. Limited street parking. Bus: 128, 474. *In room:* A/C, TV, kitchen.

3 São Conrado

The only good hotel in São Conrado, the Sheraton, sits on a thin sliver of land between a hillside *favela* (shantytown) and its own little private beach. (See the "Where to Stay in Ipanema, Leblon & Copacabana" map on p. 45.) There are no services or shops except for those in the hotel. However, the location is stunning, the area is safe, and it's just a 30-minute stroll or quick cab ride to Leblon.

VERY EXPENSIVE

Sheraton Rio Hotel & Towers 🐾🐾🐾 *Kids*   Nowhere are Rio's societal divisions more visible than from the luxury suites at the Sheraton. Located directly on its own beautiful pocket beach (the only Rio hotel with so privileged a position), the Sheraton also sits in the shadow of a hillside favela. Guests in the south-facing rooms awake to the calls of roosters roaming around the small brick shacks across the road. The hotel itself is the ultimate in luxury, featuring the best leisure area of any hotel in Rio: three large swimming pools in a beautiful parklike setting, beachfront access, and sweeping ocean views. The rooms are spacious and very bright. All have verandas with a partial or full ocean view and the interiors have recently been upgraded with new light fixtures, large desks, and dual phone lines. The location is very suitable for children and the hotel staff offer a range of activities to keep the young ones busy. The only drawback of this privileged location is that the shopping or nightlife scene of Ipanema and Leblon are at least a 30-minute walk away. However, taxis are aplenty and inexpensive, and the hotel also operates a free shuttle service.

Av. Niemeyer 121, São Conrado, Rio de Janiero, RJ 22450-220. ⓒ **0800/11-1345** or 021/2274-1122. Fax 021/2239-5643. www.sheraton-rio.com. 559 units. R$440 ($220) standard; R$480 ($240) deluxe; R$560 ($280) full oceanview double; R$680 ($340) executive suite. Extra person add 25%. Children 10 and under stay free in parents' room. Breakfast not included. AE, DC, MC, V. Free parking. **Amenities:** 3 restaurants, bar; disco; 3 outdoor pools; tennis courts (extra charge); health club (extra charge); sauna; children's center; game room; concierge; tour desk; car-rental desk; courtesy shuttle service; business center; shopping arcade; salon; 24-hr. room service; massage; babysitting; laundry service; dry cleaning; nonsmoking floors; executive-level rooms. *In room:* A/C, TV, dataport, minibar, fridge, hair dryer, safe.

4 Glória, Catete & Flamengo

These older neighborhoods just outside of downtown offer a range of excellent accommodations while providing glimpses into Rio's fascinating history.

EXPENSIVE

Hotel Florida ★★ *(Finds)*   A gem of a hotel, the Florida is very popular with business travelers from São Paulo who know a good deal when they see one: On top of a reasonable room rate, the Florida offers free parking, free local calls, and free Internet access. Built in the 1940s, the hotel doesn't suffer from the modern "small room" syndrome, and thanks to a recent renovation, the spacious and pleasant rooms offer dataports and a fresh, clean look. The standard rooms overlook the rear or the side of the building and come with shower only. Both the superior and deluxe rooms offer views and have bathrooms with jetted tubs. The nicest rooms are those overlooking the lush gardens of the Palácio do Catete, Brazil's former presidential palace. The deluxe rooms are the most spacious, each with a large entrance hall, king-size bed (very unusual in Brazil), sitting area, and desk. The hotel offers excellent discounts on weekends when its regular business travelers stay home.

Rua Ferreira Viana 81, Flamengo, Rio de Janeiro, RJ 22210-040. ⓒ **021/ 2556-5242.** Fax 021/2285-5777. www.windsorhoteis.com.br. 225 units. R$214–R$240 ($107–$120) standard; R$268 ($134) superior; R$280 ($140) deluxe. Extra person add 25%. Children 10 and under stay free in parents' room. AE, DC, MC, V. Free parking. Metrô: Catete. **Amenities:** Restaurant, bar; outdoor rooftop pool; weight room; sauna; concierge; tour desk; business center; 24-hr. room service; laundry service; dry cleaning; nonsmoking floors. *In room:* A/C, TV, dataport, minibar, fridge, hair dryer, safe.

Where to Stay in Glória, Catete & Flamengo

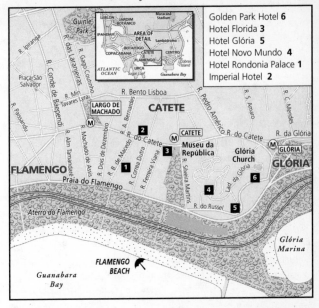

Golden Park Hotel **6**
Hotel Florida **3**
Hotel Glória **5**
Hotel Novo Mundo **4**
Hotel Rondonia Palace **1**
Imperial Hotel **2**

Hotel Glória *⚜⚜*   Truly the grande dame of Rio hotels, the Hotel Glória was built in 1922 (a year before the Copacabana Palace) to provide luxury accommodations for dignitaries attending Brazil's centennial celebrations. An annex was added in the '70s in the same style, making the 630-room Glória one of the largest hotels in the city. The cheapest rooms are in the annex. All standard, these rooms are small with garden views and dated furnishings. Renovations are currently underway, however—the already completed ninth floor looks fabulous, though that doesn't change the size or the view. Rooms in the original building reflect the rather higher standards of that bygone era: Ceilings are high, bathrooms are spacious, and the furnishings are truly elegant. Standard and superior rooms in this section are not to be scoffed at, but if you can afford it, it's worth splurging on one of the spacious deluxe rooms—the views of the marina and the Sugar Loaf are worth it. Or book a lovely junior suite—located in the hotel's corners—featuring a large living room, elegantly furnished with lovely antiques, and a spacious master bedroom.

Rua do Russel 632, Glória, Rio de Janeiro, RJ 22210-010. (℃ **0800/21-3077** or 021/2555-7272. Fax 021/2555-7283. www.hotelgloriario.com.br. 630 units (standard units in annex have shower only). R$180–R$280 ($90–$140) standard; R$260–R$360 ($130–$180) superior and deluxe; R$660–R$780 ($330–$390) junior suite. Extra person R$50 ($25). Children 10 and under stay free in parents' room. AE, DC, MC, V. No parking. Metrô: Glória. **Amenities:** 4 restaurants; bar; 2 outdoor heated pools; health club; sauna; concierge; tour desk; car-rental desk; business center; salon; 24-hr. room service; massage; babysitting; laundry service; dry cleaning; nonsmoking rooms or floors. *In room:* A/C, TV, dataport, minibar, fridge, hair dryer, safe.

Hotel Novo Mundo ⚑⚑ Built to accommodate VIP guests during the 1950 soccer World Cup held in the brand-new Maracanã stadium, the completely renovated Hotel Novo Mundo offers modern standards combined with '50s elegance. After the Hotel Glória, this is the nicest hotel in the area, with a location that makes the most of the view over the bay and the Parque do Catete. Perhaps the only drawback is the heavy traffic along the Aterro and Flamengo beach but at night it calms down enough that it's not a factor for those trying to snooze. All the front-side view rooms are spacious, comfortably furnished, and come equipped with large desks. Some have full waterfront views of Guanabara Bay and the Pão de Açúcar (Sugar Loaf Mountain), others offer views of the wide green space of the Parque do Catete. Can't decide which one is better? Go for both! The Suite Mar—the large corner suite on each floor—allows for views both ways; the higher the floor the better. Absolutely worth the money.

Praia do Flamengo 20, Flamengo, Rio de Janeiro, RJ 22210-030. (℃ **0800/25-3355** or 021/2557-6226. www.hotelnovomundo-rio.com.br. 230 units. R$144 ($72) standard; R$190 ($95) oceanview standard; R$220 ($110) oceanview suite. 10%–20% discount in low season. AE, MC, V. Valet parking R$14 ($7) per day. Metrô: Catete. **Amenities:** Restaurant, bar; business center (R$5/$2.50 for 30 min. of Internet access); salon; 24-hr. room service; laundry service. *In room:* A/C, TV, dataport, minibar, fridge, safe.

MODERATE

Golden Park Hotel   Located just outside of Rio's historic downtown, the six-story Golden Park Hotel offers affordable accommodations a few steps from the large Parque do Flamengo and a 15-minute metrô ride from the beaches of Copacabana. The hotel offers three types of rooms. All are clean and bright, and though currently a little beat up here and there, ongoing renovations should soon take care of that. Standard rooms offer showers only and a view of the alley. Superior rooms also offer only showers, but come with either street or partial park/ocean views. Deluxe rooms come with a bathtubs—some have jetted tubs—and a view of the park or ocean. Deluxe rooms ending in 01 (for example, 201) are the most spacious and each comes with a couch as well as a small desk. Prices are the same for all rooms, so book ahead to reserve a prime one. The higher the floor, the more glimpses of park and ocean you will have. At R$100 ($50) a night including breakfast, it makes a fine home base for those who would rather spend their money exploring Rio.

Rua do Russel 374, Glória, Rio de Janeiro, RJ 22210-010. ℂ 021/2556-8150. Fax 021/2285-6358. gparkrio@pontocom.com.br. 71 units. R$100–R$120 ($50–$60) double. Extra person R$20 ($10). Children 7 and under stay free in parents' room. AE, DC, MC, V. Parking R$5.50 ($2.75) per day. Metrô: Glória. **Amenities:** Restaurant, bar; tiny rooftop pool; limited room service; laundry service. *In room:* A/C, TV, minibar, fridge, safe.

Hotel Rondônia Palace ⨁   For a little bit of luxury at a budget price, try the Hotel Rondônia, located on a quiet side street off the waterfront park in Flamengo. Each of the deluxe rooms come with a tiny sauna right in the bathroom, as well as a large Jacuzzi tub. A number of the standard rooms also have saunas, though if you want one, you should ask for it specifically when making a reservation. There are no views to speak of, as the rooms either look out over the buildings behind the hotel or the narrow street in front, but the rooms themselves are comfortably furnished and very clean. Just note that rooms ending in 07 and 08 (for example, 207 and 208) are a bit smaller than the others. The Rondônia's location is another plus, near but not on the bustling Rua do Catete, within easy walking distance of either the waterfront Flamengo Park or the cafes of the Largo do Machado, and a 15-minute subway ride to either Centro or the beaches of the Zona Sul.

Rua Buarque de Macedo 60, Flamengo, Rio de Janeiro, RJ 22220-030. ℂ 021/ 2556-0616. Fax 021/2558-4133. www.hotelrondonia.com.br. 62 units (standard units have shower only). R$110 ($55) standard; R$120 ($60) deluxe with sauna and Jacuzzi. Small seasonal discount. Children under 5 stay free in parents' room. 5 and over, extra bed R$30–R$40 ($15–$20). AE, DC, MC, V. Free parking. Bus: 119. **Amenities:** Restaurant, bar; limited room service; laundry service. *In room:* A/C, TV, minibar, fridge, safe.

Imperial Hotel   It's impossible not to notice the elegant white colonial-style Imperial Hotel in the heart of Catete. Built in 1896, the mansion was once just one of many lining the Rua do Catete. The others are now all gone, and even the Imperial has been unobtrusively modified. Lurking behind the lovely original mansion is a modern hotel, built in American motel style with units overlooking the parking lot. The combination of old mansion and new motel provides some worthwhile variety. Those who want to pretend they are reliving Rio's glory days when it was the national capital and the president lived in the palace across the street can book a room in the mansion. Though a bit dated—the plumbing in particular has seen better days—and a tad close to the street noise of the Rua do Catete, these rooms are positively steeped in character. For those who prefer modern plumbing and a quiet night's sleep, there's the annex. Though character's been sacrificed, the rooms are spotless and brand spanking new. Also in the annex, the suites are a bit more spacious and come equipped with joyfully modern plumbing, including jetted tubs.

Rua do Catete 186, Catete, Rio de Janeiro, RJ 22222-000. ℂ **021/2556-5212.** Fax 021/2558-5815. www.imperialhotel.com.br. 80 units (shower only, except suites). R$82 ($41) standard; R$95 ($47.50) deluxe; R$110 ($55) suite. Extra person add 25%. Children 5 and under stay free in parents' room. AE, DC, MC, V. Free parking. Metrô: Catete. **Amenities:** Outdoor pool; tour desk; laundry service. *In room:* A/C, TV, minibar, fridge.

Where to Dine

Cariocas love to eat out. Better yet, they love to linger over their meals. A waiter in Rio would never dream of coming by to ask you to "settle up" so he can go off shift. For Brazilians, that would be the height of bad manners. So take your time. Dawdle. Savor. Enjoy.

There are countless places to dine. Literally. There are the *chopperias,* the place for cold beer and casual munchies. There are hundreds of food kiosks, each with their own specialty, be it barbecued prawns, Bahian finger food, or vegetarian sandwiches. And on top of all that, there's a wide variety of restaurants in all neighborhoods, ranging from inexpensive to very expensive, from simple sandwiches to delicious steaks, from firm fresh sushi to the complicated stews and sauces of Brazil's northeast. There's no excuse for going hungry in Rio.

Keep in mind that portions often serve two people, especially in more casual restaurants. Always ask when in doubt or you may well end up with an extraordinary amount of food. In Portuguese ask, *"Serve para dois?"* (*sair*-vee *pa*ra *doe*-is), or "Does it serve two?"

Brazilian food is hard to define, but what we consider the generic Brazilian menu comes close to what some restaurants label as international cuisine: pasta, seafood, beef, chicken. Except in Brazil, these are served with a local or regional twist. The pasta may be stuffed with catupiry cheese and *abóbora* (a kind of pumpkin), the chicken could have *maracujá* (passion fruit) sauce. Brazilian beef comes from grass-fed cows, making for a very lean beef that comes in uniquely Brazilian cuts such as *picanha* (rump steak) or *alcatra* (top sirloin). And, of course, for side dishes, no Brazilian meal is complete without farofa (see box below) and rice or black beans.

Most restaurants are open from around 11am until 4pm and then again from 7pm until midnight or later. However, there are also quite a few establishments that will stay open all day, especially on the weekends when people leave the beach at 4pm to go eat lunch. Sunday is often the busiest day for lunch as extended families get together for a meal. Because Sunday lunch is so busy, many restaurants close on Sunday evening.

> ### *Tips* Tips on Tipping
>
> The bill usually includes a 10% service charge and you are not expected to tip on top of this amount, unless service was exceptional, in which case you may want to leave another 5%.

The main exception on the hours mentioned above is in Rio's downtown. The restaurants in Centro cater primarily to the business and office crowd and only a few of them are open in the evening or on Saturday or Sunday.

These days you will find more and more kilo (*quilo* in Portuguese) restaurants. The food is laid out in a large buffet, and at the better ones, there's a chef behind a grill at the back whipping up freshly cooked steaks, chicken, sausage, or what have you. Kilos aren't all-you-can-eat. Rather, you pay by weight (which means quality is much better than at American lunch buffets). If you're not familiar with Brazilian food, it's a great way to see all the dishes laid out in front of you; you can try as little or as much as you like. Even better, there are often a variety of salads and vegetables, which are oftentimes hard to find in Brazil. The system works as follows: when you enter the restaurant, you're given a piece of paper on which all your orders are recorded. Don't lose this slip or you'll have to pay some ridiculously high fine. You grab a plate, wander by the buffet and grill filling up on whatever catches your eye (all items have the same per/kg cost, which is usually advertised both outside and inside the restaurant), and then take the plate to the scale to be weighed. The weigher records the charges on your bill, after which you find a table. Normally, a waiter will then come by and take your drink order, adding these charges to your tally. On your way out, the cashier sums it all up.

Tip: Small cups of strong, dark coffee (called *cafezinho*) are usually served free on the way out. Look for a thermos and a stack of little plastic cups by the cashier or doorway.

1 Centro & Santa Teresa
EXPENSIVE

Brasserie Europa *⋆* BRAZILIAN/STEAK Surrounded by many classic buildings, Brasserie Europa's sleek modern room with chrome and black decor is guaranteed to stand out. The restaurant is packed during lunch and often after work as well, when people

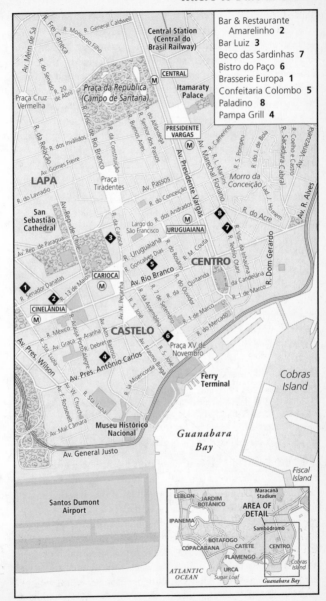

Where to Dine in Centro

Bar & Restaurante
Amarelinho **2**
Bar Luiz **3**
Beco das Sardinhas **7**
Bistro do Paço **6**
Brasserie Europa **1**
Confeitaria Colombo **5**
Paladino **8**
Pampa Grill **4**

Central Station
(Central do
Brasil Railway)

CENTRAL Ⓜ

Itamaraty
Palace

Praça da República
(Campo de Santana)

Praça Cruz
Vermelha

R. Frei Caneca
R. Monronço Filho
R. General Caldwell
Av. Mem de Sá
Av. do Senado
R. 20 de Abril
R. da Relação
R. dos Inválidos
Av. Gomes Freire
R. Vgc. de Rio Branco
R. Senhor dos Passos
R. da Alfândega
R. Buenos Aires
R. da Constituição

PRESIDENTE
VARGAS Ⓜ

Av. Marechal Floriano
R. Camerino
R. L. Martins
R. R. Pompeu
R. Coelho e Castro
R. Sádurra e Cabral
R. J. de Bola
R. Coelho e Castro
Av. R. Alves

Morro da
Conceição

LAPA

Praça
Tiradentes

Av. Passos

R. do Conceição

Av. Presidente Vargas

R. do Acre

R. Visc. da Inhaúma

R. Dom Gerardo

San
Sebastião
Cathedral

R. do Lavradio
Av. Rep. de Paraguai
Av. Rep. de Chile

Largo de
São Francisco

R. dos Andradros Ⓜ

URUGUAIANA

8
7

R. do Teófilo Otoni

R. da Candelária

R. 1 de Março

3

R. da Carioca

R. Uruguaiana
R. Gonçalves Dias

5

R. do Rosário
R. M. Couta

R. do Ouvidor

CENTRO

CARIOCA Ⓜ

Av. Rio Branco

R. do Carmo
R. da Quitanda

1

R. Senador Dantas
R. 13 de Maio

2

R. N. Peçanha
R. S. José

R. 7 de Setembro
R. da Assembleia

R. 1 de Março

CINELÂNDIA Ⓜ

Av. Pres. Wilson
R. México
R. Sta. Luzia
Av. Graça Aranha
R. Araújo Porto Alegre
R. Debret
Alm. Barroso

CASTELO

4

R. do Mercado

6

Praça XV de
Novembro

R. Erasmo Braga
R. S. José
R. la Misericórdia

Ferry
Terminal

Cobras
Island

Av. Pres. Antônio Carlos
R. N. W. Churchill
Av. F. Roosevelt
R. Sta. Luzia
Av. Mal. Câmara

Museu Histórico
Nacional

Guanabara
Bay

Av. General Justo

Fiscal
Island

Santos Dumont
Airport

LEBLON
JARDIM
BOTÂNICO
IPANEMA

Maracanã
Stadium

AREA OF
DETAIL

Sambódromo

BOTAFOGO
COPACABANA
FLAMENGO
CATETE
CENTRO

ATLANTIC
OCEAN

URCA
Sugar Loaf

Cobras
Island

Guanabara Bay

linger for a drink and a snack. Unlike many European brasseries where the menu specializes in light meals such as salads or sandwiches, here the emphasis is on meat. The menu lists a number of delicious cuts, among them filet mignon, baby beef, and Argentinean steak. Each comes with a choice of sauce and two side dishes. Beer connoisseurs will be pleased to find Duvel and Stella Artois, two imported Belgian beers that are hard to find anywhere else in Brazil. Happy hour with live music (usually bossa nova or MPB, *musica popular brasileira*) takes place Monday through Friday from 6 to 8pm.

Rua Senador Dantas 117, Centro. ✆ **021/2220-2656.** R$14.80–R$25.80 ($7.40–$12.90). AE, V. Mon–Fri 11:45am–10:30pm. Metrô: Cinelândia.

Confeitaria Colombo ✫✫✫ BRAZILIAN/DESSERTS Tucked away in a narrow side street off the busy Avenida Rio Branco, you'll find a stunning ornate tearoom. Except for the stained-glass window that was added in a 1920s renovation, the room hasn't changed much since this elegant restaurant opened in 1894. The spacious room is divided into three sections. Two large deli counters flanking either side of the entrance serve up sweets and savory snacks with coffee or other refreshments for those who can't be bothered to sit down. The remainder of the ground floor is taken up by the elegant tearoom, where a variety of teas, sandwiches, salads, and sweets are served on fine china underneath a 1920s stained-glass window. The upstairs room is reserved for full lunches—on Saturdays the *feijoada* (bean stew) alone is worth a trip downtown.

Rua Gonçalves Dias 32, Centro. ✆ **021/2221-0107.** Main courses R$27–R$39 ($13.50–$19.50), feijoada buffet R$26 ($13), including dessert. Tea service R$5–R$20 ($2.50–$10). AE, DC, MC, V. Mon–Fri 8:30am–7pm, Sat 9am–5pm. Metrô: Carioca.

MODERATE

Bar Luiz *Finds* GERMAN One of Rio's most beloved little restaurants, Bar Luiz has been around since 1887. Originally located on the Rua Assembleia and called Bar Adolf (after the owner), it moved to its current location on the Rua da Carioca in 1927. Then, as now, the bar was a popular hangout for intellectuals and politicians, which may have been why the owner was so quick to change the name in 1942. Name aside, the bar hasn't changed much over the years. The long room is simply furnished with wooden tables and chairs and a lovely tile floor. The walls are plainly adorned with old photographs of Rio, while overhead big Casablanca fans whirl to keep the heat down. Even the menu has stayed much the same, in honor of the first German owner. Cariocas flock here to gorge themselves on generous portions of sausage and sauerkraut, Wiener schnitzel, Kassler ham, and potato salad. (Health craze, what health craze?) The draft beer—lager and dark—is pumped through a 2,376-foot-long (720m) refrigerated hose before finding its way into your glass. *Prosit!*

Rua da Carioca 39, Centro. © 021/2262-6900. Main courses R$7.50–R$23 ($3.75–$11.50). AE, DC, V. Mon–Sat 11am–11pm. Metrô: Carioca.

Bar & Restaurante Amarelinho *Finds* BRAZILIAN   The prime patio on the prettiest square in Rio, the Amarelinho is the place to come to have a cold *chopp* (draft beer) and gaze on the Parisian beauty that is the Praça Floriano, particularly in the evening when the Biblioteca Nacional and the Teatro Municipal are lit up and the square begins to buzz with the energy that only Brazilians can give. The menu offers a huge selection of appetizers, sandwiches, grilled chicken, and meats served with standard Brazilian side dishes of rice, fries, or farofa. Nothing too special, most people are here for a drink and a good chat with friends after a long day at the office.

Praça Floriano 55B, Centro. © 021/2240-8434. Main courses R$10–R$22 ($5–$11). AE, DC, MC, V. Daily 11am–midnight. Metrô: Cinelândia.

Bistro do Paço *Finds* BRAZILIAN   Looking for a quiet spot to escape the heat and noise in downtown Rio? Duck into this little oasis inside the historic Paço Imperial. The restaurant serves up mostly bistro fair as well as a daily lunch special that will set you back R$12 to R$15 ($6–$7.50) for a plate of roast beef with a side order of pasta, spinach crepes with a ricotta-and-mushroom stuffing, or a chicken filet with applesauce and sautéed vegetables. For a light snack, try one of the quiches, the freshly made sandwiches with grilled vegetables, or cold-cut plates. Desserts are strictly European: Austrian Linzer tortes and German fruit strudels and Black Forest chocolate cakes, all of which go so well with the omnipresent Brazilian cafezinho.

Praça XV 48 (inside the Paço Imperial), Centro. © 021/2262-3613. Main courses R$12–R$15 ($6–$7.50), sandwiches and quiches R$6–R$9 ($3–$4.50). AE, DC, MC, V. Mon–Fri 10am–8pm, Sat–Sun noon–7pm. Bus: 415, 119.

Pampa Grill *Finds* KILO   A great kilo restaurant in the center of Rio, Pampa Grill is always absolutely packed during lunch with white-collar workers from offices downtown. The main floor serves as a rodízio restaurant—all you can eat meat brought to your table, as well as unlimited access to the buffet. Down the stairs on your right-hand side is where you'll find the kilo restaurant. The selection of salads, pasta, cold cuts, sushi, and more is top quality, and with so many customers, nothing sits on the counter for very long. In the back there's a large grill with a selection of just about any cut of beef, chicken (try the chicken hearts, they're delicious), fish, or sausage your brain could imagine or your taste buds desire.

Av. Almirante Barroso 90, Centro. ✆ 021/2220-7816. All-you-can-eat buffet R$28 ($14), or per kilo R$19.50 ($9.75). AE, DC, MC, V. Daily noon–5pm. Bus: 119, 415.

INEXPENSIVE

Bar do Mineiro ✪ *Finds* BRAZILIAN   The inland state of Minas Gerais is looked on as a culinary capital of sorts in Brazil, the source of down-home hearty comfort food. Bar do Mineiro is a little piece of Minas in Santa Teresa. Not limited to food only, this combo restaurant/art gallery/antique shop also serves up an amazing variety of *cachaça,* Brazil's national drink, a rum-like hard liquor made from sugar cane. The meals are hearty and portions generous. Appetizers include sausages and *pasteis*—savory pastries with a variety of stuffings, including sausage, cheese, or cabbage. Very popular is the *frango com quiabo* (stewed chicken with okra). *Feijão tropeiro* is another favorite and always appreciated by homesick *mineiros.* Much thicker than the feijoada, this bean dish is made with brown instead of black beans. (To locate this restaurant, see the "Where to Dine in Glória, Catete, Flamengo & Botafogo" map on p. 71.)

Rua Pascoal Carlos Magno 99, Santa Teresa. ✆ 021/2221-9227. Main courses R$10–R$18 ($5–$9). No credit cards. Tues–Thurs 11am–2am, Fri–Sat 11am–4am, Sun 11am–7pm. Bus: 214 or take the tram, getting off at the Largo dos Guimarães.

Beco das Sardinhas (Rei dos Frangos Maritimos) ✪ *Finds* BRAZILIAN   Known as "sardine alley" or "the sardine triangle," this corner in Rio's historic downtown is the perfect place to spend a Friday afternoon as locals gather to unwind from the workweek. It started in the '60s when the Portuguese owners of three small restaurants began selling fried sardines. They would cut open the fish and fry them like a filet, dubbed *frango maritimo* (chicken of the sea) by a jesting customer, and the name stuck to one of the restaurants. These days the triangle has expanded to include six restaurants in a pedestrian area between Rua do Acre and Rua Mayrink Veiga. Every Friday after 6pm, it transforms into a giant TGIF party. The patio tables and counters fill up almost as quickly as the fried sardines—salted and breaded in cassava flour—come piping hot off the grill. Accompanied by a *loura gelada* (literally "icy blond," the local nickname for draft), it's the perfect way to start a weekend. Once the

Moments You Say *Farofa*, I Say . . . Blech

Shawn says: I never got *farofa*. What I mean is, I got it with *every* meal; that was the problem. Really, what is the point? *Farofa* (flour taken from ground manioc root, then baked with oil) has the dry and crumbly consistency of sawdust—and not coincidentally, that's pretty much what it tastes like. Brazilians painstakingly disguise the flavor, sometimes adding raisins and dried fruit, but the end result tastes like . . . sawdust with raisins or dried fruit. Eating it made sense in the days when Brazilians lived in peasant huts; farofa was the sole source of carbohydrates. Like potatoes for the Irish, farofa kept you going. But Brazilians have long since evolved into a nation of city dwellers. Brazilian cooking now incorporates lots of carbs—like rice. Potatoes. French fries. Sometimes all three at once. But no matter how many starches are piled on your plate, farofa will be there to top it off. Often Brazilians sprinkle it on steak, or rice, or potatoes, or french fries. Because you can never get enough carbohydrates.

Alexandra says: Farofa—what's not to like? The coarsely roasted flour of the manioc root is the perfect companion to a Brazilian meal. Served plain, farofa's unique nutty flavor stands up, while allowing it to soak up the sauces or juices on your plate only enhances its flavor. What makes it really delicious are the additions and modifications of each cook. Every Brazilian has his or her favorite farofa recipe. My mother makes the best sweet farofa with bananas and raisins; it tastes as delightful as some of the best stuffings I've had. Other cooks prefer a savory version, adding spicy chorizo sausage, olives, or bacon. A feijoada is just not the same without farofa. Next time, skip those greasy french fries and add some farofa to your plate. Bon appetit!

crowd reaches critical mass, someone will inevitably strike up some samba or pagode and the party will ignite.

Rua Miguel Couto 139, Centro. ✆ 021/2233-6119. Everything under R$8 ($4). No credit cards. Mon–Fri 11am–10pm. Metrô: Uruguaiana.

Paladino BRAZILIAN Enjoying yourself at Paladino is much easier than deciding where it is you are: Is it a liquor store, as the hundreds of glass bottles lined up in gleaming wooden cases seem to suggest? Is it a deli, then, with racks of spices and jars of capers and artichoke hearts? Or is it, as the crowds seem to indicate, a bustling lunch bar with some of the best draft beer in town? Is an exact definition really important? Probably not. What matters is that the beer is clear and cold and comes at the wave of a finger, the atmosphere is that of Rio in the Belle Epoque, and the sandwiches and snack plates are delicious. *Pratinhos,* as the latter are known in Portuguese, cost next to nothing—R$3 to R$6 ($1.50–$3)—and come loaded with sardines (whatever you do, order the sardines!), olives, cheese, or great heaping stacks of smoked sausage. For about the same price, there are also sandwiches, or if you really feel like lashing out, an R$13 ($6.50) smoked-salmon omelet that is said to be the best in the city. All of this delectable nosh is served up by old-fashioned waiters in black pants and white shirts. Since 1907 an eclectic mixture of lawyers, shopkeepers, workers, and executives have come here, and though none has ever succeeded in defining exactly what it is, neither have they ever stopped coming.

Rua Uruguaiana 224, Centro. ⓒ 021/2263-2094. Reservations not accepted. Main courses R$3–R$13 ($1.50–$6.50). No credit cards. Mon–Fri 7am–8:30pm, Sat 7am–noon. Metrô: Uruguaiana.

2 Glória, Catete, Flamengo, Botafogo & Urca

VERY EXPENSIVE

Alcaparra ⓕ BRAZILIAN Very popular among the political elite, this is one restaurant where reservations are required; the elegant bright dining room overlooking Flamengo's waterfront is almost always packed for lunch and dinner. The restaurant's signature dish is the *mignonettes á alcaparra*—succulently grilled filet mignon with a melt-in-your-mouth lemon-and-capers sauce served on a bed of pasta. No less delicious and a bit more unusual is the *marreco ao poivre*—duck breast and leg served with a green-pepper sauce and slices of caramelized onions. A classic dish perfect for those cooler months of June and July is the *coelho ao champagne,* rabbit in champagne sauce sautéed with peppers and potatoes. Unusual for a Brazilian restaurant, the wine list covers a fair bit of territory: Chile, Argentina, California, Portugal, Italy, and a lot of French reds. Prices range from R$30 to R$200 ($15–$100) per bottle, but there is plenty of choice in the R$30 to R$50 ($15–$25) price range. The restaurant also has a nice bar, if you only want to

Where to Dine in Glória, Catete, Flamengo & Botafogo

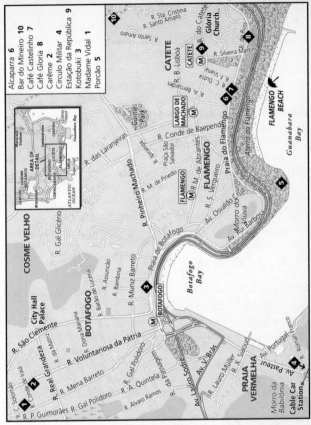

Alcaparra **6**
Bar do Mineiro **10**
Café Castelinho **7**
Café Gloria **8**
Carême **2**
Círculo Militar **4**
Estação da República **9**
Kotobuki **3**
Madame Vidal **1**
Porção **5**

schmooze or maybe track down that cabinet minister who's been ducking your calls.

Praia do Flamengo 150, Flamengo. ☎ **021/2558-3937.** Reservations required. No shorts and sandals. R$18–R$46 ($9–$23). AE, DC, MC, V. Daily noon–midnight. Metrô: Flamengo.

Carême ✦✦✦ *Finds* BRAZILIAN   The hottest chef in town has Rio's foodies flocking to her establishment en masse. Or they would flock en masse, but Flavia Caresma's cozy Botafogo bistro is a tad too tiny for en masse anything, so instead they flock in ones and fours and exult with massive oohs and aahs over her creations.

What's behind all the fuss? Partly, it's that macho Brazilian culture still finds a top female chef something of a novelty. And then there is the food: no boring, predictable a la carte menu here. Every other month Caresma puts together a tasting menu offering a range of outstanding choices. Her cuisine is classically inspired, her ingredients always top quality and fresh. On our visit we tried the delicious warm salad of tender grilled veal, rabbit, and duck served on a bed of mushrooms and greens, and the asparagus and marinated salmon with quail eggs and a beurre blanc sauce. For our main courses we chose the chicken breast stuffed with duck paté, sage, and dried-mushroom sauce, and a grilled entrecôte with mashed potatoes in a juniper-and-thyme sauce. Desserts are the creations of the patisserie chef who does an amazing job with fresh fruits and chocolate. The wine list is conservative with a small selection of well-chosen merlots, cabernet sauvignons, and Chilean chardonnays.

Rua Visconde de Caravelas 113, Botafogo. © 021/2537-5431. Reservations required. Tasting menu (includes appetizer, main course, and dessert) R$70 ($35). DC, MC. Tues–Sat 7pm–1am. Dinner is usually served in 2 seatings, 8:30 and 11pm. Bus: 176, 178.

Madame Vidal ★★ BRAZILIAN/ITALIAN   Don't hate her because she's beautiful. In a calculated attempt to attract the artistic, the trendy, and the well-heeled who tag along after them, Madame Vidal has gone over the top, first by locating her lovely old mansion restaurant in Botafogo, second by tarting up the exterior in blue and gold colonial kitsch, and third by putting customers into total culture shock as they enter this baroque wedding cake to find New York SoHo minimal. The menu offers an amazing selection of risottos, pastas, and meat dishes including a signature veal. It's all pretty good: simply prepared with quality ingredients. The ravioli stuffed with mozzarella and sun-dried tomato is fresh and delicious, as is the quail, grilled and stuffed with nuts and served with wild rice. As you'd expect from a place that aspires to attract the bohemian, Madame Vidal's is open late, daily until at least 2am, 3am on weekends.

Rua Capitão Salomão 69 (corner of Visconde da Silva), Humaitá, Botafogo. © 021/2539-2396. Main courses R$18–R$34 ($9–$17). AE, MC, V. Mon–Thurs 7pm–2am, Fri–Sun 7pm–3am. Bus: 178.

EXPENSIVE

Café Glória ★★ (Finds) BRAZILIAN   Tucked away in a Gaudí old mansion (pun intended) overlooking the Parque do Flamengo is this tasteful little gem of a restaurant. To reach the dining room, you walk in the main doors, then up a spiraling wrought-iron staircase; keep a grip on the way up, as your eyes are likely to be drawn either to the stained-glass window overhead or the colorful floor mosaic below. Once at the top, you'll have a choice between the dining room—its small tables and candlelight perfect for a romantic evening—or a table on the large deck overlooking the park. The cuisine here is modern Brazilian—fresh ingredients in interesting combinations. Definitely worth trying are the penne with fresh salmon and pepper, or the fusilli with a tomato basil sauce served with chicken breast in rosemary butter. Seafood lovers will enjoy the grilled tuna with a Japanese salad or the grilled fish of the day in a passion-fruit sauce. Meat dishes are not as creative but will keep steak lovers happy. The wine list is small and leans heavily on Chileans. As compensation, most vintages are available by the glass, so have some fun and explore.

Rua do Russel 734, Glória. ⓒ 021/2205-9647. Reservations recommended. Main courses R$17–R$28 ($8.50–$14). AE, DC, MC. Mon–Sat noon–midnight, Sun noon–6:30pm. Metrô: Glória.

Kotobuki 𝄄 JAPANESE The food at Kotobuki is good, very good even, but it's not really better than the food at a number of other Japanese restaurants around Rio. What is outstanding is what you're watching while you eat. Kotobuki offers a sweeping view of Botafogo beach, the bay with the pretty boats at anchor in the marina, and backstopping it all, the soaring Pão de Açúcar. Located in the seventh-floor food court of the Botafogo Praia Shopping mall (I know, but food court food is *different* in Brazil), Kotobuki offers lunchtime specials that include the *"prato executivo"*: 15 pieces of sushi and sashimi with a miso soup (called *misoshuri* in Brazil), or beef stir-fry with rice and miso and a sunomuno salad, for R$12.90 ($6.45). A favorite lunch special, particularly on the weekend, is the Japanese buffet. It offers a variety of sushi, sashimi, appetizers, tempura, and yakisoba for R$27.90 ($13.95). The teppanyaki for two is skillfully prepared at your table, as the chef cooks up thin slices of beef, tofu, and vegetables.

Praia de Botafogo 400, 7th floor, Botafogo. ⓒ 021/2559-9595. Reservations accepted, but window tables are on a first-come, first-served basis. R$12.90–R$49 ($6.45–$24.50). AE, DC, MC, V. Daily noon–midnight. Metrô: Botafogo.

Porcão 𝄄𝄄 BRAZILIAN/STEAK A mass carnivorous orgy. Porcão is where you go not to sample or taste or nibble, but to munch and stuff and gorge yourself on some of the best beef the world has to offer, in this case served up with some of the best views

---

Value **A Gourmet Deal for Lunch**

Striking while the stove is hot, Flavia Caresma has opened up a lunchtime restaurant in downtown Rio to lure in the business crowd. Eça, Av. Rio Branco 128 (inside the H. Stern building), Centro (**②** 021/2524-2300), is a great spot to check out Caresma's culinary skills without committing to the more formal evening event. Main courses cost R$16 to R$30 ($8–$15). Most credit cards accepted. Open Monday through Friday from noon to 4pm. Metrô: Cinelândia.

---

in the world. Porcão is a churrascaria (a chain in fact) operating on the rodízio system. It's one price for all you can eat (dessert and drinks are extra), and once you sit down, an onslaught of waiters comes bearing all manner and variety of meat (steak cuts, roast cuts, filet mignon, chicken breast, chicken hearts, sausage of divers kinds, and much more), which they slice to perfection on your plate. The "stop sign" card you receive is supposed to regulate this serving army—green means go ahead and red says no more—but considering how little respect Cariocas have for stop lights in general, it's hardly surprising that waiters keep coming no matter how abjectly you wave your little red surrender sign. Just go with it. And then there are the nonmeat dishes: included in your meal is a buffet with dozens of antipasto items, hot and cold seafood dishes, and at least 15 different kinds of salads and cheeses. Alas, no doggy bags allowed.

Av. Infante Dom Henrique s/n, Parque do Flamengo, Botafogo. **②** 021/2554-8535. R$39 ($19.50) per person all-you-can-eat meat and buffet. 50% discount for children under 10. AE, DC, MC, V. Daily 11:30am–1am. Bus: Any bus to Praia do Flamengo.

MODERATE

Café Castelinho *⊛ Value* ITALIAN   The Café Castelinho packs a great punch for such a diminutive location. From a tiny cafe tucked in just behind the fairy-tale Victorian Castelinho do Flamengo, Chef Carmine Carnevale's unique dishes have emerged to big applause at local seafood festivals. The *gamberi a carmine* is a grilled fish served with a shrimp-and-cheese sauce and topped with grilled prawns and a coconut farofa. The *filet de peixe ao potato crust* is a fish filet (usually *cherné*, a local fish with firm white meat), covered with rosti potatoes and grilled, served with cream of spinach and catupiry cheese. These elaborate meals certainly stand out amongst the other more simple dishes on the menu, but the latter are just as tasty. For a quick lunch, try the "make-your-own-pasta" dish. Choose the pasta, the sauce, five ingredients, and herbs for the sauce, and voilà, you have your own delicious creation, all for R$7 ($3.50). The cafe also serves an afternoon tea, and Thursday through Sunday there is live music from 6pm onward, usually MPB showcasing local musicians.

Praia do Flamengo 158, Flamengo. ✆ 021/2225-7650. R$7–R$22 ($3.50–$11). No credit cards. Mon–Wed noon–8pm, Thurs–Fri noon–10pm, Sat 5pm–midnight, Sun noon–9pm. Metrô: Flamengo.

Circulo Militar *(Finds* BRAZILIAN   The best view of the Sugar Loaf Mountain, and one of the best in all Rio, comes courtesy of the Brazilian armed forces (hey, if you're gonna run the country, you may as well take the best views). From the tree-shaded patio of a military club in Urca called the Circulo Militar, you look out across Praia Vemelha and a tiny bay full of fishing boats to the sheer solid sides of the Pão de Açúcar. Come in the evening and you also get the lights of Niterói twinkling far off across the waters of Guanabara Bay. Civilians are completely welcome at the club (though some of the prime tables are sometimes reserved for officers). The view certainly outshines the food, but the menu provides k-rations enough to accompany a drink or two. There's Bella Praia pizza with shrimp, squid, and octopus, or for a more substantial meal, try the mixed churrasco for two with beef, sausage, chicken, and pork served with fries and rice (R$26/$13). Live music Tuesday through Sunday from 8pm onward.

Praça General Tiburcio s/n, Praia Vermelha (on the far right, inside the military complex), Urca. ✆ 021/2295-6079. Main courses R$12–R$26 ($6–$13). No credit cards. Tues–Sun 10am–midnight. Bus: 107 from downtown, 512 from Ipanema and Copacabana.

Estação da República *(Kids* KILO   The Estação is top of the heap in that unique Brazilian category, the kilo restaurant. The place is so popular that the food is always fresh. It offers a daily selection of at least 20 salads, a range of pastas, and many favorite Brazilian dishes such as feijoada, *vatapá* (seafood stew) and *bobó* (shrimp stew). Fancier dishes include carpaccio and sushi. The pièce de résistance, however, is the grill in the back of the restaurant where skilled chefs fire up the barbeque and serve you a choice of beef, chicken, and a wide assortment of fish. It's a great place for children; they can see the food and try as much or as little as they like. Make your selection, weigh your plate, and find yourself a seat; drinks are served at your table. If the ground floor looks packed, take the escalator up to the second floor for more tables.

Rua do Catete 104, Catete. ℰ 021/2225-2650. Reservations not accepted. Main courses R$6–R$12 ($3–$6) per person, R$17.90 ($8.95) per kilo. AE, DC, MC, V. Daily 11am–midnight. Metrô: Catete.

3 Copacabana & Leme

VERY EXPENSIVE

Cipriani ✦✦✦ ITALIAN   For an elegant evening out, there's no place like the Copacabana Palace. At Cipriani, always a top contender for Rio's best restaurant, every dinner guest receives five-star treatment. The elegant dining room overlooks the hotel's swimming pool and courtyard, both magically illuminated at night. Reserve early to book a window table. The menu is mostly classic Italian with a few contemporary twists. A signature dish showing off the chef's talents is the potato ravioli with black truffle, so simple yet so satisfying. Equally scrumptious was the tagliatelle in a cream-and-coconut sauce with succulent sweet prawns. My favorite, however, was the duck breast in a balsamic sauce with blueberries—the perfect balance between sweet and savory. Another noteworthy entree is the ravioli with eggplant and mozzarella—my pasta dishes never turn out this brilliantly. To try the best of chef Carli's cuisine, opt for the tasting menu. Though not cheap at R$98 ($49), or R$150 ($75) with wine pairings, you'll savor the experience long after the last bite.

Copacabana Palace Hotel, Av. Atlântica 1702, Copacabana. ℰ 021/2545-8747. Reservations required. Semiformal dress. Main courses R$32–R$46 ($16–$23). AE, DC, MC, V. Daily 12:30–3pm and 8pm–1am. Metrô: Arcoverde.

Le Pré-Catalan ✦✦✦ FRENCH   Ever since French chef Roland Villard took over the kitchen in 1998, it's been raining awards at Le Pré-Catalan. Fortunately, Villard and his staff haven't had the time to become complacent, instead continuing to challenge themselves by creating exquisite French cuisine with just a bit of a Brazilian twist. Updated every 2 weeks, the menu offers a selection of appetizers, main courses, and dessert for R$75 ($37.50), a steal considering the quality of the ingredients, the preparation, and the service. The chef himself comes to each table to review the menu and explain the evening's dishes. Some of the best we've tried so far include the langoustines soup with coconut milk and tomato confit,

Where to Dine in Copacabana & Leme

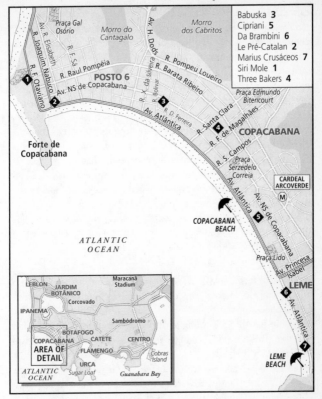

Babuska	3
Cipriani	5
Da Brambini	6
Le Pré-Catalan	2
Marius Crusáceos	7
Siri Mole	1
Three Bakers	4

the terrine of foie gras with fresh truffles and a side of chutney, and the tournedos with wild mushrooms and a vegetable sautéed with sweet potato. All dishes are beautifully presented. Desserts are made from scratch. Look for the trio of tropical fruit sorbets on a bed of warm Madeleines or the *chocolat fondant* served with a coulis of orange and passion fruit. Enjoy, indulge, and with a smile on your face, walk off the calories along Copacabana's beach boulevard.

Hotel Sofitel, Av. Atlântica 4240, Copacabana. ℰ **021/2525-1232.** Reservations required. Business casual dress. Main courses R$35–R$48 ($17.50–$24). AE, DC, MC, V. Mon–Wed 7:30–11:30pm, Thurs–Sat 7:30pm–midnight. Bus: 415.

Marius Crustáceos ℰ SEAFOOD/BRAZILIAN If the all-you-can-eat rodízio system works for meat, the successful owner of Marius restaurants asked himself one day, why wouldn't it work for seafood? And thus was Marius Crustáceos born, a must-eat stop for every seafood lover. Most people start off with a trip to the buffet, helping themselves to the feast of antipasto; cold seafood such as prawns, oysters, and crab; as well as warm seafood favorites such as paella, pasta with seafood, and popular dishes from Bahia, including *moqueca* (traditional stew) and vatapá. As hard as it may be, exercise restraint and save your appetite for the prime catch the waiters will bring to your table: lobster, prawns, tuna steaks, salmon, crab. Don't be shy about asking for your favorite seafood if you don't see it out in the dining room. Chances are, they will be able to provide it. Some of our Brazilian friends find that the waiters at Crustáceos aren't aggressive enough about pushing their seafood wares, but we found it a pleasant change of pace from some of the overeager churrascaria waiters.

Av. Atlântica 290A, Leme. ① 021/2543-6363. All-you-can-eat seafood and buffet R$48 ($24) per person. AE, DC, MC, V. Mon–Fri noon–4pm and 6pm–midnight, Sat–Sun noon–midnight. Bus: 472.

EXPENSIVE

Da Brambini ⋒ *Finds* ITALIAN   For traditional Italian food in a cozy little bistro, look no further than Da Brambini. Decorated with family photos of the Brambinis, who hail from northern Italy, the restaurant has the welcoming and friendly atmosphere of an Italian trattoria. To start with, indulge in the *couvert*—a tasty antipasto platter with olives, salami, tuna paste, grilled eggplants, and freshly baked breads. Other worthwhile appetizers include the polenta with fresh funghi or Gorgonzola. The main courses include veal with mushrooms, traditional *osso buco* (veal shanks stewed in wine), and a number of outstanding pasta dishes. Da Brambini certainly doesn't skimp on ingredients; the handmade ravioli with shrimp is just swimming with the little critters, all smothered in a creamy seafood sauce. The linguine with mussels, *sururu* (a tiny clam), and *vongole* (small clams) are equally tasty. An Italian restaurant is bound to have a halfway decent wine list and Da Brambini doesn't disappoint, with a good selection of Italian reds starting at R$24 ($12) a bottle, while Frascati or Pinot Grigio whites start at R$27 ($13.50). The service is unhurried and the staff is happy to let you linger over your dinner.

Av. Atlântica 514, Leme. ① 021/2275-4346. Reservations recommended. Main courses R$17–R$28 ($8.50–$14). AE, DC, MC, V. Daily noon–1am. Bus: 472.

Siri Mole ⋒ BAHIAN   One of the best Bahian restaurants in town, Siri Mole is named after the signature ingredient in northeastern cuisine, the soft-shell crab. Not only are the little critters in the name, they're also on the appetizer menu. Look for crunchy fried soft-shell crabs with tons of garlic, perfect for munching with a cold beer or a caipirinha. Not so good for sharing but equally delicious to start with is the *caldo de sururu,* a rich and delicately flavored chowderlike soup, brimming over with tiny clams. On the main menu you will find more siri mole in the moqueca stew. However, if this slightly crunchy crustacean ain't your thing, you can choose from a number of other moquecas made with lobster, cod, prawns, octopus, or squid. For a lighter alternative, Siri Mole also serves seafood from the grill. Save a little bit of room for dessert. A cool and smooth favorite is the *quindim,* a creamy coconut pudding often served with a plum sauce. For a bigger sugar hit, try the *cocada*—pure coconut mixed with pure cane sugar—then wash it down with a hot and black cafezinho.

Rua Francisco Otaviano 50, Copacabana. ℂ 021/2267-0894. Main courses R$18–R$38 ($9–$18). AE, DC, MC, V. Mon 7pm–midnight, Tues–Sun noon–midnight. Bus: 415.

INEXPENSIVE

Babuska ⒜ ⒦ⁱᵈˢ DESSERTS   Top-quality ice cream, made from scratch with only the freshest ingredients. Babuska has a large variety of flavors—50 at least—including many wonderful tropical treats such as mango, pumpkin with coconut, papaya, passion fruit, and, for those hide-bound traditionalists—even chocolate.

Rua Constante Ramos 13, loja A, Copacabana. ℂ 021/2255-1741. All items R$6 ($3) or less. Daily 9am–10pm. Bus: 415.

Three Bakers QUICK BITES/DESSERTS   Three Bakers offers the perfect combination of American-style sandwiches and Brazilian sweets and desserts. The sandwich menu includes a variety of breads not often seen on Carioca menus, including ciabatta, eight grain, whole wheat, and challah. The Al Pacino sandwich comes with Parma ham, mozzarella, sun-dried tomatoes, and a Mediterranean dressing. The Romeo and Juliet is a delicious combination of chicken breast, herb-flavored catupiry cheese, greens, and an apricot dressing. Once you've chewed through one of those, you can move on to dessert. Choose from a mouthwatering selection of cakes and pies such as the "ecstasy," a chocolate cake with fresh strawberries, whipped cream, and chocolate sauce, or for something more nutty, the chocolate mousse cake with cashews. The bakery also serves up a mean brew of cappuccino with a rich and luscious layer of foam.

Rua Santa Clara 86, Copacabana. ℂ 021/2256-7000. www.thebakers.com.br. All items under R$9 ($4.50). No credit cards. Mon–Fri 9am–8pm, Sat 9am–6:30pm, Sun 9am–4pm. Bus: 415.

Tips **Where to Find the Finest Feijoada**

For the best feijoada in town, try one of the following restaurants (on a Saturday, of course—lunch only). **Confeitaria Columbo,** Rua Gonçalves Dias 32, Centro (© 021/2221-0107), serves an outstanding feijoada in the loveliest dining room in town. **Galani,** Av. Vieira Souto 460, on the 23rd floor of the plush Caesar Park Hotel, Ipanema (© 021/2525-2525), is famous for its Saturday buffet. Even fancier is the spread served at the Sheraton's **Mirador** restaurant, Avenida Niemeyer, São Conrado (© 021/2274-1122), with its privileged oceanview. After lunch you will welcome the 30-minute walk back to Leblon. For a hearty feijoada any old day of the week, visit **Casa da Feijoada,** Rua Prudente de Moraes 10, Ipanema (© 021/2523-4994). Brazil's most famous dish is served for lunch or dinner.

4 Ipanema

VERY EXPENSIVE

Madame Butterfly 🐱🐱 JAPANESE   Rio's favorite Japanese restaurant, Madame Butterfly has in its 12 years seen Japanese cuisine in Brazil evolve from exotic novelty to just another part of the Rio dining scene. So now that Japanese has arrived, the two sisters who guide the Butterfly have decided it's time to spread their wings and get a bit more creative. Some of this involves going back to Japan to capture, tag, and re-export dishes that never seemed to make it to the West. Tops so far in this category is *umewan* soup, a rich broth made with Japanese plums, algae, and horse radish. Their other thrust is developing delicious new Brazilian-Japanese hybrids such as gyoza with Brazilian abóbora pumpkin– or ginger-flavored lobster served on a cheese risotto. Another interesting twist is the *casquinha de siri,* a Japanese-inflected version of the traditional Bahian appetizer. As done in the Butterfly, the dish features crabmeat and spices on a half shell sprinkled with fresh fish eggs. All of these new taste combinations seem to be paying off, for even with all the new competition in Rio, *Veja Magazine* just awarded the restaurant top honors for best Japanese restaurant for the second year in a row.

Rua Barão da Torre 472, Ipanema. © 021/2267-4247. Reservations recommended on weekends. Main courses R$28–R$55 ($14–$27.50). AE, DC, MC. Daily noon–2am. Bus: 415.

Where to Dine in Ipanema & Leblon

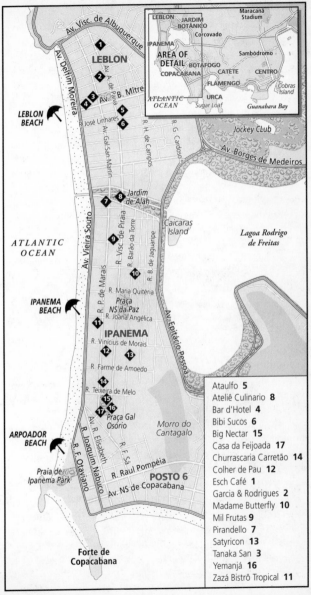

Ataulfo **5**
Ateliê Culinario **8**
Bar d'Hotel **4**
Bibi Sucos **6**
Big Nectar **15**
Casa da Feijoada **17**
Churrascaria Carretão **14**
Colher de Pau **12**
Esch Café **1**
Garcia & Rodrigues **2**
Madame Butterfly **10**
Mil Frutas **9**
Pirandello **7**
Satyricon **13**
Tanaka San **3**
Yemanjá **16**
Zazá Bistrô Tropical **11**

Satyricon ✸✸✸ SEAFOOD   Just for fun, don some dark shades and cop an attitude when you walk up to Satyricon. Depending on the quality of your movie-star swagger, you might well find a paparazzi or two leaping out, camera in hand, to snap off candid shots of your arrival. This is, after all, one of Rio's most select hangouts, and the society columnists and snap-happy photogs are never far away. Fame and fortune certainly weren't amassed overnight by owners Marly and Miro Leopardi, however, who started the restaurant 20 years ago with an emphasis on seafood Italian-style. Over the years, the Italian focus has faded somewhat, supplanted by a total devotion to seafood itself. Dinner should certainly start with the three-fish carpaccio, made fresh every day with an always-changing variety of fish. If you're feeling hungry or have brought the entourage along, you could also go for the seafood platter. Not only is it outstanding, it's humongous. One of the restaurant's trademark dishes is the *pargo,* a firm white fish that comes with filets crusted in a layer of kosher sea salt. For a heartier dish, try the codfish stew in red wine, olives, tomatoes, and peppers. And if Madonna is in town, better get there early. This is her favorite Rio restaurant, and she's not known for sharing.

Rua Barão da Torre 192, Ipanema. ✆ 021/2521-0627. Reservations required. Main courses R$26–R$48 ($13–$24). AE, DC, MC, V. Mon 6pm–2am, Tues–Sun noon–2am. Bus: 415.

EXPENSIVE

Pirandello ✸✸ ITALIAN   If life is but a stage, Pirandello has done a fabulous job setting the scene: masks of Tragedy and Comedy hang over the entranceway, while inside the hushed red velvet chairs and sparkling silver serve only to highlight the expanse of elegant white table linen, the stage for the drama to come. The curtain rises on appetizers such as oysters (raw or au gratin) and tuna salad with radicchio and bruschetta. For main courses, Pirandello offers 14 types of risotto and 15 kinds of pasta, as well as osso buco, saltimbocca, and other Italian favorites. Seafood takes center stage in most dishes. Look for appearances of risottos with oysters and goat cheese or shrimp with arugula. The Don Fernando spaghetti combines shrimp and baked oysters with pencil-thin strips of pumpkin and eggplant. Before the final curtain, leave some room for the coffee ice cream with amaretto biscuit, a fine farewell to an elegant evening out. Valet parking is available.

Rua Paul Redfern 37, Ipanema. ✆ 021/2274-2986. Main courses R$13.90–R$39 ($6.95–$19.50). AE, DC, MC, V. Mon–Fri 7pm–midnight, Sat–Sun and holidays noon–1am. Bus: 415.

Yemanjá ✿✿ BAHIAN   If your beach and sightseeing schedule is getting too hectic, step into this little piece of Bahia in the heart of Ipanema's busiest shopping district. The name and decor pay homage to the sea goddess Yemanjá, and with her blessing, the menu showcases the best and freshest the sea has to offer. To whet your appetite, order the couvert—not your usual bread, butter, and olives, but a delectable combination of Bahia's best flavors including grilled squid, tapioca pancake, and a dollop of vatapá fish stew. You may want to skip more appetizers as the dishes are hearty and portions are large. Prominently featured on the list of main are the moquecas, a traditional Bahian stew made with coconut milk, red palm oil, peppers, cilantro, and a generous amount of lime juice. Other Bahian favorites include bobó—a stew made with succulent shrimp—and vatapá—the richest stew of all, made with fish, ground-up peanuts, and sauce thickened with bread. All main courses serve two with lots left over. Service is laid-back and unhurried and the staff is friendly and helpful; the perfect timeout for a tired traveler.

Rua Visconde de Pirajá 128, Ipanema. ✆ 021/2247-7004. Main courses R$18–R$30 ($9–$15). AE, DC, MC, V. Mon–Thurs 6pm–midnight, Fri–Sat and holidays noon–midnight, Sun noon–10pm. Bus: 415.

Zazá Bistrô Tropical ✿✿ BRAZILIAN/FUSION   Dishes at Zazá blend South American cuisine with Oriental flavors, making Zazá one of the few fusion restaurants in Rio de Janeiro. Appetizers include deliciously sautéed shrimp with palm hearts in a sweet-and-sour sauce and crisp little fall (not spring) rolls with shiitake mushrooms and caramelized vegetables. Main courses often lack the cute names but don't disappoint when it comes to mixing up the flavors. The tuna steak comes grilled in a soy-and-passion-fruit sauce on a bed of cardamom rice. Also popular is the filet mignon with palm heart and mushroom sauce served with a balsamic reduction. Vegetarians always have a daily special to choose from, made with seasonal produce and interesting spices.

A seating tip: The folks lined up at the door every night aren't there for a seat on the veranda or at one of the ground-floor tables. The "in" place to eat is upstairs, where everyone sits on the floor leaning back on masses of silk-covered pillows. Surrounded by candlelight and lanterns, the room feels like a palace from *Arabian Nights*.

Rua Joana Angelica 40, Ipanema. ✆ 021/2247-9101. R$20–R$29 ($10–$14.50). AE, DC, MC, V. Sun–Thurs 7:30pm–1am, Fri–Sat 7:30pm–2am. Bus: 415.

MODERATE

Churrascaria Carretão *(Kids)* *(Value)* BRAZILIAN/STEAK   For a
churrascaria meal without breaking the bank, try Carretão. The system is similar to many rodízio restaurants: Meats are delivered right
to your table by a constant parade of waiters carrying a variety of
cuts, and you can help yourself to a large buffet with a selection of
20 salads, various types of sushi, and some fish dishes. Among the
latter, the *bacalhau a bras* is especially good. This traditional
Portuguese dish consists of a codfish stew with potatoes, olives, and
egg. On the meat side, in addition to beef, Carretão also serves up a
variety of pork, sausage, chicken, and turkey cuts. Children under 5
eat free and those ages 5 to 9 pay only half price. Just keep them
away from the fancy fruit smoothies and desserts that the waiters
eagerly push on you; these jack up the bill pretty quickly.

Rua Visconde de Pirajá 112, Ipanema. ✆ 021/2267-3965. R$16.90 ($8.45) all you
can eat; drinks and desserts extra. AE, DC, MC, V. Daily 11am–midnight. Bus: 404,
474 (corner Teixeira de Melo).

Colher de Pau *(Finds)* BRAZILIAN   For a light lunch or a snack, stop
in at Colher de Pau. Delicious salads such as the *salpicão* (thin
potato chips with carrots, chicken breast, and raisins in light
mayonnaise dressing) or *palmito* (greens and palm hearts in a
Parmesan dressing) can be a small meal on their own or combined
with a grilled sandwich. For a more substantial lunch, the restaurant
serves grilled fish or filet mignon with a choice of sauce and rice or
potatoes. At R$12 ($6) the afternoon tea is quite a treat, served with
juice, various breads and jellies, cookies, a slice of cake, and a sweet.
Whatever you do, don't skip dessert: Bite-size Brazilian sweets with
coconut, chocolates, and nuts, or a three-chocolate or cheesecake-
with-mango minitorte will provide just the right sugar high to take
you through the afternoon.

Rua Farme de Amoedo 39, Ipanema. ✆ 021/2523-3018. Main courses
R$8–R$16.90 ($4–$8.45). No credit cards. Daily 10am–8pm. Bus: 415.

INEXPENSIVE

Big Nectar *(Value)* QUICK BITES   One of Rio's best *lanchonetes*,
Big Nectar is a bit like a magician's top hat. You glance into this
hole-in-the-wall diner and think there's nothing there, then the guy
behind the counter conjures up any kind of fruit juice you care to
name, all of it made fresh and to order. Actually, the menu in this
standing-room-only spot lists just over 25 different kinds of fruit
juice. In addition to the standards such as passion fruit (*maracujá*),
pineapple (*abacaxi*), or cashew fruit (*caju*), there's *carambola* (star

fruit), *goiaba* (guava), *jaca* (jack fruit), and *açerola* (red juice from the tiny açerola fruit). This is where things get fun. You mix anything with anything else. Try *laranja com açerola* (orange juice with açerola, a very popular combination), maracujá with mango, or pineapple and guava, cashew, and açerola.

Teixeira de Melo 34A, Ipanema. No phone. All items under R$9.50 ($4.75). No credit cards. Daily 7am–midnight. Bus: 404, 474.

5 Leblon

VERY EXPENSIVE

Bar d'Hotel ⭐⭐ *Finds* ITALIAN   On the first floor of the Marina Hotel in Ipanema, this hip eatery overlooks the most famous beach in the world yet doesn't even try to cash in on the view. Instead, what attracts the trendy crowd here to eat, drink, and be merry is each other. Artists, actors, soccer players, designers, and others too cool to look at the ocean compete for each other's attention, all the while trying not to look like they're looking. Fortunately, above and beyond the posing, the food is also great, so we mere mortals can remain happily oblivious to the star-spying and just have fun. If you have to wait at the bar for a table (very likely if you don't make reservations) try a lemon kir royal (champagne with lemon sorbet) or a saké caipirinha. Once seated, the waiter will come over with a black board listing the daily specials. The cuisine is sort of Italian. Appetizers include four types of bruschetta; the sampler plate comes with one of each. Main courses range from a delicious goat-cheese ravioli in tomato sauce to a grilled salmon served with a rich and creamy artichoke risotto. The restaurant is also open for breakfast and lunch, but the cool people don't show up until after 10pm.

Av. Delfim Moreira 630, 2nd floor (inside the Marina All Suites Hotel), Leblon. © 021/2540-4990. Reservations recommended. Main courses R$12–R$30 ($6–$15). MC, V. Thurs–Sat 7am–2am, Sun–Wed 8am–midnight. Bus: 415.

Esch Café ⭐ BRAZILIAN   While many Brazilian restaurants are starting to inch smokers out, this gorgeous bistro embraces them with open arms, providing a stylish refuge for cigar aficionados and other smokers. (There is a small nonsmoking section.) The cafe safeguards regulars' stogies in humidor lockers and operates a cigar store on the premises that sells the world's finest: habanos, and habanos only.

Even for many of the nonaddicted, the attractions of the Esch seem to outweigh the slightly smoggy atmosphere—the cafe has become a very popular nightspot in Leblon. Befitting a small bistro, the menu is uncomplicated, offering delicious sandwiches with cold cuts, Swiss cheese, or smoked salmon. There's also a variety of homemade salads, including a chicken Caesar salad and a tomato-and-mozzarella salad—and for mains, a few well-prepared pasta dishes such as a penne with spinach and Gorgonzola or pasta arrabiata. Grilled meats and fish are served with a side dish and sauce of choice: the filet mignon with a port-and-saffron sauce and grilled vegetables is a good option and reasonably priced at R$21 ($10.50). And for dessert, how about a cigar?

Rua Dias Ferreira 78, Leblon. © **021/2294-3173.** Reservations recommended in the evening. Main courses R$16–R$28 ($8–$14). AE, DC, MC. Mon–Fri noon–5pm and 6–10pm. Bus: 415.

Garcia & Rodrigues ✿✿ BRAZILIAN/FRENCH When Garcia & Rodrigues first opened in 1997, it became an instant success, leaving other deli and gourmet stores scratching their heads on just how to compete with this veritable food mega-complex. Encompassed within its walls are a delicatessen, bakery, cafe, patisserie, ice-cream parlor, and wine bar. And if that isn't enough, there's also a restaurant with fine dining. In the capable hands of chef Christophe Lidy, the kitchen makes use of Brazil's freshest ingredients to create dishes with a very French accent. Much to the delight of many regulars, the menu changes frequently, adjusting to the ingredients available seasonally. One recurring menu favorite, however, is the *galinha d'angola,* a roasted chicken stuffed with a compote of pears and spices. The garlic-roasted swordfish is a dish I wouldn't mind seeing again someday, and I have equally fond memories of the duck breast with figs—a perfect marriage of tender, slightly fatty duck meat and the sweet, meaty flavor of figs. Definitely leave room for dessert; the patisserie chef and ice-cream makers do not disappoint.

Av. Ataulfo de Paiva 1251, Leblon. © **021/2512-8188.** Main courses R$30–R$52 ($15–$26). Reservations recommended. AE, DC, MC, V. Mon 8pm–midnight, Tues–Sat noon–3:30pm and 8pm–midnight, Sun 1–4pm. Deli opens at 10am. Bus: 415.

EXPENSIVE

Ateliê Culinario ✿ BRAZILIAN More form than substance, the Ateliê Culinario lives in a beautiful two-level loft. Rustic decorations in wood and iron work well with the tall windows and soaring ceiling. The menu covers mostly light meals such as savory pastries stuffed with prawns and catupiry cheese. Miniquiches are another good starter option. Main courses include grilled cherné fish served with an herb pesto and vegetable ratatouille. There are also pasta dishes—the ravioli with goat cheese is very nice. For dessert, the kitchen makes excellent cakes and minicakes. Overall, however, the food doesn't quite soar to the same heights as the interior. This is the perfect place for a light snack and a caipirinha or a coffee and dessert.

Rua Paul Redfern 41, Ipanema. ℂ 021/2529-6856. Main courses R$18–R$40 ($9–$20). AE, V. Mon–Thurs noon–midnight, Fri noon–1am, Sat 1pm–1am, Sun 1pm–midnight. Bus: 415.

Tanaka San ℛ JAPANESE Even your basic Japanese sushi bar goes upscale in Leblon. The decor at Tanaka San is modern and sleek with pastel colors and carefully selected pieces of modern art. The large sushi bar offers a great view of the master himself, Yasuto Tanaka, at work. (That is if he is not busy at some of his other restaurants.) Those who prefer to can still sit on the floor, but there are only very limited number of these traditional tables; the well-heeled Zona Sul customer prefers to sit on a chair. The menu includes many standard dishes such as sushi, sashimi, and tempura as well as a delicious *robata*—grilled skewers with seafood, squid, sweet potato, shiitake mushrooms, or chicken. If there are two of you, consider sharing the teppanyaki stir-fry. Made right at your table, with a choice of squid, prawns, or pork, and fresh vegetables and sauce, it makes for a satisfying meal.

Rua Bartolomeu Mitre 112, Leblon. ℂ 021/2239-0198. Reservations recommended on weekends. Main courses R$9–R$38 ($4.50–$19). AE. Mon 7pm–midnight, Tues–Fri 7pm–1am, Sat noon–1am, Sun noon–midnight. Bus: 415.

MODERATE

Ataulfo (Value) BRAZILIAN/DELI A large restaurant and deli, Ataulfo offers something for any time of the day. Walk in for a quick coffee and a sweet, a light sandwich, a delicious buffet lunch, or a more leisured dinner for two. The lunchtime buffet is a bit different from most others; instead of paying by the kilo or an all-you-can-eat feast, you choose per dish, combining one, two, or more dishes into the meal of your choice. For example, you could pick up a quiche and a salad, or a chicken filet with sun-dried tomato and basil sauce and a side dish of sautéed potatoes. All dishes are priced R$2.90 to R$9.90 ($1.45–$4.95) and vary every day. For those who resist the urge to order dessert, the deli section provides one last temptation on the way out. Strategically placed by the door, its glass cases contain a cornucopia of pastries, sweets, and sorbets. Go ahead, you can always get it to go.

Av. Ataulfo de Paiva 630, Ipanema. ℂ **021/2540-0606.** Reservations for groups only. Small dishes under R$10 ($5), main courses R$12–R$31 ($6–$15.50). AE, MC, V. Daily 11:30am–5:30pm and 7:30pm–midnight; deli and cafe daily 9am–midnight. Bus: 415.

Mil Frutas ℛ DESSERTS   Already famous for its luscious ice cream, Mil Frutas has now added salads, quiches, and wraps to its menu. The latter is still something of a novelty in Brazil, so there are some interesting combinations available: Cowboy wraps with red-pepper cream cheese, egg, ham, and mushrooms, and Arabesco wraps with sun-dried tomatoes, fresh cheese, radicchio, and olives. If the wrap trend doesn't take root in Rio, Mil Frutas will always have a role selling the best ice cream in town.

Rua Garcia d'Avila 134, Ipanema. ℂ **021/2521-1584.** All items under R$12 ($6). No credit cards. Daily 10:30am–1am. Bus: 415.

INEXPENSIVE

Bibi Sucos ℛ *Value* QUICK BITES   The overhead menu at this popular neighborhood juice bar is refreshingly straightforward: juice, juice, and juice. You pick one or more fruit combinations and into the blender they go. It's trendy in newly health-conscious Rio to add on a scoop of protein powder for strength, *guaraná* for energy, or pollen for general health. In addition to providing for your liquid needs, Bibi also sells hamburgers, grilled cheese sandwiches, and a variety of Brazilian savory pastries.

Av. Ataulfo de Paiva 591, Leblon. ℂ **021/2259-4298.** All items under R$10 ($5). No credit cards. Daily 8am–2am, later on weekends if busy. Bus: 415.

Exploring Rio

Most visitors to Rio de Janeiro stay in the beachfront neighbor-hoods of Copacabana and Ipanema. They're great places to soak up the sun and to people-watch. But even if your time is limited, it's worth making the effort to explore further. In the historic down-town neighborhoods of Centro, Lapa, and Santa Teresa, there are narrow cobblestone streets and grand plazas, gold-covered churches, and buildings in the baroque, beaux arts, and Art Deco styles. Shoppers will be in heaven; browse the craft markets for souvenirs or check out the small shops in downtown's pedestrian streets. Upscale shoppers will love the Rio Sul mall and the fancy boutiques in Rio's tony Ipanema. If you have the energy, Rio's stunning setting offers numerous recreational activities: hiking, hang gliding, surfing, and kayaking are just a few options. Taking in a game of soccer is an adventure in itself. Nowhere are the crowds larger or livelier than at Rio's Maracanã stadium. The city's vibrant cultural scene comes to life in the evening and never disappoints: See some of the local samba bands or emerging talents at the city's many live-music venues or splurge to see a big national star such as Caetano Veloso.

SUGGESTED ITINERARIES FOR THE FIRST-TIME VISITOR

If You Have 1 Day

On your first day in Rio, **hit the beach early.** Enjoy the clear air and an hour or so of tanning in the softer morning rays. Then head up to the **Corcovado** and see Rio laid out below you in all its glory. Stop in for a quick lunch at any of Rio's countless kilo restaurants, then in the afternoon head in to **Centro** to explore what you've seen from on high. Wander **old Rio,** making sure to check out the Uruguaiana shopping district and to poke your head in any one of the baroque churches. Finish your walk with a nice cold chopp (beer) at a sidewalk cafe in **Cinelândia,** or in the countless patios in the **Arco do Teles.** Have dinner back in the Zona Sul, at one of the top-notch restaurants in **Leblon.** If it's a Saturday in pre-**Carnaval** season, go see a **samba school rehearsal.**

If You Have 2 Days

On your second day get some culture. Go see the **Museum of Modern Art,** or if painting's not your thing, see the **Historical Museum,** the **Copacabana Fort,** or **Ilha Fiscal.** Have lunch overlooking the **Sugar Loaf** at the **Círculo Militar** in Urca. Afterwards, work off those calories by climbing up to the **Pão de Açúcar**'s peak. Reward yourself for your efforts by having dinner at the **Porcão** on **Flamengo beach**—all-you-can-eat Brazilian barbecue with a view of the bay and the Sugar Loaf thrown in. In the evening, go for a drink, some dancing, and some live Brazilian music at any of a number of spots in **Lapa.**

If You Have 3 Days

In the morning, take the old streetcar across the **Arcos de Lapa** to the quirky hilltop neighborhood of **Santa Teresa.** See the **Chácara do Céu museum,** or clamber up the catwalks in the **Ruin Park.** Enjoy the view. In the afternoon, go **hang gliding.** Soar above the beach, feeling the wind and admiring the mountains and the waves below. Or take a hike in the rain forest in **Tijuca National Park,** or stroll amid the stately palm trees in the **Jardim Botânico.** In the evening, stroll around the edge of the **Lagoa.** Have a beer or dinner at one of the many kiosks and enjoy the music and the prime people-watching.

If You Have 4 Days or More

See how the other half lives. Take Marcelo Armstrong's **Favela Tour** through the huge and hidden neighborhood of **Rocinha.** Or check out the sights in **Niterói** across the bay. Try some extreme sports like **rappelling** or **rafting.** Or take a gentle tour down the coast to the **Casa do Pontal** and **Grumari beach.** If you've got several days to spare, go inland to the summer capital of **Petrópolis,** or the pretty historical cities of Ouro Prêto and **Mariana.** Or else head up the coast to **Búzios** or **Cabo Frio** and do some **scuba diving** or just hang out on the long white **ocean beaches.** Of course, you could even spend more time on the beach in Rio.

1 The Top Attractions

CENTRO

Ilha Fiscal 🐦🐦   If you ever take the ferry to Niterói, you'll see a blue-green ceramic castle afloat on its own little island in the bay off Praça XV. It looks like the dwelling place of a fair elfin princess but

What to See & Do in Centro

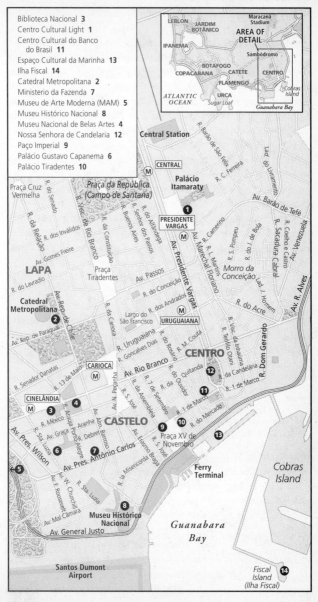

Biblioteca Nacional **3**
Centro Cultural Light **1**
Centro Cultural do Banco
  do Brasil **11**
Espaço Cultural da Marinha **13**
Ilha Fiscal **14**
Catedral Metropolitana **2**
Ministerio da Fazenda **7**
Museu de Arte Moderna (MAM) **5**
Museu Histórico Nacional **8**
Museu Nacional de Belas Artes **4**
Nossa Senhora de Candelaria **12**
Paço Imperial **9**
Palácio Gustavo Capanema **6**
Palácio Tiradentes **10**

in fact was built for a more mundane task: as the headquarters for the Customs service. Initially a quite prosaic building was planned, but Emperor Pedro II intervened, demanding that the gem of a site be given a jewel box of a building. Designer Adolpho Del-Vecchio complied, making charming use of the Gothic-revival style then sweeping Europe. It's curious how the fate of the palace and the emperor seemed to intertwine. When construction was finally finished in 1889, the normally reclusive Dom Pedro II decided to have a grand ball on Ilha Fiscal, hoping that ingratiating himself to Rio's elite would help vitalize his very shaky rule. Arriving by boat on the night of November 9, 1889, Dom Pedro stumbled on the stone steps of the quay. Quick with words if not on his feet, the emperor quipped, "The monarch may have slipped, but the monarchy remains in place." Six days later the empire collapsed.

Visitors to the island get to see some of this history, notably a large oil painting entitled "The Last Ball of the Monarchy," and they get to see the building itself, which is a gorgeous piece of work. Much of the rest of the interior is given over to a reasonably interesting, small museum focused almost solely on the Brazilian navy (it is their island). The tour lasts about 2½ hours.

Tip: The navy also offers a 90-minute boat tour of four small islands in the Bahia Guanabara bristling with destroyers, aircraft carriers, and lots more military hardware. The voyage to Ilha Fiscal, Ilha das Cobras, Ilha dos Enxadas, and Ilha Villagagnon takes place aboard a World War I–era tugboat. The cost is R$6 ($3) for adults, R$3 ($1.50) for children and students. Call ℰ **021/2233-9165** or 021/3870-6992 to confirm departure times.

Av. Alfredo Agache s/n, Centro. ℰ 021/3870-6025. Admission R$4 ($2) adults, R$2 ($1) children 12 and under. Guided tours only. Departures Thurs–Sun 1–4pm, Sat–Sun additional 2:30pm departure. Bus: 119, 415 (Praça XV).

Museu de Arte Moderna (MAM) ✶✶   It's impossible to miss the MAM. Located in the large waterfront Flamengo park, it's a long, large, rectangular building lofted off the ground by an arcade of concrete struts, giving the structure the appearance of an airplane wing. The elegance of the design is marred somewhat by the dirt streaks and cracks in the concrete, but once you enter into this elevated space (via a spiral stairway just beyond the turnstiles), you realize the architect was onto something. In this city, in this setting, one cannot ignore the surroundings. Like the arches of a Gothic cathedral, the concrete struts do all the load-bearing work, allowing for walls of solid plate glass that welcome in both city and sea. Not incidentally, the structure also provides a vast interior display area free of pillars and other obstructions, one easily adapted to whatever new art should arrive. Displays change constantly—check their website to see what's on—but at all times the MAM presents the best of what's happening in Brazil and Latin America, as well as providing a temporary home to the big traveling international exhibits. Signage—a rare bonus—is in both English and Portuguese. Allow an hour to 90 minutes.

Tip: At the end of your visit, make your way out to the second-floor patio and look down: The garden, including the lawn with the cascading wavy shapes, is the work of Brazil's great landscape architect Roberto Burle Marx. The MAM also has a cafe, a bookstore, and a film archive containing over 20,000 Brazilian titles.

Av. Infante Dom Henrique 85, Parque do Flamengo (Aterro), Centro. (© 021/ 2210-2188. www.mamrio.com.br. Admission R$8 ($4) adults, R$6 ($3) students and seniors, free for children 12 and under. Tues–Fri noon–6pm, Sat–Sun noon–7pm. Metrô: Cinelândia. Bus: 472, 438 (get off at Av. Beira Mar by the museum's footbridge).

Museu Histórico Nacional 🏛🏛 The place for anyone looking for a good overview of Brazilian history, from Cabral's arrival in A.D. 1500 to the events of the present day. Housed in the former national armory, the National History Museum features seven permanent exhibits on themes such as Early Exploration, Coffee Plantations, and Modernism, each of which is illustrated with abundant maps and artifacts. Even better, much of the Portuguese signage comes with English translation. Keep in mind that Brazilian museums haven't bought into the "interactive learning" idea. Instead, displays consist of glass cases and explanatory text. They're carefully curated—one case shows a mattock used in an 18th-century peasant rebellion juxtaposed with a bright red banner of the modern Sem-Terra movement, a telling evocation of the land distribution problem that has plagued the Brazilian countryside for 400 years and counting. Allow 2 hours (longer if you're a serious history buff). The museum is only a 10-minute walk from the Praça XV (Bus: 119, 415), unfortunately under the elevated Avenida Presidente Kubitschek. Its crumbling concrete pilings make the street below look like a set from a Dirty Harry movie, but thanks to a significant police presence, it's actually quite safe.

Praça Marechal Âncora s/n. (© 021/2550-9224. www.visualnet.com.br/mhn. Admission R$4 ($2) adults, R$3 ($1.50) seniors and children 12 and under. Tues–Fri 10am–5:30pm, Sat–Sun 10am–6pm.

Museu Nacional de Belas Artes   A classic museum in the European tradition, the Museu das Belas Artes houses a vast collection of European and Brazilian art, with an emphasis on 18th- and 19th-century European work. Up the grand staircase is the Rodin reading room with a statue of Rodin's *Meditation Sans Bras* in bronze. Though the floor layout is confusing, the art itself is beautifully displayed. For those looking for something distinctly Brazilian, the highlight is definitely the collection of Frans Post. Brazil's first landscape painter, Post came to Brazil in 1637 when the Dutch forces under Maurits van Nassau conquered Pernambuco. Also worth seeing is the beautiful collection of Italian baroque, some of these brought to Brazil in 1808 by the fleeing Portuguese King D. João VI. The center rooms are used for temporary exhibits, usually of Brazilian artists. No English signs. Expect to spend an hour and a half.

Av. Rio Branco 199, Centro. ⓒ 021/2240-0068. R\$4 (\$2) adults, free for children under 10 and seniors. Tues–Fri 10am–6pm, Sat–Sun 2–6pm. Metrô: Cinelândia.

Paço Imperial   For 155 years, this was the administrative nerve center of Brazil, serving as the governor's palace and then as the home and office of Brazil's emperors from 1808 until the fall of the monarchy in 1888. It's a pleasingly simple structure, long and low and rectangular, its many high-ceilinged rooms arranged around a pair of cool interior courtyards. Nowadays it serves as an exhibition hall for traveling cultural exhibits, some of which are excellent, but most of which, alas, are in Portuguese only. Still, it's an extremely pleasant and interesting building to walk through. One room on the ground floor at the back charts the history of the palace, with maps showing its location in old Rio, and paintings and engravings depicting the important moments in Brazilian history to which the building served as a backdrop. Allow about an hour.

Tip: The cafe in the courtyard on the ground floor is a great place to take refuge on hot afternoons in Rio (open the same hours as the museum).

Praça XV, Centro. ⓒ 021/2533-4407. Admission R\$5 (\$2.50) adults, R\$3 (\$1.50) students and seniors, free for children 7 and under. Tues–Sun noon–6:30pm. Bus: 119, 415 (and many others).

SANTA TERESA

Museu Chácara do Céu   A wealthy man with eclectic tastes, Raymundo Castro Maya had this mansion built in the hills of Santa Teresa, then filled it with all manner of paintings and pottery and sculpture. The house itself is a charmer, a stylish melding of hillside and structure that evokes Frank Lloyd Wright's work in the American West. Not surprisingly, the views from the garden are fabulous. Inside, you'll get a glimpse into the eccentric mind of a collector. Though he made short forays into books and silver, Castro Mayo seems to have had three chief interests: European painters (impressionists like Monet and Matisse, and more daring stuff like Picasso and Dali); Brazilian art, particularly 19th-century landscapes; and Chinese pottery. He also seems to have felt some kinship between the three; certainly he displayed them together. Thus on an upper floor landing do we find a cubist painting by Dutchman Kees Van Dongen next to an 18th-century Brazilian landscape, both of them hung over an antique Chinese vase. Why? Search me. But when you're done puzzling over that, there are lots of maps and paintings, particularly of Rio in its early years, a room of Brazilian art in sliding storage cabinets, some antiques and silver, and that great back-patio view of Centro.

Rua Murtinho Nobre 93, Santa Teresa. (*) 021/2507-1932. Admission R$2 ($1) adults, free for children under 12. Free admission Wed. Wed–Mon noon–5pm. Tram: Curvelo (Chácara do Céu).

CATETE, GLORIA & FLAMENGO

Museu da República—Palácio do Catete 🏛🏛   It's gratifying to find a museum that works so hard to grab your interest. Located in a gorgeous baroque palace that from 1897 to 1960 served as the official residence of Brazilian presidents, the three floors of exhibits in this museum try to engage visitors on the history and politics of the Brazilian republic. True, sometimes the attempts don't quite come off. One third-floor display had assorted busts of Brazilian presidents on one wall, an oversize sketch of Superman in flight on another, and between them a glass case with a nasty-looking AR-15 assault rifle wedged upright between a pair of black Nike high-tops. I think this was meant to make us cogitate deeply on the myth and violent reality of power, but mostly it got us wondering at the immaturity of certain curators. More traditional displays preserve the air of the palace in its administrative days—a formal ballroom with a long, leather-covered table was where the cabinet used to meet (ho hum). The best—and most biased—exhibit is the three-room hagiography of President Getúlio Vargas. It's a curious treatment for this museum, given that Vargas launched the coup that brought the first republic to an end in 1930. Still, they do a fabulous job, creating a multimedia sensory experience of Getúlio's life and times. Allow an hour to 90 minutes.

Tip: The formal gardens surrounding the palace are well worth a walk. There's a cafe in an artificial grotto, and next to that a small branch of the Folklore Museum containing puppets and folk art from around Brazil. Admission is free.

Rua do Catete 153, Catete. ✆ 021/2558-6350. Admission R$5 ($2.50) adults, free for seniors and children 11 and under. Free for everyone Wed. Tues–Fri noon–5pm, Sat–Sun 2–6pm. Metrô: Catete.

BOTAFOGO & URCA

Museu do Indio ✦✦ *Kids*   Housed in an elegant 19th-century mansion in a quiet part of Botafogo, the Indian Museum's exhibits are some of the most innovative and artistic we have come across in a Brazilian museum, including striking wall-size black-and-white photos adorned with colored feathers, and a display on kids' toys where the objects dangle from the ceiling at various heights. The symbolism of the hunt is portrayed in a dark room with just a ray of light illuminating the floor, casting an eerie glow on spears and animal skulls. There are no English signs, but the exhibits are so vivid, they speak for themselves. For kids there is a gallery with (washable) body paint and a large selection of stamps, so they can practice adorning themselves as warriors or hunters, or chiefs or shamans. It's a great spot for children and an easy place to spend 2 hours. As a good portion of the displays are outside, avoid going on a rainy day.

Rua das Palmeiras 55, Botafogo. ✆ 021/2286-8899. www.museudoindio.org.br. R$2 ($1) all ages (free for children in strollers). Tues–Sun 10am–5:30pm, Sat–Sun 1–5pm. Metrô: Botafogo.

Sugar Loaf Mountain (Pão de Açúcar) ✦✦✦   Along with samba, beaches, and beautiful women, the Sugar Loaf remains one of the original and enduring Rio attractions. Deservedly so. Standing on its peak, the entire *Cidade Maravilhosa* lays at your feet: the beaches of Ipanema and Copacabana, the favelas of Babylonia, the Tijuca Forest, Christ the Redeemer on his mountain, the old downtown, the bridge, the Bay of Guanabara, and the fortresses at the edge of far-off Niterói. It's a truly beautiful sight. The cable car leaves every half hour from 8am to 10pm, more frequently if there's enough people waiting. The ascent takes two steps, the first from the ground station in Urca to the 726-foot (220m) Morro de Urca, the second up to the 1,307-foot (396m) Sugar Loaf itself. Trams are timed so it's next to impossible to make both trips without spending transition time on the Morro, so better to relax and enjoy life.

The Morro offers excellent views, as well as a cafe, snack bar, restaurant, souvenir stands, and children's play area.

Av. Pasteur 520, Urca. ℂ 021/2546-8400. Admission R$18 ($9) adults, R$9 ($4.50) children 6–12, free for children under 6. Daily 8am–10pm. Bus: 107. Note that this bus goes by only infrequently. Better to take any of the hundreds of buses that stop at the Rio Sul shopping center. From the bus stop it's a R$4 ($2) cab ride to the cable car station. *Tip:* Coming back, you can catch an expensive tourist cab outside the cable car ground station, or else walk out to Av. Pasteur, turn left, and walk 330 ft. (100m) to Rua Ramon Franco and get one of the normal city cabs for half the price.

LAGOA

Jardim Botânico 𝕽𝕽   A photograph of the main avenue of the Botanical Gardens—a procession of stately imperial palms punctuated by a splashing classical fountain—graces nearly every tour brochure of Rio. Fortunately, the reality lives up to the photos. In the nearly 2 centuries since Emperor Dom João VI founded the original, the botanical garden has grown to 141 hectares and added 6,000 species of tropical plants and trees to its collection. It's now one of the few places near Rio to see standing Brazilwood (*Pau Brasil*) and other species from the Atlantic rain forest. Unfortunately, managers of the Jardim don't do much to explain the collection. Visitors get a basic map (though the cashiers can be stingy unless you ask), and many trees and shrubs are labeled with common and Latin names, and that's about it. Either bone up before you go, bring along someone who knows plants, or else do what most do and just enjoy the peace and beauty of a meander along the many little paths and garden trails and greenhouses. There's a cafe and a small bookshop on-site. The botanical museum/cultural center has been closed with no foreseen reopening date.

Rua Jardim Botânico 1008. ℂ 021/2294-9349. Admission R$2 ($1) adults, free for children 7 and under. Daily 8am–5pm Bus: 170 (from Centro), 571 (from Glória-Botafogo), 572 (from Zona Sul).

ZONA SUL

Forte de Copacabana 𝕽𝕽   Simply massive. Built on the eve of World War I by the German arms maker Krupp, Copacabana Fort boasts walls of reinforced concrete 40 feet (12m) thick. They protect a whacking great cannon (305mm) that could fire a deadly shell 14 miles (23km) out to sea. The army has done an excellent job presenting the interior as it was when it was a working bastion. One of the first things you see as you enter is the commander's quarters, preserved pretty much as it was in 1930 when it was used to lock up president Washington Luis after a bloody coup. Other rooms contain then-state-of-the-art instruments (lots of brass wheels and finely scaled calipers) for targeting and aiming the great guns. And down in the very bowels of the fort, the cannon are still in place. Best of all, the bored soldiers guarding the place never leave the gate, so you're free to touch and fiddle and play as much as you want. Allow about an hour.

Praça Coronel Eugênio Franco 1, Copacabana. © 021/2521-1032. Admission R$3 ($1.50) adults, free for children 8 and under and seniors. Tues–Sun 10am–4pm. Bus: 415 to far end of Copacabana beach.

COSME VELHO

Corcovado 🎦🎦🎦   The price is a bit steep but then so is the rail line, its narrow gauge winding upward past hillside shacks, through trees and tangled rain-forest creepers, up and ever up, yea unto to the very feet of Christ. A stylish Art Deco Christ, 99 feet (30m) high on a mountaintop 2,343 feet (710m) above sea level. The view from His toes is definitely worth the money. The mountains, the bay, and the city all lay revealed beneath your feet. It's enough to give you feelings of omniscience. For those who want the touristic nitty-gritty, the statue was designed by Carlos Oswald (with head and hands sculpted by Paul Landowski), while the overall complex was the work of architect Heitor da Silva Costa. It was originally intended to mark the 100th anniversary of Brazilian independence in 1922, but due to a funding shortfall didn't get opened until 1931. At the peak station, there's a small refreshment and souvenir stand but not much else. Allow about 2 hours round-trip, including time spent gazing at the glory that is Rio. Note that touts at the ground station will almost certainly approach you offering a bus trip to this lookout plus another viewpoint a little lower down for R$20 ($10). There's nothing dishonest about them and it's not a bad deal (except that you'll likely have to wait around while they fill up a bus), but you do miss out on the nifty train ride.

(Train Station) Rua Cosme Velho 512, Cosme Velho © 021/2558-1329. Admission R$20 ($10) adults, R$10 ($5) children 6–12, free for children 5 and under. Trains going up depart every 30 min. 9am–6pm. Last train down 7:30pm. Bus 422, 583, or 584 to Cosme Velho.

Museu Internacional de Arte Naïf do Brasil 🎦🎦   Don't miss the Museu de Art Naïf, located just a few hundred yards from the Corcovado tram station. Sometimes known as primitive or ingénue art, its practitioners paint from the heart, portraying the daily life of common folks. Whatever they may lack of technical skill, they more than make up for by the cheerful and expressive drawing and the vibrant use of color. The top floor is exclusively reserved for local artists. Visitors will recognize many popular scenes from Cariocas' daily life such as a Flamengo-Fluminense soccer game at the Maracanã stadium, the samba parade, the beach, and the small neighborhood botequim cafes. The lower level is reserved for international artists, with constantly changing exhibits. A number of pieces are for sale, but be aware that *naïf* don't mean cheap. Prices range from R$200 to R$6,000 ($100–$3,000). Expect to spend 45 minutes.

Rua do Cosme Velho 561, Cosme Velho. ℂ 021/2205-8612. www.museunaif. com.br. R$5 ($2.50) adults, R$2.50 ($1.25) children. Tues–Fri 10am–6pm, Sat–Sun noon–6pm. Bus 422, 583, or 584 to Cosme Velho.

FURTHER AFIELD

Jardim Zoológico—Rio City Zoo 🦁 (Kids)   If you haven't got time to get to the Amazon, this may be the place to come. Though not huge, the zoo is green, leafy, and pleasant, and has about 2,000 different species on display, most of them Brazilian. It's particularly good for sighting birds. There are toucans (of Fruit Loops fame), macaws, and other colorful tropical species, some in an open aviary so you can walk amongst them while they fly around. (That doesn't apply to the harpy eagle: The zoo's example of the world's largest raptor sits caged and alone, looking both ominous and forlorn.) The reptile house and primate displays are also quite good. Some displays are inevitably small and cramped, which may produce cries of pity from your budding environmental activist, but all in all, the zoo does a creditable job reproducing habitats while providing access to the public.

Quinta da Boa Vista s/n, São Cristóvão ℂ 021/2568-7400. Admission R$4 ($2) weekdays, R$5 ($2.50) weekends. Free for children less than 3½ ft. (1m) tall. Tues–Sun 9am–5pm. Metrô: São Cristóvão.

Museu de Arte Contemporânea—Niterói 🦁🦁   Oscar Niemeyer's spaceship design for Niterói's new Contemporary Art Museum has done for this bedroom city what Gehry's Guggenheim did for Bilbao: put it on the map (at least in Brazil). Set atop a promontory with a stunning view of Rio, the all-white flying saucer says clearly yet elegantly that here stands a landmark structure. The magic continues inside with an observation gallery following a band of picture windows around the outside circumference, inviting

patrons to gaze on Rio, the Sugar Loaf, Guanabara Bay, and the city of Niterói itself. As a gallery, however, the museum has drawbacks. Circular buildings are inherently difficult to make functional, on top of which the finishing on the inside seems extraordinarily cheap, as if most of the budget had gone on architectural fees, leaving money enough only for tatty carpeting and bubbling drywall work. Still, curators do their best, bringing in a constantly changing selection of the best of Brazilian contemporary art (think abstract sculpture, textiles, and painting). Even so, one can't help thinking the best piece of work on display is the building itself. Allow about an hour.

Mirante de Boa Viagem s/n. Niterói. ℂ 021/2620-2481. Admission R$5 ($2.50) adults, R$3 ($1.50) students and seniors, free for children 7 and under. Tues–Fri and Sun 11am–6pm, Sat 1–9pm. From Praça XV take the ferry to Niterói, then take a short taxi ride to the museum.

Museu Nacional (Quinta da Boa Vista) 🗡🗡 In the center of a grand romantic park, approached by a long tree-shaded boulevard lined with statuary, stands the pretty pink baroque palace that was once the royal palace and is now home to the National Museum. Inside, the collection is vast and incredibly varied; many items were originally acquired by Emperor Pedro II and Empress Teresa, who dabbled respectively in botany and archaeology. Assembled in the grand entrance hall are many of the more exotic items: mastodon trunks, a saber-toothed tiger skull, the full skeleton of a giant Pleistocene sloth (16½ ft. or 5m long!), and a huge multiton meteorite cut in cross-section so visitors can run their hands across its polished iron-nickel surface. Beyond that main hall, the collection becomes a bit more ordered. One vast wing is devoted to the works of man (mostly *Homo brazilienses*). On display are dolls dressed in regional costumes, weapons and masks of aboriginal tribes, whips and saddles from interior cowboys, and much more. The other wing attempts to present all of life—from the smallest protozoa through the various orders of sponges and crustaceans to arthropods and mammals. Signage is all in Portuguese, but is not essential to see and enjoy. We spent a good 2 hours here; others less keen on natural history could probably do it in an hour.

Quinta da Boa Vista s/n, São Cristóvão. ℂ 021/2568-1149. Admission R$3 ($1.50) adults, free for children 10 and under and seniors. Tues–Sun 10am–4pm. Metrô: São Cristóvão.

2 Other Museums & Cultural Centers

CENTRO

Biblioteca Nacional ⍟ Neoclassical at its most gracious, the National Library is worth poking your head in just to see the grand entrance hall with staircases extending up through a lofty atrium five floors high. Guided tours are offered twice a day, but if you just want to look around and don't mind a small fib, simply show some ID to the front-desk person and claim you're doing research. The reading rooms are lovely, and in the ground-floor reference room, there's a not-bad selection of magazines.

Av. Rio Branco 219, Centro ⓒ **021/2262-8255**. www.bn.br. Free admission. Mon–Fri 9am–5pm. Guided visits at 1 and 4pm. Metrô: Cinelândia.

Centro Cultural do Banco do Brasil ⍟ It's worth stepping inside this gorgeous neoclassical building just to gaze up at the soaring domed atrium. Once the HQ of Brazil's national bank, the building was converted in 1989 into one of the city's premier cultural spaces. Inside (in lovely cool air-con), there's a pleasant mezzanine cafe and a small bookstore on the ground floor with an excellent selection of art and architecture books (many in English). Several small galleries on higher floors feature changing exhibits on art and culture. Three theaters sometimes hold concerts but normally stage Portuguese-language theater. And should you be feeling book-starved, there's a fairly decent research library. Allow anywhere from 15 minutes to several hours, depending on what you're interested in.

Rua Primeiro de Março 66, Centro. ⓒ **021/3808-2000**. Free admission. Tues–Sun 1–7:30pm. Bus: 136, 415.

Centro Cultural Light ⍟ Once the head office for the city electric utility and the main garage for city streetcars, this grand 1911 building has been converted into a fascinating display space. Inside, there's a gallery with some great historic photos of old Rio and another smaller gallery with a rather esoteric exhibit on the history of the city's electrification. A third room containing four large canvases of Rio by the famed Brazilian artist di Cavalcanti is currently closed (*sem previsão* as Brazilians say, meaning who knows when it will reopen). Best of all, much of the building's interior has been gutted to create a sizable atrium that is often used for concerts. An old tram car serves as the stage. Call for programming details, but the music is often MPB (*musica popular brasileira*).

Rua Marechal Floriano 168, Centro. ⓒ **021/2211-2911**. Free admission. Mon–Fri 10am–7pm, Sat–Sun 2–6pm. Metrô: Presidente Vargas.

Espaço Cultural da Marinha With a destroyer, a submarine, and some great ship models, the Navy Cultural Center is guaranteed to delight naval and maritime buffs. The display space is located on the old Customs dock on the waterfront (from Praça XV turn right—north—and walk underneath the elevated freeway for about 330 ft./100m). That means it's narrow and thin, the exhibits extending ever backwards to the end of the pier. On display are countless ship models, including a full-size replica of the royal barge and countless small-scale models of everything from the *Golden Hind* to primitive Brazilian sailing rafts. More interesting for nonmodel freaks are the displays at the very back on underwater archaeology, including a wide variety of relics—coins, Delft blue china; jewelry— from the 1648 wreck of the *Nossa Senhora do Rosario*. Moored outside the museum are the *Riachuelo,* a 1970s-era submarine, and the *Bauru,* a small World War II destroyer. Self-guided tours of these ships (also free) run from noon to 5pm. This is also the place from which one departs for tours of **Ilha Fiscal** ⟆⟆.

Av. Alfredo Agache s/n, Centro. ☏ 021/3870-6879. Free admission. Tues–Sun 10am–4pm. Bus: 119, 415 (Praça XV).

BOTAFOGO

Museum Carmen Miranda ⟆ If Carmen Miranda could see her museum, she'd roll over in her grave (spilling pineapples and bananas just everywhere). A concrete bunker in a postage-stamp park surrounded by four lanes of traffic hardly seems a fitting tribute to the flamboyant '40s film star. Inside the banana bunker, however, the small collection does a fine job illustrating Carmen Miranda's star appeal. A large number of her publicity photos are on display, blown up to near life-size, along with smaller photos showing the story of her life and career, including her 1939 American breakthrough in the Broadway musical *Streets of Paris.* Also on display is the outfit she wore to the 1941 Academy Awards ceremony, as well as jewelry and accessories, including the trademark tall fruit hats. The museum also has a large collection of video documentaries, biographies, the movies in which she starred, and a compilation of her songs. The receptionist is delighted when visitors ask to have these put on—a number are in English.

Av. Rui Barbosa s/n (in front of No. 560), Flamengo. ☏ 021/2551-2597. R$2 ($1) for adults and children 5 and over, free for children under 5 and seniors. Tues–Fri 10am–5pm. Bus: 172 from Ipanema or Copacabana or 433 from Centro.

FURTHER AFIELD

Maracanã Stadium The largest soccer stadium in the world and the temple of Brazilian soccer, the Maracanã got off to an inauspicious start at the 1950 World Cup when close to 200,000 spectators in the brand-new stadium saw Brazil lose the cup final to arch-rival Uruguay. (The loss still hurts—if you want to taunt a Brazilian soccer fan, just mention the 1950 Cup. Fortunately this was only a temporary setback—Brazil went on to win four World Cups). The best way to experience the Maracanã stadium is with a couple hundred thousand other fans at one of the big games (see "Spectator Sports," later in this chapter). For those who don't have that opportunity or want a behind-the-scenes look, there are guided tours. An English-speaking guide takes visitors through all floors of the stadium, including the dressing rooms, all the while delivering a seemingly endless stream of Brazilian soccer trivia.

Rua Profesor Eurico Rabelo s/n São Cristovão. ℂ 021/2569-4916. Mon–Fri 9am–5pm, Sat–Sun and holidays 9am–3pm. No tours during events or games. R$3 ($1.50), free for children under 12. Metrô: Maracanã. Enter through gate 18.

3 Architectural Highlights

HISTORIC BUILDINGS & MONUMENTS

Rio's a great place for architecture buffs, and an even better place to watch what happens when overconfident urban designers set their hands to the task of urban renewal. For a city so blessed with mountains, ocean, and historical roots several centuries deep, Rio's movers and shakers have suffered from a striking sense of inferiority. As a result, various well-meaning Cariocas have since the early 1900s taken turns ripping out, blowing up, filling in, and generally reconfiguring huge swaths of their city in order to make Rio look more like Paris or Los Angeles or, lately, Miami Beach. The results of these various movements are—for better and worse—now and forever on permanent display.

CINELÂNDIA

"Rio Civilizes Itself!" Armed with this slogan and a deep envy of what Baron Haussman had done in Paris, engineer-mayor **Pereiro Passos** set to work in 1903 ripping a large swath through Rio's Centro district to create the first of the city's grand boulevards, the **Avenida Central.** So efficient was "knock-it-down" Passos that the old colonial Rio he set out to demolish can now be found only in the few square blocks around the **Travessa do Commércio** to the north of **Praça XV.** Accessed via the **Arco do Teles**—an arch built in 1790 to allow passage through a commercial building facing the square—it's a charming area of narrow cobblestone streets and gaily painted colonial shops, now much missed by civilized Cariocas.

The boulevard Passos created in its stead, however, was also quite graceful. Now renamed the **Avenida Rio Branco,** the 109-foot (33m) boulevard runs from **Praça Mauá** south past the grand neoclassical **Igreja de Nossa Senhora da Candelária** to what was then waterfront at the **Avenida Beira Mar.** The four-story Parisian structures that once lined the street are now found only in photographs, replaced by tall and modern office towers. The best place to witness the handiwork of these turn-of-the-century Paris-izers is on the **Praça Floriano,** referred to by most Cariocas by the name of its subway stop, **Cinelândia.** Anchored at the north end by the extravagant beaux-arts **Teatro Municipal,** and flanked by the equally ornate **Museu de Belas Artes** and neoclassical **Biblioteca Nacional,** the praça beautifully emulates the proportions, the monumentality, and the glorious detail of a classic Parisian square.

CASTELO

The next stage in urban reform came in the early '20s, when a group encouraged by public health advocate **Oswaldo Cruz** and backed by a development consortium decreed that the hilltop castle south of Praça XV had to go; the 400-year-old castle was a breeding ground, they said, for pox and plague and other infectious diseases. In 1922, the castle was blown up, the hill leveled, and—starting in the early '30s—construction begun on a series of government office towers inspired by the modernist movement then sweeping Europe. The first of these—then the Ministry of Education and Health but now known as the **Palácio Gustavo Capanema** (Rua da Imprensa 16)—listed among its architects nearly all the later greats of Brazilian architecture, including **Lucio Costa, Oscar Niemeyer,** and **Roberto Burle Marx,** with painter **Candido Portinari** thrown in for good measure. International architects sat up and took note; other less avant-garde government departments commissioned architects with different ideologies, resulting in a **War of the Styles** that raged through the remainder of the 1930s. Perhaps the most bombastic counter-volley was the overblown neoclassical **Ministerio da Fazenda** building (Presidente Carlos at Almirante Barroso). The resulting enclave of office towers, known as Castelo, lies on the patch centered on the **Avenida Presidente Antonio**

Carlos. Chiefly of interest to architectural buffs, it should be toured only during office hours.

CIDADE NOVA

"Knock-it-down" Passos had nothing on **Getúlio Vargas.** On the national scene, the Brazilian dictator was creating a new quasi-fascist political structure called the Estado Novo; in his capital city, he set about creating a **Cidade Nova** to match. In 1940, on Vargas's personal order, a monster 12-lane boulevard was cut through the city fabric from the beautiful **N.S. de Candelaria** church out through the **Campo de Santana** park to the northern edges of downtown. Anchoring this new mega-boulevard was the **Central Station** (known officially as the Estação Dom Pedro II, a graceful Moderne building with a 446-foot (135m) clock tower that still stands overlooking the city. Vargas's plan called for the entire 2½-mile (4km) street to be lined with identical 22-story office blocks. Fortunately, only a few were ever built; they can be seen on the block crossed by Rua Uruguaiana. As a silver lining, however, there was lots of space left for architect Oscar Niemeyer to build the **Sambodromo,** the permanent samba-parade ground. Designed in typically Niemeyer all-concrete style, it stands in the shadow of an elevated freeway, about half a mile (1km) along Presidente Vargas.

ATERRO

The next great reconfiguration of Rio came 2 years after the federal capital fled inland to Brasilia. City designers took the huge high hill—**Morro Sto. Antonio**—that once dominated the Largo Carioca, scooped away the earth, and dumped it on the beach from Lapa to Flamengo, creating a vast new waterfront park. On the rather raw spot where the hill once stood, there arose the innovative cone-shaped **Catedral Metropolitana** (Metropolitan Cathedral), and at the intersection of the new avenidas **República do Chile** and **República do Paraguai,** a trio of towering skyscrapers, the most interesting of which is the "hanging gardens" headquarters of Brazil's state oil company **Petrobras.** On the waterfront park—officially called Parque do Flamengo but most often referred to as *Aterro,* the Portuguese word for landfill—designers created new gardens and pathways, a new beach, and a pair of modernist monuments: the **MAM (Modern Art Museum),** and the impressive **Monument to the Dead of World War II.** Not incidentally, the park also bears two wide and fast roadways connecting Centro with the fashionable neighborhoods in the Zona Sul.

CHURCHES & TEMPLES

Rio is awash with churches, with some 20 in Centro alone. Likely the most impressive church in Rio is **Nossa Senhora de Candelaria** ⚑ (open Mon–Fri 7:30am–4pm, Sat–Sun 7:30am–noon), set on a traffic island of its own at the head of Avenida Presidente Vargas. The very clean and simple neoclassical design dates from a renovation begun in 1775. Particularly worth noting are the huge and ornate cast-bronze doors, the ceiling panels telling the story of the church, and the two large Art Nouveau lamps on either side of the pulpit; they look like cast-iron Christmas trees.

Still impressive, if not quite worth the hype or the long trek, is the **Mosteiro São Bento,** located on a hill on the far north corner of downtown (access is via an elevator located in Rua Dom Gerardo 40; open daily 8am–11am and 2:30–6pm). The main church itself is a shining example of the Golden Church, utilizing the high baroque practice of plastering every inch of a church's richly carved interior in gold leaf. Somewhat disappointing is the way the church forecourt has been transformed into a car park, and the total absence of view from the monastery's strategic hilltop. *Tip:* Sunday morning Mass features Gregorian chanting by the monks. Service begins at 10am, but arrive early if you want a seat.

The reason (we believe) tour guides so long suggested going to the Mosteiro São Bento is that the **Igreja da Ordem Tercebira de São Francisco da Penitencia** ⚑ (Largo da Carioca 5; open Wed–Fri 11am–4pm) was long closed. Set on a hilltop overlooking Largo Carioca, this and the next-door Church of Santo Antônio form part of the large Franciscan complex in the city center. While both are worth visiting, the São Francisco church is simply outstanding: Interior surfaces are filled with golden carvings and hung with censors of heavy ornate silver. Last and most innovative of Rio's significant churches is the **Catedral Metropolitana** ⚑⚑, Av. República de Chile 245, open daily from 7am to 6pm. At each of the four cardinal compass points, a rectilinear latticework of concrete and stained glass soars upwards, tilting inward as it rises. Where they meet at the ceiling, there's another stained-glass latticework—a cross—shining softly with light filtered in from the sky. The form is ultimately modern; the feeling is soaring High Gothic.

4 Neighborhoods to Explore

CENTRO 𝄞𝄞

The place where it all began, Rio's **Centro** neighborhood contains most of the city's notable churches, squares, monuments, and museums, as well as the modern office towers where Rio's white-collar elite earn their daily bread. Roughly speaking, Centro stretches from the **Morro de São Bento** in the north to the seaside **Monument to the Dead of World War II** in the south, and from **Praça XV** on the waterfront east, more or less, to the **Sambodromo.** It's a compact, pleasantly walkable area; crossing from one side of downtown to the other on foot takes no more than 45 minutes.

Rio's (and Centro's) first and most important square is **Praça XV,** located in the center of the city's old waterfront. This is the place where governors and emperors resided, and the site where the Brazilian republic was proclaimed on November 15, 1889. Notable sights around the square include the **Paço Imperial,** the **Palácio Tiradentes,** and, on the north side of the square, the **Arco do Teles.** Walk through this unobtrusive old archway and you come to a tiny remnant of **old colonial Rio,** complete with narrow shop fronts and cobblestone streets. The area's main street, the **Travessa do Commércio,** transforms into a lively outdoor patio/pub in the evenings.

Forming the back edge of Praça XV is **Rua Primeiro de Março,** a busy commercial street with a number of churches, including the **Ordem Terceiro do Carmo,** the **Santa Cruz dos Militares,** and near the far end of the street, the massive yet lovely **Nossa Senhora de Candelaria.** Continue along Primeiro de Março to the end and you come to the foot of the hill upon which rests the **São Bento Monastery.**

Continuing west from Praça XV along either **Rua Ouvidor** or **Rua Sete de Setembro** takes you to Centro's prime upscale shopping enclave. Its far border is marked (more or less) by the **Avenida Rio Branco.** Created in 1905 as an answer to Paris's Champs-Elysées, Rio Branco is still the city's most desirable commercial address. It runs from the cruise ship terminal on the **Praça Mauá** southwards to the pretty Parisian square known as **Cinelândia** (more on that later). About halfway along, a block to the east of Rio Branco, lies the large irregular **Largo de Carioca.**

Though not very interesting in itself, the square is useful as a landmark. Above it on a hilltop stands the glorious golden **Igreja de**

Santo Antônio. To the north of the square, from **Rua da Carioca** to the vast, traffic-choked wasteland known on maps as the **Avenida Presidente Vargas,** and from **Avenida Rio Branco** in the east to the **Campo de Santana** park in the west, lies one of Rio's prime walking, shopping, and sightseeing areas. It's an area of narrow, irregular streets, two-story shops, little square and charming small churches. Shopaholics will enjoy the **informal market** centered on the **Uruguaiana** metrô stop and the bargains to be had elsewhere in the neighborhood.

Looking southward, the Largo Carioca marks the transition from old Rio to new, and from low-rise to very, very high-rise. Towards the east, **Avenida República de Chile** boasts many of the city's most important commercial skyscrapers, including the landmark **Petrobras** building, and the distinctive conical ziggurat that is the **Metropolitan Cathedral.** Just south of the modern concrete cathedral, the past makes a token resurgence in the form of the **Arcos da Lapa,** a Roman-style aqueduct that now carries trams south from the city center up to the hilltop neighborhood of **Santa Teresa.**

South and west of Largo Carioca lies **Cinelândia** (officially called **Praça Floriano**), a Parisian city square faithfully reproduced all the way down to the opera house (or **Teatro Municipal** as its called) and the many sidewalk cafes. Many of the high-rises surrounding the square show the Art Deco and Moderne touches of buildings from the '30s and '40s.

South again from Cinelândia, making use of a pedestrian overpass to cross a pair of wide and busy roads, you come to the man-made **Parque do Flamengo.** The chief sights in the park are the **Museum of Modern Art** and the soaring concrete **Monument to the Dead of World War II.**

LAPA

A tiny, funky little neighborhood once known as the Montmartre of the Tropics, Lapa is dead easy to find. It's centered around the **Largo da Lapa** at the foot an old and very picturesque aqueduct known as the **Arcos da Lapa.** In addition to those two sights, Lapa offers some lovely old colonial buildings and—in recent years—a very active nightlife scene.

SANTA TERESA 🐧🐧

Santa Teresa is special, an anomaly if you will. Most hilltop neighborhoods in Rio are favelas—unsanctioned shantytowns. Santa Teresa is anything but—it's a respectable, slightly bohemian neighborhood with a number of sights to lure visitors. Chief among these is the *bonde,* the old-fashioned streetcar that whisks passengers from downtown over the **Arcos da Lapa** into Santa Teresa. The other two chief sights are the **Museu Chácara do Céu** and the **Ruin Park,** located side by side on a tall hilltop. Both are worth a visit, and when you're done, wander the neighborhood enjoying the fabulous views and the mix of modern, colonial, and Art Deco architecture. *Tip:* The Santa Teresa tram station is not at all easy to find. It's behind the big "hanging gardens" Petrobras building, on Rua Profesor Lélio Gama, a little street that runs off Rua Senador Dantas.

GLORIA/CATETE/FLAMENGO ⊛

Extending south from the Glória metrô stop to the top end of Botafogo Bay, these three neighborhoods once comprised Rio's toniest residential area—that is until the tunnel to Copacabana opened in 1922. Things weren't really helped by the Aterro landfill project in the 1950s, which relieved much of the neighborhoods' traffic congestion, but at the same time cut off easy access to the sea. The main north-south street—known variously as the **Rua da Glória,** the **Rua do Catete,** and the **Rua Marquis de Abrantes**—is well worth an afternoon or evening stroll. Particularly pretty is the **Largo do Machado,** located at the metrô stop of the same name. For visitors, the chief attractions in this area include the lovely hilltop **Church of Our Lady of Glória,** the funky Art Nouveau **Café Glória,** and the **Catete Park and Palace,** home to the **Museum of the Republic.**

BOTAFOGO

Botafogo reacted to the rise of Copacabana and Ipanema by reinventing itself as a secondary commercial center. Its broad streets contain a number of office high-rises and big retail shopping malls, including the **Shopping Rio Sul,** the first mall to open in the city. Though not an especially rewarding place to stroll, Botafogo does have a couple of worthwhile sights of its own, including the **Indian Museum** (see "The Top Attractions," earlier in this chapter) and the bustling food-fair and nighttime-music jam in the **Cobal Public Market.**

URCA

Urca is the pretty little neighborhood nestled around the foot of the Pão de Açúcar. Partly residential, partly home to a naval training college, the area was built on fill during the 1920s, thus accounting for the Art Deco and Moderne style of many of the neighborhood's buildings. Architecture aside, for nonresidents the only reason to visit Urca is for the views—three of them in fact, all worthwhile.

The first is from the peak of the **Pão de Açúcar,** reached by cable car from Urca's Avenida Pasteur. The second view is obtained by strolling the seawall on **Avenida Portugal.** And for those who think views go best with something cold, the third and final view spot is from a table at the **Círculo Militar** (see p. 75), on the edge of **Praia Vermelha.** The view of the Sugar Loaf is quite simply the best in town.

COPACABANA 𝔸𝔸

Beach! This one word comprises everything there is to say about Copacabana, but then it's a word that contains within it an endless variety of human behavior. Two and a half miles (4km) long and bright sandy white, Copacabana beach is the stage upon which people swim, surf, jog, preen, make sand castles, suntan, and volley. The broad and beautifully landscaped **Avenida Atlântica** runs along the beach's entire length. Running parallel two streets inland, **Nossa Senhora de Copacabana** is the main shopping and commercial street.

IPANEMA 𝔸𝔸

The famous stretch of beach immortalized in Tom Jobim's song "The Girl from Ipanema" nestles in between Copacabana, Leblon, and Lagoa. No more than 8 blocks wide in some areas, it is one of the more coveted residential neighborhoods in all Rio. Built mostly after Rio's Art Deco boom, there are very few landmark buildings to speak of; most apartment buildings are nondescript, some are downright ugly. What Ipanema does offer is great shopping on **Rua Visconde de Pirajá** and its side streets, an excellent nightlife scene (especially around the **Rua Paul Redfern**), some terrific restaurants, and then, of course, there is the beach. The major recreation area for residents and locals alike, Ipanema beach is full of sun worshipers almost every day of the year, not to mention the people playing volleyball and soccer. Joggers and walkers stroll the black-and-white–patterned sidewalk every day of the week, but Sunday is the day to see and be seen when the beachside **Avenida Vieira Souto** is closed to traffic, and people cycle, in-line skate, and scooter along, at all times showing tans and tight form to advantage.

LEBLON

A smaller and, if anything, trendier version of Ipanema. Leblon sits directly to the east of Ipanema; the dividing line is the drainage canal for the Lagoa, now landscaped into a park called the **Jardim de Ala.** The most significant difference between the two neighborhoods is

Favelas: Rio's Hidden Neighborhoods

The Rio neighborhood of Rocinha is home to 150,000 people, is served by two bus lines (nos. 591 and 546), two banks, two radio stations, three nightclubs, a post office, a TV station and a samba school. Yet, though located on the hillside above São Conrado beach, it appears on few if any maps. Why? It's a *favela,* an informal community of mostly poor people squatting on land that ostensibly belongs to the state.

The first favela was created in the 1800s by demobilized soldiers who'd been promised land and, when the government reneged on the deal, occupied it anyway. Since then the term has come to mean any community occupied without official government sanction. There are close to 600 of them in Rio, often located in close proximity to the city's wealthiest neighborhoods. Middle-class Brazilians tend to ignore their existence, though the family maid will often commute in from one every day.

In recent years, the Rio city government—having come to the conclusion that eradicating favelas is no longer an option—has been working to integrate them into the city fabric. Sewer and water lines are being extended, and formal title is being given to owners of favela dwellings. If the process continues, these neighborhoods may someday even show up on the map.

the street names. The beachside avenue in Leblon is known as **Avenida Delfim Moreira,** while the main shopping street is **Avenida General Martin.** Most of the best restaurants cluster around the end of **Avenida Ataulfo de Paiva** where it meets **Rua Dias Ferreira.**

LAGOA

Lagoa is an odd neighborhood, as the focus is the big lagoon (**Lagoa Rodrigo de Freitas**) that drains into the ocean between Ipanema and Leblon. For the majority of Cariocas, this is primarily a recreation area. They come to walk, cycle, in-line skate, or run the 5-mile (8.5km) pathway that circles the lagoon. In the afternoon and evening, the neighborhood's pleasures become more hedonistic as people come to the many waterside kiosks to grab a drink, have some food, or listen to a group play live music.

BARRA DE TIJUCA

The Brazilian envy of things American has finally expressed itself in architecture. Though ostensibly part of Rio de Janeiro, Barra (as it's usually called) looks and feels much like an American beach city, like L.A. or Miami Beach. Streets are wide and filled with 4x4s, because in Barra—as in L.A.—only a nobody walks. Instead, folks out here drive—to the beach, to their penthouse apartment, to the full-size replica of Studio 54 at the **American Center** mall.

5 Beaches, Parks & Plazas

BEACHES

Beaches are to Rio what cafes are to Paris. And while each beach has its own particular traits, there are some general rules to help you take the waters like a true Carioca.

BE PREPARED   First and foremost: **Get a Brazilian bikini** (though perhaps not if you're male). No matter how funky or fashionably teeny your swimsuit looked up north, on a Rio beach it's guaranteed to scream *gringo*. And if you're thinking the figure's not quite bikini-ready, relax. In Brazil everybody and their grandma wears a two-piece. (Note, however, that however small they may shrink that top, Brazilian women *never* go topless—that's for the heathen French).

Second: **Don't be a pack rat.** If you carefully observe your fellow beachgoers, you'll note that Brazilians bring neither picnic basket nor backpack full of stuff and gadgets. All you really need is a towel, sunscreen, and a little bit of cash for beer, food, and other incidentals. (One final argument for traveling light is security: The odds of getting mugged on a Rio beach in daytime approach zero, but leaving that Discman, wallet, or pocket camera on the sand while you head off for a swim *is* an open invitation for someone to relieve you of your valuables.)

Third and most important: **Relax.** The Brazilian beach is not a high-stress hangout. Go for a little swim, chat with the one what brung ya or the cutie on the towel next door, have a beer and some snacks, and soak up those rays.

WATER CONDITIONS   The only other thing to consider before heading for the beach is the condition of the water. The beaches facing Guanabara Bay (primarily Flamengo and Botafogo) are nearly always too polluted for swimming. Thanks to a substantial current, the ocean beaches (Copacabana, Ipanema, Barra) are much cleaner, but even so, sometimes after a heavy rain the coliform count rises beyond acceptable levels. The newspaper *Globo* prints a daily beach report listing all beach closings. Consult the paper or ask at your hotel.

THE BEACHES   As mentioned above, the older bay beaches such as **Botafogo** and **Flamengo** are now unfortunately quite polluted. They're fine and picturesque places for an afternoon stroll, but a poor spot if your heart is set on swimming. Off by itself out in Urca, the **Praia Vermelha** faces out enough towards the ocean that its waters are often fine.

The first of the ocean beaches to see development back in the '20s, **Copacabana** 🏖🏖 remains a favorite. The wide and beautifully landscaped Avenida Atlântica is a great place for a stroll (the wavy landscaped sidewalk mosaic is the work of landscape designer Roberto Burle Marx). The area at the far end of the beach near the Forte Copacabana is where fishermen beach their small craft. For those with other fish to fry, the area in front of the Copacabana Palace around the Rainbow kiosk is a well-known gay area.

The *postos* (lifeguard stations) along Copacabana and Ipanema beaches are open daily from 8am to 8pm. They offer first aid (free if needed) and changing and toilet facilities for a charge of R$1 (50¢). Postos are numbered one through eleven starting from Leme and ending in Leblon. Cariocas will often use them as a reference point instead of the cross streets.

Ipanema beach 🏖🏖 was famous amongst Brazilians even before Tom Jobim wrote his famous song about the tall and tan and lovely girl he saw and sighed over. Stretching almost 2 miles (3.25km) from the foot of the Pedra Dois Irmãos to the Ponta Arpoador, the beach at Ipanema is a strand like nowhere else. Part of the attraction does involve observing the self-confident sensuality with which the Ipanema *garotas* stroll the sands (Equal opportunity purists should note that there's an equivalent amount of beefcake on hand—it just doesn't inspire songs or poetry.). But more than anything, Ipanema is a carnival. Watch the games of volleyball or *footvollei* (like volleyball, but no hands allowed), beach soccer, surfing, and wake boarding. The section just around the point from Copacabana—called **Praia do Arpoador**—is a prime surf spot and a great location for watching the local dudes take to the waves. One of the surf schools also runs lessons for kids from the local favelas. The area around Posto 8 (opposite Rua Farme de Amoedo) is Ipanema's gay section.

Further down into **Leblon** (still the same beach, just a different name once you cross the canal), you will find the **Baixo Baby.** This play area, equipped by corporate sponsors with lots of playground equipment and beach toys, is a popular gathering place for nannies and parents to watch their kids run around and do what kids do on a beach: play with sand.

Off on its own and surrounded by mountains, **São Conrado** beach offers some fine scenery and a (relative) sense of isolation. Its other main claim to fame is as a landing strip for all the hang gliders (*asa delta* in Portuguese) who leap from nearby peaks.

Farthest from the city is the beach at **Barra de Tijuca.** The only reason to go out here is if you're a surf-head desperate for a wave. The surfing is said to be the best in Rio, particularly right in the middle near Barraca do Pepê (Pepe's Shack).

PARKS & GARDENS

In addition to numerous beaches, Rio is also blessed with a variety of parks. On the waterfront near Centro, there's **Flamengo Park,** a good place to stroll in the late afternoon if you're looking for a nice view of the Sugar Loaf.

Out in the other direction, just past the northern edge of downtown, lies the **Quinta da Boa Vista,** the royal family's former country residence (open daily 7am–6pm; located a short walk from the Sao Cristóvão metrô stop). Designed in the Romantic style by French landscape architect Auguste Glaziou, the Quinta da Boa Vista has all the tricks of the gardeners trade: tree-lined dells, small ponds and waterfalls, a grotto, a lookout, even a temple of Apollo. The park is also home to the city zoo and the national museum (see "The Top Attractions," earlier in this chapter).

Closer to the city core lies the **Campo de Santana** (open daily 7am–7pm; opposite the Central metrô stop). A pretty, formal park, its fence and four iron gates protect 50 species of trees, four ponds, and a grotto. The fence also encloses numerous *agoutis* (a bizarre-looking mini-capybara), ducks, peacocks, and marmosets, as well as a large collection of stray cats that Cariocas seem to dump here.

Last and best, the **Parque Nacional Da Tijuca** (Tijuca National Park) is a wonder. At 3,300 hectares, it's the biggest urban forest in the world, and one of the last remnants of Atlantic rain forest on Brazil's southern coast. Among its more special points are the Pico de Tijuca, the Corcovado, the Vista Chinesa, and the Pedra da Gávea. For more information on the park, visit the website of the recently formed Friends of Tijuca National Park.

Moments   Spectacular Views

Views in Rio come at a premium. The two best—from the **Sugar Loaf** and the **Corcovado**—are both ticket-charging attractions. But in a city with so much geography, it's impossible to fence off everything. What follows are views you get for free.

One of the best spots to look for free is from the **Ruin Park** 🎭🎭 in Santa Teresa. Located right next to the Museu Chácara do Céu (see p. 94), the park was once a sizable mansion belonging to Laurinda Santos Lobo, one of Rio's leading socialites. When the house burned down, the city cleverly reinforced the gutted shell and then installed all manner of ramps and catwalks. Visitors can now clamber this way and that, gaining excellent views of the city in all directions; one lookout at the top of the building provides a 270° view of Rio.

Walk to the end of Leblon beach and keep going along Rua Aperana and eventually (after gaining 70m in altitude) you'll get to **Seventh Heaven Lookout** (Mirante de Setimo Céu). Part of the **Parque Penhasco Dois Irmaos,** the lookout provides an excellent view of the beach, the Sugar Loaf, and the Corcovado high above.

SQUARES & PLAZAS

What's the difference between a *largo* and a *praça?* Simple. A praça is a city square and a largo is, well, also a city square, except a largo is always bigger than a praça, except—like with the Largo de Boticario—when it isn't.

Tucked away just a few hundred meters uphill along Rua Cosme Velho from the Corcovado train station is one of Rio's prettiest squares, the **Largo de Boticario** 🎭🎭, named for the druggist Luis da Silva Souto, who settled there in 1831. It's a gem of a spot, with five gaily painted colonial houses encircling a fountain in the middle of a flagstone square. Mature fig trees overhead make for abundant shade, while traffic noise seems completely drowned out by the soft gurgling of the Rio Carioca (from which residents of Rio derive their nickname) taking its last few breaths of air before disappearing forever beneath the city streets.

The best way to arrive in **Praça XV de Novembro** is by sea—
if not on a sailing ship from Portugal, then a ferry from Niterói will
do the trick. To your right as you arrive, beyond a statue of Dom
João VI on a horse, is the **Chafariz do Mestre Valentim,** an ornate
water fountain that marks Rio's former coastline.

Perhaps the city's prettiest square (next to Cinelândia) is the
Largo do Machado in the Catete neighborhood. Perfectly propor-
tioned, the square is dominated by the **Igreja Matriz de Nossa
Senhora da Glória,** a strange but rather elegant combination of
traditional Greek temple and a three-story bell tower. As an added
bonus, there are a number of Parisian-style sidewalk cafes on the
square's northern flank.

Also well worth a visit is the **Largo São Francisco de Paula** in
Rio's old shopping district. There's an outdoor market on one side
of the square and on the other the huge baroque-style **Igreja de São
Francisco de Paula.**

6 Especially for Kids

There are few things in Rio that *aren't* for kids. Brazilians take their
children everywhere—restaurants, bars, even dances—and voice no
objection when others do the same. Still, there are a few places that
stand out as being especially kid-friendly. First and most obvious is
the **beach.** Sun and surf and sand castles have kind of an enduring
kid appeal. For younger children, the beach at **Leblon** features the
Baixo Baby, a free play area equipped with all manner of toys and
play stuff geared for toddlers. For slightly older kids, the **city zoo**
(**Jardim Zoológico**—see "The Top Attractions," earlier in this
chapter) is guaranteed to delight and just possibly educate. One of
the few museums of interest to kids is the **Museu do Indio** (see
"The Top Attractions," earlier in this chapter) in Botafogo. The
museum offers kids stamps and (washable) body paints so they can
practice adorning themselves like natives; the re-creations of Indian
houses on the grounds are fun places in which to crawl in and out.
Few kids can resist the fun of a train (or tram ride). The Santa Teresa
tram zooms over a high aqueduct, then snakes through the narrow
streets of this old neighborhood. At the top station, hop off and
make your way over to the **Ruin Park** (see "Spectacular Views,"
above), the shell of an old mansion featuring numerous stairs, a
tower, and catwalks on which to run up and down and around. The
bonus for parents is the fabulous views of Rio.

> **Tips DIY When It Comes to Tours**
>
> When booking a tour or outdoor activity, it's best to make the call yourself. (Don't worry about language; most tour operators speak English.) The concierges and desk staff in most hotels are remarkably mercenary. If they make the booking for you, it will cost you anything from 10% to 50% more and you won't necessarily get the tour you want. Rio concierges are notorious for informing guests that a tour they wanted is "full," then putting them on a tour with another company—one that offers the concierge a bigger cut.

7 Organized Tours

BUS TOURS CityRio (© 0800/25-8060) operates three integrated bus lines that cover the city's main tourist attractions. Buy a ticket on one of the air-con buses and you can then step on and off any RioTur bus for the next 24 to 72 hours. Cost is R$16 ($8) for 24 hours, R$30 ($15) for 48 hours, R$40 ($20) for 72 hours. Price includes a booklet that shows bus routes and provides basic tourist information.

Gray Line (© 021/2512-9919) offers a number of tour itineraries: the R$60 ($30) afternoon tour of the Sugar Loaf and Rio's historic downtown is a reasonable value; the R$60 ($30) half-day tour (morning or afternoon) of the Corcovado is really a bit of a racket; all they're providing is transfer to and from the train station at a markup (above the train ticket cost) of R$42 ($21). You can also combine these two tours to make a full-day itinerary for R$140 ($70), lunch included.

For a smaller, more personalized tour, contact **Blumar** (© 021/2511-3636). Tours can be organized for one to three people and a guide and include all of Rio's landmarks and a variety of cultural evening programs as well. Prices range from R$72 ($36) for a tour of the Tijuca Forest to R$186 ($93) for a Rio-by-Night tour, including dinner and a show (prices are per person based on two people).

BOAT TOURS A 3-hour tour. Sounds ominous, but Gilligan never made it to Rio. **Saveiros Tour** (© 021/2224-6990; www.saveiros.com.br) offers 3-hour tours of Guanabara Bay aboard an old wooden fishing schooner. Cost is R$15 ($7.50) including snacks of fresh fruit. Departure is at 9:30am Tuesday through Sunday from the Glória Marina (Metrô: Glória). The tour takes in

y yards, has a look at the Sugar Loaf from the
the bay to Niterói to look at the huge Fortaleza
guarded the mouth of Guanabara Bay.

HE̲̲̲OURS Rio is a town where taking the high
ground is rewarded. **Helisight** (© **021/2511-2141** or
021/2542-7895 for Sugar Loaf, 021/2259-6995 for Lagoa;
www.helisight.com.br) offers sightseeing tours by helicopter. Prices
range from R$86 ($43) per person for a 6-minute circuit around the
statue of Christ to R$500 ($250) per person for a 1-hour grand
tour. Minimum of two to three people per flight. Tours depart from
Urca Hill (halfway up to the Sugar Loaf) and from the shore of
Lagoa (opposite the rowing stadium in Leblon).

SPECIALTY TOURS **Marcelo Armstrong's Favela Tour** 🛈
(© **021/9989-0074** or 021/3322-2727; www.favelatour.com.br):
Rio's hillside favelas are huge, complex, and fascinating—a whole
other world in fact—but as an outsider, it's difficult to navigate your
way through this world safely. Licensed guide Marcelo Armstrong
knows the territory; he's been doing tours since '93, longer than any
of his competitors, and has an exceptional rapport with locals. A 3-
hour tour costs R$45 ($22.50), including pickup and drop-off. A
portion of the fee goes to fund a school that tour-goers get to visit.

Cultural Rio (© **021/9911-3829** or 021/3322-4872; www.
culturalrio.com) is owned and operated by Professor Carlos
Roquette, a native-born Carioca and self-educated expert on pretty
much anything to do with his home city. If you have a pet interest,
no matter how arcane, odds are Roquette can put together a tour
that'll keep you interested. His more common tours include
Colonial Rio, Baroque Rio, Imperial Rio, Art Deco Rio, Black Rio,
A Night at the Opera, Styles in Rio, and Modern Rio, but there are
lots more.

TRAM TOURS Rio has far more tram track than gets used by the
daily tram to and from Santa Teresa. Every Saturday, some of this
track gets put to use for two special tram tours. The **Historical Tour**
departs at 10am, while the **Ecological Tour** begins at 2pm. Both
tours are guided and run about 3 hours. For further information, call
the Museu do Bonde at © **021/2242-2354.** *Note:* The tram station's
behind the big "hanging gardens" Petrobras building, on Rua
Profesor Lélio Gama, a little street that runs off Rua Senador Dantas.

WALKING TOURS **Gray Line** (© **021/2512-9919**) offers a
very pricey walking tour covering Praça XV, the Arco do Teles,
Candelaria Church, the São Bento Monastery, and a few other

Finds **Unseen Rio**

Two of Rio's more interesting museums and its last semi-wild beach are unfortunately so far south most people never visit. **Rio Hiking** (© 021/9721-0594; www.riohiking.com.br) offers a 1-day tour, taking in all three of these sites: the **Burle Marx Estate, Grumari Beach,** and the **Casa do Pontal Museum.** Burle Marx was Brazil's most famous landscape designer (responsible for the wavy lines on the Copacabana sidewalk, among other things). At his 100-acre estate, he assembled more than 3,500 species, which he grouped according to their shapes and textures. The tour spends 2 hours at the estate, then heads to the red sand of Grumari Beach for 3 hours of relaxing, including a grilled-fish lunch at a beachside restaurant, followed by a visit to the Casa do Pontal (see "The Top Attractions," earlier in this chapter). Cost, not including lunch, is R$110 ($55).

sights in Rio's historic downtown. Price for the afternoon tour is R$75 ($37.50). Departures Tuesday through Friday.

8 Outdoor Activities

ADVENTURE SPORTS Aventuras Rio (© 021/9195-8462; www.aventurasrio.com.br) offers a couple of 1-day adventure sport options from Rio. On the **rappelling** trip, you drive past Barra de Tijuca to beautiful Guaratiba, hike for an hour to a cliff overlooking an undeveloped beach, then rappel down a 115-foot rock face. Then you hang out, swim for bit, and head back. Cost is R$90 ($45).

The **white-water** rafting trip takes you to a small river an hour north of Rio with Class III (and sometimes Class IV) rapids. The descent takes about 3 hours. Cost is R$90 ($45).

GOLFING There's some fine golfing at the **Gávea Golf Club,** Estrada da Gávea 800, São Conrado (© 021/3332-4141). However, the club—like virtually every golf course in Brazil—is private. The Copacabana Palace Hotel and the Sheraton Hotel have an arrangement allowing their guests to tee off. Others have to be invited by a club member.

HANG GLIDING Flight instructor Paulo Celani of **Just Fly Rio** *RR* (© 021/9985-7540 (cell), 021/2268-0565 (land); www. justfly.lookscool.com) used to be an agricultural engineer, until he decided he'd much prefer to fly for a living. That was 15 years ago.

Since then Paulo has soared in tandem with hundreds of people aged 5 to 85, no experience necessary. It's one of the most exciting things you can do in Rio. Well worth the R$160 ($80) per flight, pickup and drop-off included.

HIKING   The largest urban forest in the world, **Tijuca National Park** offers some fabulous hiking opportunities within the city limits. **Pico de Tijuca** (3,373 ft./1,022m) makes an excellent 2-hour hike; the trail head is at the end of Caminho do Pico da Tijuca. The more **demanding Pedra da Gávea** (2,732 ft./828m) usually takes a full 6 hours. **Rio Hiking** 🕮🕮 (✆ **021/9721-0594;** www.riohiking.com.br) offers guided hiking trips to all of these peaks and more. The 4-hour Sugar Loaf trip, which includes a short stretch of rock climbing, costs R$80 ($40). Less strenuous is the Tijuca Forest tour, which involves a jeep tour of the forest, stops at a waterfall and a couple of lookouts, and a 2-hour hike to Pico de Tijuca. Cost is $R110 ($55), with the option of returning via the fascinating hilltop neighborhood of Santa Teresa. Guides Denise Werneck and Gabriel Barrouin know Rio well, speak excellent English, and are a delight to be with.

SEA KAYAKING   **Simone Miranda Duarte** (✆ **021/9954-9632**) runs guided sea-kayak trips from Praia Vermelha in Urca out and around some of the small islands. The fiberglass kayaks aren't quite up to North American quality, but it's nice to be on the water. Cost is R$15 ($7.50) per hour.

SURFING   California's not the only hot surfing spot in the world. Rio has a number of good spots to catch the waves. The surfing beach closest to the main part of Rio is **Arpoador** beach in Ipanema. Waves are between 3¼ and 10 feet (1m and 3m). Out in Barra de Tijuca, the main surf beach is **Barra-Meio,** a half-mile long (1km) stretch in the middle of the beach (around 3100 Avenida Sernambetiba). Waves average around 6½ feet (2m). If you've brought your board and just need transport, there's a **Surf Bus** that departs the Largo do Machado at 6am and 2pm daily, going along Copacabana, Arpoador, São Conrado, and Barra de Tijuca before returning. If you need a board, **Spirit,** Galeria River, Rua Francisco Otaviano 67, loja 4, Ipanema (✆ **021/2267-9943**), rents short boards, fun boards, and long boards for R$20 to R$30 ($10–$15) a day. If you're looking for **lessons,** there are a couple of instructors in Rio. However, like true surf dudes, they neither have nor answer phones; you have to go find them. In Barra, go to **Pepe's shack** (Barraca do Pepê) and look for **Pedro Muller** or **Gagu,** both of whom operated surf schools around there. Price of a private lesson is around R$20 ($10) an hour.

9 Spectator Sports

AUTO RACING Nearly all races in Rio are at the **Nelson Piquet International Car Race Track,** Avenida Embaixador Abelardo Bueno, Jacarepaguá (✆ **021/2441-2158**). The schedule of races can be obtained by calling the track.

FUTEBOL 𝄐𝄐𝄐 The best and only true way to experience the world's largest soccer stadium is to come during a big game. What an experience! Fans arrive at **Maracanã,** Rua Profesor Eurico Rabelo s/n (✆ **021/2569-4916;** Metrô: Maracanã), hours beforehand, literally—for a 4pm game they arrive at 1pm *at the latest*—and the world's biggest party begins. Outside, folks drink ice-cold beer. Inside, the *torcedores* (fan club members) bring out the samba drums and pound away for a good half-hour, psyching themselves up before parading in the banners—huge flags in team colors—to the wild applause of their fellow fans. Then the other team parades in their flags, and your team boos. Then your side sings a song insulting their team. Then their team sings a song insulting your team. Then they unveil a massive *banderão* covering half the stadium. Then your side unveils your *banderão*. Samba drums beat all the while. Eventually, after several hours of this silliness, a soccer game breaks out. And the best thing about the Brazilian game is they have utter contempt for defense; it's attack, attack, attack for the full 90 minutes. The four best teams in Rio are Flamengo, Fluminense, Botafogo, and Vasco de Gama. Scheduling is incredibly complex, but guaranteed your hotel clerk (or bellhop) will know about the next big game. Tickets are quite affordable, ranging from R$15 to R$40 ($7.50–$20)

Tip: Organized trips to the big games are a scam. They often charge R$100 ($50) or more for a ticket and bus transport (to a stadium that's right on the subway line). Even if you took a cab there and back, you'd still come out ahead.

HORSE RACING Horse races are held at the Jockey Club in Lagoa, officially known as the **Hipódromo Do Jockey Club Brasileiro,** Praça Santos Dumont 31, Gávea (✆ **021/2512-9988**). Races take place on Monday from 6:30 to 10:45pm and on Friday from 4 to 9pm. Grand-Prix and Classics racing is on Saturday and Sunday from 1 to 7pm.

7

Shopping

If Cariocas had to list their primary joys in life, shopping certainly wouldn't come out on the very top—there are, after all, beaches and music and sex to consider—but it'd certainly be in the top five. Cariocas shop anywhere and everywhere: Even on the beach, vendors will peddle an enormous range of products. Elsewhere, clothing, shoes, arts and crafts, musical instruments, and other souvenirs can all be had at good prices.

1 The Shopping Scene

The old downtown neighborhood of Centro offers great deals for clothes and shoes. Fun to explore are the pedestrian streets around **Rua da Alfândega, Rua Uruguaiana,** and **Rua Buenos Aires,** jam-packed with hundreds of merchants in side-by-side small shops. The best days for shopping are Monday through Friday when the downtown core is full of office workers. The area around **Largo da Carioca** has a number of market stalls and street vendors. More upscale clothing can be found around the **Rua Gonçalves Dias,** with many stores selling Brazilian brand names and local designers.

Copacabana, Ipanema, and Leblon don't have any large malls, just boutique malls known as *galerias* in Brazil. The prominent shopping areas are the main streets of the neighborhood. In Copacabana, **Nossa Senhora de Copacabana** is the main shopping street, with many souvenir shops, music, clothing, and sporting-goods stores. The beachfront area also houses a street market on Saturdays and Sundays, selling souvenirs and arts and crafts from various regions of Brazil. For upscale and exclusive shopping in Ipanema, try **Rua Visconde de Pirajá,** especially between the **Rua Anibal de Medonça** and **Rua Vinicius de Moraes.**

Hours for small stores and neighborhood shops are typically Monday through Friday from 10am to 7pm, and 9am to 1pm on Saturday. Malls are usually open from 10am to 10pm Monday through Saturday and have limited hours on Sunday (2–8pm). In tourist areas, shops will often be open on weekends.

Most shops accept one or more types of credit card. Often you can negotiate a discount for paying cash instead of by credit card. In many stores you will also see two prices listed on items: *á vista* (the lower price) refers to cash payments, *cheque ou cartão* is the price for payments made with a check or credit card. Please note that there is a difference between *Credicard* (a brand of credit card) and *cartão* or *cartão de credito* (the generic word for any kind of credit card).

2 Shopping from A to Z

ARTS & CRAFTS

Brumado   This store in Laranjeiras has an excellent collection of Brazilian arts and crafts from across the country, including some indigenous art and toys. Rua das Laranjeiras 486, loja 924, Laranjeiras. ✆ 021/2285-0699. Bus: 584.

Jeito Brasileiro   Just next to the Corcovado station, Jeito Brasileiro is geared to the average tourist who is looking for a little souvenir, but the collection includes some better-than-average pieces such as ceramics, leather, and wooden craftworks. Rua Ererê 11 A, Cosme Velho. No phone. Bus: 584.

Pé de Boi   Also in Laranjeiras, on your way to the Corcovado, Pé de Boi's collection is enormous. Going beyond just Brazilian arts and crafts, it also includes works from popular Peruvian, Ecuadorean, and Guatemalan artists. It's also a great spot to browse for arts and crafts from other Brazilian regions such as the Amazon, Pernambuco, and Minas Gerais. Rua Ipiranga 55, Laranjeiras. ✆ 021/2285-4395. Bus: 584.

BEACHWEAR

Blue Man   Our favorite swimwear store, Blue Man is known for its original designs and prints. Bathing suits and bikinis can be found in various styles, often allowing you to mix and match tops and bottoms for your preferred look. Also with outlets in the Rio Sul and Fashion Mall shopping centers. Visconde de Pirajá 351, loja 108, Ipanema. ✆ 021/2247-4905. Bus: 474.

Sal & Seda   Everything you need for the beach and beyond. Sal & Seda offers beautifully designed bikinis (not just the itsy-bitsy, teeny-weeny kind, though they have those, too) and bathing suits, some with lovely embroidery. There's also a selection of tops and tunics made out of high-quality white cotton with delicate embroidery, cool enough to wear to the beach, yet beautiful enough to wear for an evening out. Rua Visconde de Pirajá 540, Ipanema. ✆ 021/2294-0791. www.saleseda.com.br. Bus: 415.

BOOKS

Dantes Editora e Livraria For an excellent collection of inexpensive used pocket books in English (just what the doctor ordered for reading on the beach), try this bookstore in Leblon. For the more intellectually motivated, there are also more serious tomes through which to browse. Rua Dias Ferreira 45b, Leblon. ✆ 021/2511-3480. Bus: 415.

Letras e expressoes For a large selection of foreign magazines and newspapers, check out this bookstore in Ipanema. In the travel section, you will also find a number of excellent books on Rio, including some beautiful coffee-table photo books. Rua Visconde de Pirajá 276, Ipanema. ✆ 021/2521-6110. Bus: 415.

Livraria da Travessa Nothing's better than losing yourself in a good bookstore every now and then. With its lovely wooden floor-to-ceiling shelves and black-and-white–checkered floor tiles, this beautiful store positively invites browsing sessions of several hours or more. Good collection of English-language books. Av. Rio Branco 44, Centro. ✆ 021/2242-9294. Bus: 128. Rua Visconde de Pirajá 462 A, Ipanema. ✆ 021/2521-7734. Bus: 474 and 128.

CARNAVAL COSTUMES

Casa Turuna For those creative types who would like to make their own Carnaval costume instead of buying it from a samba school, Casa Turuna is your spot. Established in 1920, this little store in Rio's downtown sells everything you can think of and more. Let your imagination run free. Odds are they've seen it all over the years. Rua Senhor dos Passos 122, Centro. ✆ 021/2224-0908. Metrô: Central.

A DEPARTMENT STORE

Lojas Americanas For inexpensive clothing, candies, appliances, and toiletries, check out the Lojas Americanas department store chain. Some locations (including the store in Ipanema) also have a small grocery department. The music department often has great deals on CDs. Visconde de Pirajá 526-532, Ipanema. ✆ 021/2274-0590. Bus: 474.

FASHION
FOR CHILDREN

Pituca Brazilians spoil their children shamelessly, with the result being that children's clothing is fashionable and stylish. Pituca offers the most variety in the 2- to 10-year-old age range, but other sizes are also available. Sizes for children's clothing in Brazil are measured by the child's age: months for babies and years after the age of 2. Recall, however, that on average, Brazilians tend to be a little smaller than North Americans. Rua Visconde Pirajá 180-C, Ipanema. ℭ 021/ 2267-2734. Bus: 415.

FOR MEN

Sandpiper Check out Sandpiper for trendy casual wear. Especially if you are in the market for shirts or informal jackets, this is a great spot. And like most of the men's clothing stores in Brazil, they usually add a few more splashes of color than you might be used to. Rua Santa Clara 75, Copacabana. ℭ 021/2236-7652. Metrô: Arcoverde.

Toulon Excellent spot to pick up some smart casual wear. Good-quality jeans, khakis, colorful long-sleeve cotton dress shirts, and T-shirts are available at reasonable prices. Toulon also sells necessities such as belts, underwear, and socks. There is another branch at Av. N.S. de Copacabana 978, lojas B/C, Copacabana (ℭ 021/ 2247-1051; Bus: 474). Rua Visconde de Pirajá 135, Ipanema. ℭ 021/ 2247-8716. www.toulon.com.br. Bus: 474.

FOR WOMEN

Dimpus The words young and trendy come to mind when describing the Dimpus collection. Pieces are colorful and hip but still quite wearable for work or evening wear. A popular store with Rio's 18- to 35-year-olds. Rua Maria Quiteria 85, Ipanema. ℭ 021-523-1544. www. dimpus.com.br. Bus: 415.

Lelé da Cuca One of the more elegant and upscale shops in Ipanema's tony shopping district, Lelé da Cuca caters to many of Rio's society women. Its collections include elegant evening and glamour wear, with a variety of European designer labels such as Chanel. The store also has a large collection of accessories such as belts, purses, and shoes. Rua Visconde de Pirajá 430 B, Ipanema. ℭ 021/ 2287-5295. Bus: 474.

Rabo de Saia Elegant women's clothing for those who like simple and clean styles with just a dash of color. Santa Clara 75, Copacabana. ℭ 021/2255-7332. Bus: 415.

FOOD

Garcia & Rodrigues A restaurant, bar, deli, and gourmet store. Garcia & Rodrigues tries to be everything to all people and does it all amazingly well. If you don't have time to stop in for a dinner or lunch, pick up some items to go. Just keep in mind that anything imported is especially expensive. Yes, that small box of European chocolates really costs R$24 ($12)! Av. Ataulfo de Paiva 1251, Leblon. (C) 021/2512-8188. Bus: 474.

GALLERIES

Ateliê Selaron   Working out of his atelier just behind the Sala Cecilia on the Lapa Square, Selaron is well known for his paintings and the interesting frames he creates. Escadaria do Convento 24 (enter off the Rua Joaquim Silva), Lapa. (C) 021/2242-0922. Metrô: Cinelândia.

Ateliê Tetê Cappel and Eduardo Fallero Studio   The smaller the better—this duo has made their fame creating tiny reproductions of well-known landmarks. Not just the famous touristy Rio sites, but also small-scale versions of bars, houses, and heritage buildings. Rua Vinicius de Moraes 190, Ipanema. (C) 021/2522-1141. Bus: 415.

HB-195   Named after the abbreviation of the street name, this gallery in Santa Teresa exhibits work from a variety of local contemporary artists. A bonus is the nice view you get from this lovely house. Follow the signs for the Chácara do Céu museum and instead of turning a sharp left on Rua Murtinho Nobre, continue straight ahead for another 200 yards (182m) to get to Rua Hermenegildo Barros. Open Wednesday through Sunday from 2 to 7pm. Rua Hermenegildo Barros 195, Santa Teresa. (C) 021/2508-9148.

GIFTS & SOUVENIRS

Ely's Gems and Souvenirs   One of the largest souvenir stores in Rio, Ely's consists of two sections. On the left you will find all the typical souvenirs: woodcarvings, Bahian dolls, T-shirts, and mugs, as well as a large array of gifts made with precious stones. On the right-hand side is the jewelry section of the store, selling beautiful creations in silver and gold, as well as loose stones. Av. Nossa Senhora de Copacabana 249, loja D. (C) 021/2541-2547. Metrô: Arcoverde.

Lido Souvenirs   Just a block from the Copacabana Palace Hotel, you will find a wide range of souvenirs, from the ultra-tacky to the exquisitely tasteful. The store's specialty is semiprecious and precious stones, sold loose as well as in a variety of trinkets such as teaspoons with stone handles, stone birds, and jewelry. Rua Adolfo Dantas 26 B, Copabana. (C) 021/2541-8098. Bus: 415. Metrô: Arcoverde.

JEWELRY

Amsterdam Sauer   The best-known name in Brazil for gems, jewelry, and souvenirs made with semiprecious and precious stones. The Ipanema location houses both the store and museum, and both are worth a visit even if you are not in the market to buy. The museum shows off many of Mr. Sauer's original finds when he first came to Brazil in 1940 and started working as a miner, gemologist, geologist, and finally as a jeweler. The store offers a wide range of jewelry and loose gemstones such as emeralds, aquamarines, imperial topaz (mined only in Brazil), tourmalines, citrines, and Brazilian opal. Rua Visconde de Pirajá 484, Ipanema. (*C* **0800/26-6092** or 021/2512-9878. www.amsterdamsauer.com. Bus: 474.

H. Stern   It is hard to miss the H. Stern advertisements in hotels around Rio (and the rest of Brazil), and it is only a matter of time before you will receive an invitation to visit the store, transportation complimentary. If you do not receive such an offer, just phone the store and they will be pleased to arrange this for you. Specializing in precious and semiprecious stones, the company also owns mines and polishing shops, guaranteeing the quality of their products from start to finish. Rua Garcia D'Avila 113, Ipanema. (*C* **021/2259-7442**. Bus: 474.

LEATHER GOODS

Mala Amada   Ran out of luggage space for all your souvenirs? Mala Amada has an excellent selection of handbags, purses, briefcases, and wallets. All are made with high-quality Brazilian leather and produced locally in the store's own factory. Also located at Rua da Carioca 13, Centro (*C* **021/2262-0676;** Metrô: Carioca). Rua Visconde de Pirajá 550, Ipanema. (*C* **021/2239-8648**. Bus: 474.

MALLS & SHOPPING CENTERS

Botafogo Praia Shopping   This mall has an excellent selection of clothing stores such as Dimpus, Folic, Corpo and Alma, Exchange, Old Factory and Madame MS. For your photo needs, check the Kodak Rio photo shop on the ground floor. The food court on the seventh floor has a few fast-food options as well as three excellent restaurants (Kotobuki, Emporium Pax, and Enseada) with gorgeous views of Botafogo beach and the Pão de Açúcar. Praia de Botafogo 400, Botafogo. (*C* **021/2559-9559**. Metrô: Botafogo or Bus 512 (to Alfredo Gomes). Please note that all buses marked VIA ATERRO take the express route and have no stops along Botafogo beach.

Rio Sul   One of the most popular malls in the city, Rio Sul is very accessible, located in Botafogo just before the tunnel that goes to Copacabana. With over 450 stores, a movie theater, and an excellent food court, Rio Sul is always busy and is a great place to get a feel for Brazilian fashion and prices. Rua Lauro Muller 116, Botafogo. (*C* **021/ 2545-7200**. Bus: 119, 474.

São Conrado Fashion Mall Although it has lost of bit of its original glitter and appeal, the São Conrado Fashion Mall is still a favorite haunt for Rio's well-heeled and fashion-conscious shopper. Over 150 stores, carrying national and international designers, display their wares. Maybe it's because of its upscale clientele, but the mall's food court is the best in town. Estrada da Gávea 899, São Conrado. ✆ 021/2322-2733. Bus: 178.

MARKETS

Babilônia Feira Hype It may be spelled "hype" but it's pronounced "hippie," as in long-hair groovy cool man. Located in the Jockey Club, the Babilônia Hippy Fair is an arts-and-crafts market and more. You can listen to music, get a shiatsu massage, design a henna tattoo, buy a nose ring, get yourself pierced, and if things get really groovy, you can even turn on, tune in, and drop out. *Tip:* The market makes a great stop after touring the nearby botanical gardens. Open every other Saturday and Sunday from 2 to 10pm. Check for correct week in the newspaper, or phone ahead. Hipódromo do Jóquei Clube Brasileiro, Rua Jardim Botanico s/n. ✆ 021/2236-7195. Bus: 170, 571, or 572.

Feira Hippie Ipanema In the '60s, this square was the hippie hangout in Rio, and though the market is not quite the outstanding arts-and-crafts fair it used to be, it's still a fun place to browse on a Sunday morning if you happen to be in Ipanema. The event takes place from 9am to 5pm every Sunday in the large Praça General Osorio (intersection of Rua Teixeira de Melo and Rua Visconde de Pirajá).

Feirarte In front of the Paço Imperial on one of Rio's most historic squares, this craft market features a range of artists showcasing their handiwork. There's leatherwork, ceramics, glass, and silver, not to mention food and drink stands and less-talented vendors peddling more touristy souvenirs. Takes place every Thursday and Friday from 8am to 6pm. Praça XV, Centro. Bus: 119 or 415.

MUSIC

Toca de Vinicius *(Finds)* In the heart of Ipanema stands this small temple dedicated to the god of bossa nova, the poet and composer Vinicius de Moraes. Anything related to bossa nova can be found in this tiny store: an impressive collection of bossa nova CDs and vinyl, songbooks, and (mostly Portuguese) books and magazines on the smooth and mellow sounds of Brazil. Check out the website for bossa nova music events at the store or around town. *Tip:* The last Sunday of every month, the store usually hosts a late-afternoon music event (from 4pm onward). Rua Vinicius de Moraes 129, Ipanema. © 021/2247-5227. www.tocadovinicius.com.br. Bus: 474.

Top Sound   Even though most music shops have given up on vinyl, Top Sound still carries a good collection of LPs and provides vinyl lovers with the opportunity to expand their collections with some Brazilian tunes. The store also takes pride in stocking hard-to-find CDs and lets you listen before purchasing. Av. N.S. de Copacabana 1103, loja C. © 021/2267-9607. Bus: 415.

MUSICAL INSTRUMENTS

The *berimbau,* that wooden string instrument from Bahia, is likely one of Brazil's most popular souvenirs, but for music lovers there are many more interesting instruments from which to choose. The Rua da Carioca has turned into music-store central with at least five shops by most recent count grouped together on its short length. Look for tiny hand-held rattles or else pick up a tambourine or small set of drums. The *agôgô* is an interesting-looking double bell used to keep a beat. Guitar players will love the *cavaquinho,* a sort of Brazilian version of the ukulele. For these and more instruments, visit **Musical Carioca,** Rua da Carioca 89 (© 021/2524-6029); **Casa Oliveira Musicais,** Rua da Carioca 70 (© 021/2252-5636); or **Guitarra Prata,** Rua da Carioca 37 (© 021/2262-9659). Metrô: Largo da Carioca.

SALONS

You will see many small salons in Rio that offer very inexpensive salon services, mainly manicures and pedicures. These services are usually advertised as *pé* ("foot," pedicure) and *mão* ("hand," for manicure). Prices range from R$8 to R$15 ($4–$7.50) for a manicure and R$10 to R$20 ($5–$10) for a pedicure. Often there will be a discount for getting both at the same time. Look in Centro for less-expensive salons where a combo manicure/pedicure may cost as little as R$15 ($7.50). It is customary to tip the beautician R$2 to R$4 ($1–$2). These little salons are significantly cheaper than the fancy hotel salons, but keep in mind that you are not getting a spa treatment, just cuticle removal, buffing, shaping, and polish.

Ophicina do Cabelo   Not the cheapest but certainly worth the money. This top-quality salon offers haircuts for both men and women, manicures, pedicures, and a range of beauty treatments, including waxing, massages, and facials. Open Tuesday through Sunday from 9am to 9pm. Appointments recommended for evenings and Saturdays. Av. Delfim Moreira 630, 4th floor of the Marina Palace Hotel, Leblon. © 021/2529-2968. Bus: 474.

SHOES

Arezzo   If Carioca women had to choose their favorite shoe store, it would without a doubt be Arezzo. This company always seems to stay just a step ahead of the trends without being too avant-garde and the prices are reasonable. Also sells a great selection of high-quality leather purses. Various locations, including Rio Sul and Rua Visconde de Pirajá 295, Ipanema. ℭ 021/2521-4737. Bus: 415.

Mr. Cat   For the latest and most elegant styles in shoe fashions, have a look at Mr. Cat's collection. The store goes for classic designs—business as well as evening wear for both men and women. All shoes are made of the highest-quality made-in-Brazil leather. Prices are very reasonable, ranging from R$50 to R$150 ($25–$75) for a pair of top-quality leather men's dress shoes. Rua Visconde de Pirajá 414, loja D Ipanema. ℭ 021/2523-4645. Bus: 474.

SURF SHOPS

Atol das Rocas   Everything you need to catch those waves . . . surfboards, body boards, wet suits. Not a surfer? This Rio shop also has a great collection of shorts, Bermudas, T-shirts (for both men and women), and sunglasses. Rua Ouvidor 161, Centro. ℭ 021/2232-4965. Metrô: Uruguaiana.

Spirit   One of the few surf stores that also stocks rentals, Spirit is conveniently close to the best surf spot in Ipanema, Arpoador beach. Open Monday through Saturday only, you will have to book ahead if you want to surf over the weekend. Rentals range from R$20 to R$30 ($10–$15) for a short board, fun board, or long board. Galeria River, Rua Francisco Otaviano 67, loja 4, Ipanema. ℭ 021/2267-9943. Bus: 128.

SPORTING GOODS

Galeria River   Cool central; not just one shop but a minimall with at least a dozen sports and outdoor stores that sell skateboards, surf gear, in-line skates, and climbing equipment, as well as accessories such as clothing, sunglasses, and hiking boots. Great place to pick up tips on where to go, lessons, and local hangouts. Galeria River, Rua Francisco Otaviano, Ipanema. Bus: 128.

Wollner Outdoor   A good address for high-quality outdoor gear: backpacks, daypacks, hiking boots, rain gear, and climbing gear. Prices are comparable to those in the United States and Canada. Also offers outdoor courses and trips; see notice board in store or **www.wollner.com.br** for upcoming events. Rua Visconde de Pirajá 511, Ipanema. ℭ 021/2274-6121. Bus: 415.

8

Rio After Dark

It's an open question whether Cariocas possess some hidden nightlife gene or whether they've trained themselves for decadence through years and years of practice. Whatever the case, there's lots to do in Rio. It starts early and continues very late. Cariocas themselves don't make a big deal about a night on the town: They're happy either heading out for beers, dancing to forró music, or eating shrimp in some hole-in-the-wall botequim. However, if you as a visitor want to go for the quintessential Rio experience, you have to learn to pace yourself. Whether you spend the day seeking out sights or on the beach, head back to your hotel in the afternoon for a wee bit of a nap. Trust us, this will be the key to making it through the night.

Once you're up again, head out in the cool early evening for a coconut juice on the beach. Sip it while watching the sunset (in summer around 8pm), then around 9pm stroll over to a patio for a predinner drink. Jobi in Leblon is a great spot. On the weekends, you could walk along the pathway by the Lagoa and find a table at one of the kiosks. Plan to have dinner around 10pm and to be ready for your evening of dancing around midnight. (Most places don't even open until 11pm.) Your options at this point depend on the day and the time of year. If you're in Rio between October and Carnaval, attending one of the samba school rehearsals on Saturday night is a must. Otherwise, on a Thursday night see who's playing at the Ballroom. On a Friday night check out the dancers at one of Rio's traditional dance halls downtown, the Elite or Asa Branca. Of course, there are a number of discos and bars to choose from and then there are always the botequins, Rio's neighborhood bars. Wherever you wind up, after 3 or 4 hours dancing, you may find yourself getting peckish. For a late-night or early morning snack, stop in at the Pizzeria Guanabara in Leblon, open until at least 5am on weekends. By the time they throw you out of there, it'll just be time to wander down to the beach and watch the sunrise, ready for a new morning and another night in Rio.

To find out more about listings for arts and entertainment, check the Friday editions of the *O Globo* or *Jornal do Brasil* newspapers. Available at all newsstands (buy early in the day as they sell out quickly), both publish a detailed weekly calendar of events, including nightlife, performing arts, concerts, and other events in the city. The Rio tourism agency **Riotur** also publishes a detailed booklet of events in English and Portuguese called *Rio Incomparável,* available at their main information center at Av. Princesa Isabel 183 in Copacabana, or call **Alô Rio** at ℰ **021/2542-8080** for information on events around town; they keep an updated list and have English-speaking staff to answer any questions.

Here's some vocabulary to help you decipher the listings information from the newspapers. Under *musica* or *show,* you will find the listings for live music. Lovers of Brazilian music should look for anything under *forró,* MPB (*musica popular brasileira*), *bossa nova, choro, pagode,* or *samba.* Listings under *pista* refer to events at nightclubs or discos. Most listings will include the price of admission: *couvert* is the cover charge and *consumação* states the drink minimum. It is quite common to have two rates, one for women (*mulher*) and one for men (*homem*), the latter usually paying more. The days of the week are given in abbreviations: *seg* or *2a* (Mon), *ter* or *3a* (Tues), *qua* or *4a* (Wed), *qui* or *5a* (Thurs), *sex* or *6a* (Fri), *sab* (Sat), and *dom* (Sun).

1 The Performing Arts

The performing-arts season in Brazil runs from early April until early December. April is a particularly good time—the equivalent of the North American September—as theaters and companies unveil their programs and kick off with their season premieres.

Centro Cultural do Banco do Brasil   Housed in a gorgeous neoclassical building (former home of the Banco do Brasil), this extremely well patronized cultural center gets about 1.8 million visitors a year. Two theaters in the center host regular recitals, concerts, and dance performances, as well as Portuguese-language theater. There are also regular photography and art exhibits in the center's small exhibition rooms. Check the newspapers or the website for more information. Rua Primeiro de Março 66, Centro. ℰ 021/3808-2026. www.cultura-e.com.br. Admission varies from free to R$15 ($7.50). Exhibits are always free. Metrô: Uruguaina.

Teatro João Caetano   Named after one of Brazil's best-known 19th-century dramatists, the theater has a varied calendar, hosting many of Brazil's popular musicians as well as classical concerts.

Occasionally there are also presentations of modern dance and theater. Praça Tiradentes s/n, Centro. ℂ 021/2221-0305. Tickets R$10–R$40 ($5–$20). Metrô: Carioca.

Teatro Rival   Located in downtown Rio, the Teatro Rival is a small theater that does an outstanding job booking local and popular national acts, mostly of MPB. Ticket prices are quite reasonable, so give it a shot. You may be looking at the next Marisa Monte or one of Brazil's many talented performers who haven't made it big internationally. Rua Alvaro Alvim 33, Centro. ℂ 021/2532-4192.Tickets R$10–R$40 ($5–$20). Metrô: Cinelândia.

Theatro Municipal   Brazil's prime venue for the performing arts, the elegant Parisian-style Theatro Municipal stages everything from opera to ballet to symphony concerts. The theater's ballet corps and symphony orchestra perform regularly throughout the year, and the theater also hosts many visiting companies such as the BBC symphony orchestra, the Berlin Philharmonic, the Kirov Ballet, and the Brazilian Symphony Orchestra. Besides the formal programming, the theater also offers an inexpensive noon-hour opera series (*opera do meio-dia*) and concerts in the foyer. Check the newspapers for updated programming. Praça Marechal Floriano s/n, Centro. ℂ 021/2544-2900. www.theatromunicipal.rj.gov.br. Tickets R$15–R$40 ($7.50–$20) for most performances. Metrô: Cinelândia.

2 Music & Dance Clubs

Throughout the summer, the city of Rio organizes concerts, outdoor movies on the beach, and other events in Copacabana. Check with **Alô Rio** at ℂ 021/2542-8080 and make sure to pick up the events listing *Rio Incomparavel* from Riotur for a complete overview.

Tip: Check out the **Rio Hiking** website (**www.riohiking.com. br**) for excellent tips on where to catch live music or just grab a drink and meet people. (Click on "About Us" or "Rio Hints.") Rio Hiking's owner Denise Werneck is as passionate about Rio's nightlife as she is about exploring her city's exuberant nature trails.

In most clubs and discos, you can expect to pay a cover charge. Women usually pay less than men; you'll see the two prices listed at the door. Often there is also a drink minimum, ranging anywhere from R$5 to R$60 ($2.50–$30). In most venues you are handed a card upon entry that is to be used to record all your purchases. The bill is then settled when you leave. A 10% service charge will be included and a tip on top of that is not required. Hang on to your card for dear life. If you lose it, you'll be charge an astronomical fee.

TRADITIONAL BRAZILIAN MUSIC

Asa Branca   Located in a beautiful old mansion in the funky and only slightly shady neighborhood of Lapa, Asa Branca is one of the traditional Brazilian music venues, playing pagode, samba, choro (an offshoot of samba), and the immensely popular forró. Dancing goes until the early hours. For those who don't like burning the midnight oil, there is a Saturday-afternoon feijão (beans) and samba event. From 2 to 9pm, Adelson Alves, one of the veterans of the Carioca music scene, serves up copious amounts of samba and all the feijão you can handle. Open daily after 10pm and Saturday from 2 to 9pm. Av. Mem de Sá 17, Lapa. ℂ **021/2232-5704.** Cover R$6–R$8 ($3–$4). Bus: 409, 410.

Elite   One popular gafieira or traditional dance hall is the Elite, tucked in behind an arcade of Romanesque arches on the second floor of a little pink and plaster gem of a colonial building in Centro. Even if you can't dance, it's worth having a drink and watching in awe and admiration as some of the older folks strut their stuff. Often these couples will dress the part: men in crisp linen suits and wing-tip dance shoes and women in rustling silk dresses with ballooning '50s style skirts. Only open Friday through Sunday: Friday after 7pm, Saturday after 10pm, and Sunday from 6pm onward. Rua Frei Caneca 4, Centro. ℂ **021/2232-3217.** No cover, drink minimum of R$6 ($3). Metrô: Central.

Estudantina   Only open on Fridays and Saturdays, the gafieira Estudantina is another mainstay on the Carioca ballroom scene. Many students of the dance school come and show off, but newcomers and novices are made to feel equally welcome. A 10-piece band plays every weekend. Doors open at 11pm. Arrive early to grab

---

⸂Moments⸃ The Gafieira of Days Gone By

Though now as rare as a winning Brazilian soccer team, the traditional ballroom dance halls known as *gafieiras* once defined the Carioca nightlife scene. Still worth a visit even if you can't dance, gafieiras are a legacy of the elegant days of old, when couples would dress for the occasion and everyone knew the steps. Most folks don't show up in suits or ballgowns anymore, but couples still dance with elegance and the tunes are unmistakably Brazilian: samba and pagode, a bit of rumba or foxtrot, and nowadays lots of forró.

---

a table. Praça Tiradentes 79, Centro. © 021/2507-8067. Cover R$6–R$12 ($3–$6). Metrô: Carioca.

Plataforma 1 *Overrated*   Ah, the tourist trap. Every city has at least one. Some are even fun in a tacky kind of way. Others—and in this category one should place the Plataforma 1—should be labeled with little radioactive stickers reading AVOID. What's offered is supposedly a song-and-dance showcase of Brazilian culture. The reality is a mediocre supper served up with a glitzy Vegas-style show. Rua Adalberto Ferreira 32, Leblon. © 021/2274-4022. Admission price depends on who you book through. Minimum price R$80 ($40). Bus: 415.

Velha Guarda da Mangueira *Finds*   For an afternoon of some of the best traditional samba, check out the Mangueiran Old Guard (*Velha Guarda da Mangueira* in Portuguese). These senior members of the traditional samba school Mangueira (the winner of the very first official parade held in 1932) gather every Saturday afternoon next to the Sambodromo to make some of the best samba around. The location is casual, admission is cheap, and the beer an eminently affordable R$1.50 (75¢) a can. Don't underestimate these guys, though! With years of experience, these are some of the best sambistas around and famous guest musicians drop by on a regular basis. Starts at 4pm. Rua Frederico Silva 85, Praça XI, Centro. © 021/2255-9158. Cover R$10 ($5). Metrô: Central.

LIVE MUSIC

Aside from these listings, many small chopperias and botequins (see "Bars & Pubs," below, for longer descriptions of these two institutions) will often have a singer or small combo playing. Usually there's a small cover charge (*couvert* in Portuguese) for this entertainment. By sitting down and listening, you're agreeing to foot the bill. The fee is automatically added to your tab. If you want to know what the couvert is before deciding to stay, simply ask the waiter. The key phrase is *"Quanto e o couvert?"* (*Kwan*-toe eh oh *koo*-ver?).

ATL Hall   Latin America's largest dedicated concert venue, the modern ATL Hall is located in the far-off corners of Barra da Tijuca in the Shopping Via Parque. Most international stars and many of Brazil's big stars such as Marisa Monte, Gilberto Gil, and Ney Matogrosso favor this 10,000-seat auditorium. An evening out will undoubtedly be pricey: Public transit is almost nonexistent, making taxis your best bet for getting out there. Expect to pay at least R$40 ($20) one-way from the Zona Sul neighborhoods of Ipanema or Leblon, or negotiate a return fare with the driver. Av. Ayrton Senna

Moments New Year's Eve in Rio

Rio's annual New Year's Eve extravaganza puts all those "special millennium celebrations" to shame. Millions pack the beach for an all-night festival of music, food, and fun, punctuated by spectacular fireworks. Trust the Brazilians to throw a party where everyone is welcome and admission is free.

Arrive early and enjoy a New Year's buffet at one of the scores of restaurants or hotels along the beachfront Avenida Atlântica. Music kicks off at 8pm, as people make their way down to the beach until every square inch of sand is packed. By midnight, more than two million have joined the countdown. As the clock strikes 12, the fireworks begin. Five barges moored off Copacabana plus more in Leme, Ipanema, Flamengo, Paquetá, and the Forte de Copacabana, at the end of the beach, flood the sky with a shower of reds, greens, purples, and yellows and golds. When the last whistling spark falls into the sea, bands fire up their instruments and welcome in the new year with a concert that goes on until the wee hours. Many stay all night and grab a spot on the sand when they tire. If you ever entertained romantic notions of waking up on the sand at Copacabana, this is the night to live your dream. The event is perfectly safe.

3000, Barra da Tijuca. ✆ **021/2421-1331** or phone Ticketmaster 0800/771-2391. www.atlhall.com.br. Cover varies but these are the big-ticket shows with some acts charging up to R$100 ($50).

Canecão   It's old and tattered and the sightlines aren't terrific, but it's also got tradition. Everyone who's anyone in Brazilian music has played this aging 3,000-person auditorium, from Djavan to Milton Nascimento to Gal Costa. For his recent acoustic tour Superstar Caetano Veloso chose this venue over some of the more modern and fancy halls. A few tables are available but need to be booked well in advance Otherwise, it's standing-room only. The box office and theater are just across the street from the Rio Sul shopping center. Av. Venceslau Brás 215, Botafogo. ✆ **021/2543-1241.** Cover varies with each event, starting around R$15 ($7.50) and going up to R$60 ($30) for the larger events. Bus: 474 to Rio Sul.

During the party, followers of the Afro-Brazilian religion Candomblé mark Reveillon in their own way. New Year's Eve is an important moment in Candomblé, a time when followers make offerings to the powerful sea goddess Yemanjá. Along the beach, circles of women dressed all in white light candles and prepare small boats loaded with flowers, mirrors, trinkets, and perfumes. They launch the boats into the surf in hopes of obtaining Yemanjá's favor for the year to come.

Cariocas traditionally wear white on New Year's Eve; it's the color of peace and the color worn by devotees of Candomblé to honor Yemanjá. Don a pair of white shorts and a T-shirt, but don't forget your swimsuit. The traditional New Year's Eve "polar bear swim" will be even more tempting when the temperature is a balmy 42°C (105°F).

The best way to get there is by subway (buy tickets in advance to avoid lines). Most streets in Copacabana are closed to traffic; parking anywhere near the beach is impossible. For more details on the schedule, contact **Alô Rio** (© **021/2542-8080**).

Carioca da Gema *(finds)*   Though the Carioca da Gema is a fine little restaurant, music is really the chief thing on order. All the dishes on the menu are named after famous samba songs, while up on stage there's a nightly offering of samba, served live. The combination has turned this little bistro into one of the hottest commodities in the downtown Rio nightlife scene (see "Nightlife Zones: Lapa," below). On Friday and Saturday nights, the place is packed with people crowding in to enjoy the music. The show normally kicks off at about 8pm, but space is very limited, so come early, get a spot close to the stage, and grab a bite to eat while waiting for things to heat up. Rua Mem de Sá 79, Lapa. © 021/2221-0043. Cover R$5–R$10 ($2.50–$5) and drink minimum R$6 ($3). Metrô: Cinelândia.

Mistura Fina   Mistura Fina was clearly far ahead of its time when it opened up some 2 decades back. A restaurant, bar, piano lounge,

Tips   Nightlife Zones: Lapa

Bars and clubs have their moments, and so, over time, do neighborhoods. Lapa is definitely on the up again. In the roaring '20s, Lapa's vibrant nightlife with its many bars and nightclubs earned it the nickname "Montmartre of the tropics." It fell on hard times in the '50s and '60s, but in the last year or two, Lapa has undergone a major revival as even Cariocas from trendy Ipanema and Leblon come here to party. City and state governments have sat up and taken notice, investing money renovating some of the neighborhood's gorgeous heritage buildings, encouraging the development of restaurants and bars, and pumping US$2.5 million into the revitalization of the Rua do Lavradio. Things hop almost every night of the week, but the best days are Thursday, Friday, and Saturday. The most popular hangouts are on the Rua Mem de Sá, around the lovely Largo da Lapa, and on the Rua do Lavradio on the far side of the Arcos da Lapa. Worth checking out are **Emporium 100**, Rua do Lavradio 100 (✆ **021/2852-5904**)—a great spot for samba and choro—and the **Bar Semente**, Rua Joaquim Silva 138 (✆ **021/ 2242-5165**), for Friday-night salsa and mambo.

and dance club all in one, it's a great place to start with a drink on the large veranda overlooking the lagoon, grab a bite to eat at the restaurant, or get in the mood with some jazz at the piano bar. And when that starts to get a little too mellow, head up the stairs to the dance club. Every Saturday it hosts a live concert followed by a DJ after 11pm. Other nights have either a DJ or a live act. No teenyboppers here, Mistura Fina attracts the 30- to 50-year-olds who can afford to pay a little bit more for this classy venue. Av. Borges de Medeiros 3207, Lagoa. ✆ 021/2537-2844. www.misturafina.com.br. Cover ranges from R$10–R$30 ($5–$15). Bus: 572.

DANCE CLUBS

Ballroom   A restaurant by day, this mild-mannered location with the oh-so-generic name transforms itself into a packed and hopping dance club after 10pm, complete with lots of live music. Thursdays are forró nights, Brazil's version of upbeat country music. Fridays are reserved for Flashback Tunes, familiar hits from the '70s, '80s, and '90s, usually performed by the house band. Other programming varies. Rua Humaitá 10, Botafogo. ✆ **021/2537-7600**. Cover varies with event but usually around R$10 ($5). Bus: 178. Metrô: Botafogo.

The Bed Room   The latest hot club for Rio's buffed and beautiful is located past the Sheraton Hotel in the somewhat remote reaches of São Conrado. The gimmick luring folks out here is given away in the name—the club does indeed resemble a giant bedroom, where the young and taut can lounge and pose and generally hang out on one of 19 big soft beds surrounding the dance floor. Sheeting space is limited of course, so call to book ahead if you want a guaranteed spot on the covers. Saturday nights are particularly popular, with DJ Nino ruling the floor with his selection of techno and house. Estrada da Joá 150, São Conrado. ✆ **021/3322-6193**. Drink minimum R$20 ($10) for women and R$30–R$60 ($15–$30) for men. No public transit.

Bunker 94   Not everyone swoons to bossa nova or the upbeat sounds of samba and forró. At Bunker 94, Rio's young and pierced move to the pounding sounds of techno, trance, and house as spun by three different DJs on three different dance floors. Gay-friendly club. Open only Thursday through Sunday after 11pm. Rua Raul Pompeia 94, Copacabana. ✆ **021/2521-0367**. Cover R$10–R$15 ($5–$7.50). Bus: 415.

Melí-Meló   Rio's hottest current nightclub. Located on Lagoa, the spacious club has two dance floors with excellent DJs, a cyber café, and sushi bar. There is no cover charge but a stiff drink minimum that ranges from R$20 ($10) on weekdays to R$50 ($25) on Saturdays. Lineups are as competitive and doormen as snooty as anything south of Manhattan. That's the price you pay for rubbing elbows (or other extruding bodily bits) with Rio's beautiful people. Sightings of models, starlets, socialites, soccer players, and other assorted celebs are a dime a dozen. Av. Borges de Medeiros 1426, Lagoa. ✆ **021/2219-3132**. www.meli-melo.com.br. Drink minimum Tues–Thurs R$20–R$25 ($10–$12.50) and Fri–Sat R$25 ($12.50) for women and R$40–R$50 ($20–$25) for men. Bus: 572.

3 Bars & Pubs

Always ask when going into a restaurant or bar with live music if there is a cover, or *"couvert para a musica,"* and how much it is to avoid any surprises when your bill comes.

BOTEQUINS

Arco do Teles   Tucked away in an alley just off the Praça XV, the Arco do Teles looks like a movie set of old Rio. Perfectly preserved colonial two-story walk-ups are set on narrow cobblestone streets, lined with restaurants and cafes. Though it's a good place to go for a quick lunch, prime time is after work hours, especially on Thursday and Friday nights. Office workers flock here to grab a few cold chopps (draft beer) and catch some music before heading home. Often they forget to go home. As the evening wears on, tables and chairs take over the entire alley, creating a large impromptu patio—it's one of the best people-watching spots in town. Travessa do Comercio, Arco do Teles (from the Praça XV, facing towards the bay, you will see the arch that marks the entrance to the alley on your left). Bus: 110 or 415.

Bip Bip   Another internationally acclaimed botequim—the Parisian daily *Le Monde* featured this tiny bar on its front page—Bip Bip's owes its fame to an outstanding musical program. Tuesday and Sunday nights are the best evenings to catch some great samba or pagode; it's not unusual to see some of Brazil's best musicians join in: Beth Carvalho, Nelson Sargento, Walter Alfaiate, and others come out regularly to sing and play. Rua Almirante Gonçalves 50, Copacabana. (*C) 021/2267-9696. Bus: 432.

Bracarense   Unanimously voted the best botequim in town, the *New York Times* even went so far as to proclaim it the best in Brazil—Bracarense may be suffering a bit from its own success. Particularly on Saturdays when the botequim is packed beyond capacity, the speed of service can slow to a crawl. Considering the

---

(*Moments* The Culture of Botequins

Botequins are to Rio what pubs are to London and cafes are to Paris: The spot where locals traditionally gather, whether it be for end-of-day drinks or impassioned late-night philoso-phizing. Brazilians also refer to the botequins as *"pé sujos"*—literally dirty feet—meaning they're nothing fancy, often just plastic tables and fluorescent lights (though rich in character and local flavor). Some of the botequins have developed into popular nightlife attractions, offering live music and excellent food and drawing crowds from all over the city. Most botequins, however, remain small, not very fancy watering holes where at almost any hour of the day one can kick back with a cold beer, have some snacks, and catch up with the latest gossip. See a description of the most popular ones in this section.

overall quality, however, that may be a minor complaint. What assets are a botequim judged on? Beer quality is the No. 1 criterion. Bracarense's secret lies in an ultra-long hose—60 meters (180 ft.)—stored in ice, so as the chopp wends its way to your glass, it chills down to perfection. Food quality is also key, particularly the little munchy appetizers that go so well with beer. At Bracarense these are in the expert hands of the Minas Gerais native Alaíde, who works miracles in the small kitchen. Rua José Linhares 85, Leblon (corner of Ataulfo de Paiva). (✆ 021/2294-3549. Bus: 464.

Jobi One of the trendier botequins, Jobi is busy any day of the week, but on Fridays and Saturdays a lineup is guaranteed. You might as well make friends with the other people who are waiting, as chances are you will be seated closely together in this small and cozy bar. Conversations frequently fly across the tables. Like many botequins, Jobi has excellent beer, tasty snacks, and a great atmosphere. On top of that, Jobi stays open until 4:30am, making it a favorite post-party haunt to wind down from an evening out. Av. Ataulfo de Paiva 1166, Leblon. (✆ 021/2274-0547. Bus: 434.

Simplesmente For a night out in Santa Teresa, check out the lovely Simplesmente. Located in an old house with tall arched colonial doors, this bar reflects the somewhat bohemian flavor of this arty hill-top neighborhood. Considered by many residents as their local botequim, Simplesmente eschews fluorescent lights and plastic tables in favor of rich Persian carpets and tall green plants; and in place of the traditional smell of stale beer, there's a lingering scent of incense. Despite this yuppification, however, this little bar remains a botequim at heart, and it's a favorite gathering place for locals and visitors who love this neighborhood's atmosphere. Opens Monday through Saturday at 7pm and stays open until at least 3am. Rua Paschoal Carlos Magno 115, Largo dos Guimarães, Santa Teresa. (✆ 021/2508-6007. Taxi recommended in the evening.

OTHER BARS & PUBS

Academia da Cachaça A field trip to the Academia da Cachaça puts the concept of advanced education in a whole new light. It is here that 40 members of the Cachaça Academy meet to dispute and discuss the finer points of the fiery white cane liquor that is Brazil's national drink. For though all cachaça comes from cane juice, not all cachaças are created equal. The selection at the Academia is overwhelming. Ask the bartenders for advice and begin that lifelong intellectual quest for the perfect "white one" or "water that the birds

---

Finds Quiosques da Lagoa

They began as lowly concession stands, but the kiosks around the Lagoa Rodrigo de Freitas have evolved into a fun, casual nightlife scene. Known in Portuguese as *quiosques da Lagoa* (not surprisingly, "kiosks of Lagoa"), they're the perfect place to stroll, munch, drink, and people-watch. Set at regular intervals along the pleasant green path that girdles the Lagoa, the kiosks range in size and quality from simple snack stands to full-fledged restaurants and entertainment centers. The cuisine ranges from Brazilian basic to Lebanese, Japanese, or Italian, while the entertainment ranges from a boombox on volume "11" to excellent live bands (some of which even charge a small cover). The thickest concentration of kiosks begins opposite the Flamengo club, on Rua Gilberto Cardoso, and continues clockwise along the area opposite the Jockey Club. Another grouping clusters around the Praça Profesor Arnaldo de Moraes, at the Ipanema end of the Lagoa. The booths are open year-round, but they're especially popular in summer; weekday hours are from 6pm onward—they get busy around 10pm—and on weekends from noon onward. A full loop around the Lagoa is 5 miles (8km), making for a pleasant 2-hour walk.

---

don't drink" (as locals sometime refer to this hard liquor). Rua Conde de Bernadote 26, loja G, Leblon. ⓒ 021/2239-1542. www.academiadacachaca. com.br. Bus: 415.

Lord Jim Fun as Rio nightlife is, there are those who hanker now and again for a reprieve—this authentic British pub is where they come. Lord Jim's is the place to look for ex-pats crying in their Guinness, or else to pick up a game of darts or even watch a puzzled Carioca digging in to exotic British dishes such as shepherd's pie. Rua Paulo Redfern 63, Ipanema. ⓒ 021/2259-3047. No cover. Bus: 432.

Mercado Cobal de Humaitá *Finds* Is it a bar? Is it a restaurant? Or is it a great seething mass of people at plastic patio tables quaffing chopp, munching food, and listening to tunes from one or more live bands? That last is probably the best description of the nighttime scene at the Mercado Cobal. By day a mild-mannered (and quite fun) fruit-and-vegetable market, at night the Mercado transforms itself into a huge outdoor bar scene with seven different restaurants. All meld into one large bustling patio, with busy

Tips Late-Night Dining

Looking for a late-night bite? Given that most bars and clubs and even restaurants don't even really get going until 11pm, late in Rio really does mean late. The following are a few longtime Carioca favorites.

A classic hangout is the **Pizzeria Guanabara,** Av. Ataulfo de Paiva 1228, Leblon (✆ **021/2294-0797**). Open until at least 4am on weekdays and even later on weekends, it is the after hours meeting spot for some pizza and pasta. Open until 6am on weekends, the 50-year-old **Cervantes,** Prado Junior 335, Copacabana (✆ **021/2275-6147**), offers booze and food (the pork sandwich with melted cheese and pineapple alone is worth the trip) to attract a wide variety of clientele: tourists, clubbers on their way home, local prostitutes, transvestites, and regular neighborhood residents. As the manager likes to say, "drunks all belong to the same social class."

waiters racing up and down the aisles trying to keep their tables straight. Galeto Mania serves up a tasty grilled chicken, Pizzapark offers a full range of pizzas, Manekineko whips up tray after tray of fresh sushi, while Espirito Chopp serves the best cold draft beer. Cobal de Humaitá, Rua Voluntarios da Patria 446, Botafogo. Galeto Mania ✆ 021/2527-0616. Manekineko ✆ 021/2537-1510. Occasionally bars will add a couvert (cover) charge to your bill for live music, varying from R$4–R$10 ($2–$5). Metrô: Botafogo. Bus: 178.

Skylab Bar *Moments*   In a city of such stunning beauty, it's worth heading up to the high ground. Located by the poolside on the 30th floor of the Rio Othon, the Skylab Bar is the place to sip a caipirinha or batida cocktail while imbibing the intoxicating views of Copacabana stretched out beneath your feet. Time your visit during an evening with a full moon and the hotel throws in live music as well. The Skylab Bar is also a restaurant, but with so many more interesting food options to explore in the streets below, it's better to treat your time there as a cocktail: an exquisite and beautiful concoction that only whets your appetite for the evening ahead. Hotel Rio Othon, Av. Atlântica 3264, Copacabana. ✆ 021/2525-1500. No cover. Metrô: Arcoverde.

4 Gay & Lesbian Nightlife

Rio's gay community is fairly small, certainly smaller than one would expect from a city of 10 million people. For all Rio's reputation for sexual hedonism, the macho culture still predominates. As lasciviously as heterosexual couples may behave in public, open displays of affection—even hand-holding—between same-sex couples are still not accepted in Brazil. Many gays and lesbians prefer to stay in the closet except with their closest friends.

Nor are there really any specific gay neighborhoods in Rio, certainly nothing like San Francisco's Castro district or even Vancouver's West End. There are, however, a number of gay meeting places and nightlife areas. The current most popular nightspot is in Ipanema around the Galeria Café on the Rua Teixeira de Melo. During the day the stretch of sand close to Posto 8 (opposite the Rua Farme de Amoedo) is also popular. Copacabana has a number of gay clubs and bars (the Copa, Bunker 94, and Le Boy), as well as a popular meeting place on the beach in front of the Copacabana Palace Hotel at Rainbow's. In Rio's old downtown, there are a few popular places around the Avenida Mem de Sá and Rua do Lavradio. A good resource to pick up is the latest edition of the *Gay Guide Brazil,* a small booklet available at some of the clubs and bookstores in Ipanema, or check **http://riogayguide.com** or **www. gay-rio.com**. The Brazilian term for gay-friendly is *GLS,* which stands for gay, lesbian, and sympathizers. Often you will see this abbreviation used in listings or restaurant or bar reviews.

CLUBS

Blue Angel Venture round the corner from Le Boy and lo, there appeareth the Blue Angel, a mixed gay and lesbian bar with a small added gallery of avant-garde art. Very upscale, very classy, the Angel is populated with a host of beautiful people, among them artists and models and starlets (is there a male equivalent to the starlet?). The bar has an impressive cocktail list and the kitchen serves up appetizers and sandwiches until the wee hours of the morning. Rua Julio de Castilhos 15, Copacabana. ✆ 021/2513-2501. No cover. Bus: 415.

Bunker 94 Sunday nights the otherwise mixed but gay-friendly Bunker 94 (see description under "Music & Dance Clubs") hunkers down for the lesbian-only Discotcheka night, one of the few lesbian club events in Rio. Rua Raul Pompeia 94, Copacabana. ✆ 021/2521-0367. Cover R$10–R$15 ($5–$7.50), men pay R$30–R$45 ($15–$22.50) Sun evenings. Bus: 128.

The Copa   A bar, restaurant, club, and tea salon all in one. Certainly not the most typical gay bar, the Copa's ultra-kitsch '50s and '60s decor has quickly established a great following amongst Rio's GLS crowd since it opened in October 2000. On most nights after the clock strikes 12, the DJs start spinning tunes, the girls and boys kick up their (high) heels, and everyone's a Cinderella. Rua Alves Saldanha 13 A, Copacabana. ✆ 021/2255-8740. www.thecopa.com.br. No cover charge. Bus: 128.

Galeria Café   Forget the old college prank of how many sophomores you can fit in a VW. At the Galeria, the new game is how many gorgeous men can you squeeze into a bar. Set in a lovely small gallery stunningly decorated with a changing display of work by local artists, the Galeria Café packs them in to its combo art space, dance club, and bar. Not for the claustrophobic, people stand shoulder-to-shoulder, bicep to bicep. Both the cafe and the sidewalk get really, really hopping after 1am. Rua Teixeira de Melo 31E, Ipanema. ✆ 021/2523-8250. www.galeriacafe.com.br. Cover R$2–R$10 ($1–$5). Bus: 415.

Le Boy   The largest gay club in Rio, Le Boy has been one of the hot spots on the gay scene since it opened in 1992. Modeled on the high-end clubs of New York and London, Le Boy is glamorous and funky and extremely spacious with a soaring four-story ceiling hovering somewhere up over the dance floor. A La Girl is in the works, but nothing firm had happened as of press time. Rua Raul Pompeia 102, Copacabana. ✆ 021/2513-4993. www.leboy.com.br. Cover ranges from R$5–R$15 ($2.50–$7.50). Bus: 415.

5 Everything You Need to Know About Carnaval

What a party! What a statement of values. Anyone who's ever even remotely entertained the stereotype that South Americans are somewhat ill-acquainted with the work ethic should pause to consider Carnaval. Thousands of people—many of them of limited means or just plain poor—spend hundreds of hours practicing and preparing for the Samba School Parade that culminates this 4-day celebration. That so much effort goes into producing something as ephemeral as a single evening of joy and splendor says something about Cariocas' somewhat quirky sense of priorities, but also volumes about their abilities for perseverance.

Originally, Carnaval marked the last few days of fun before Lent—the 40-day period of fasting and penitence preceding Holy Saturday and Easter. The religious aspect of the celebration faded some time ago, but Carnaval's date is still determined by the ecclesiastical calendar. Officially, the Carnaval celebration occupies only the 4 days immediately preceding Ash Wednesday. With typical ingenuity and panache, however, Cariocas have managed to stretch this traditional last-bit-of-fun-before-Lent into an event lasting several months, culminating in the explosion of music and color that is the **Samba School Parade.** (The teams in the parade are officially called *escolas* [schools], though they're really community groups whose sole focus is the parade.) For those actively involved in the samba schools, Carnaval is a year-round occupation. As soon as the last sequins and feathers have been swept off the streets, each school starts planning the next year's theme, composing their music, building floats, sewing costumes, and finally rehearsing.

If you're not able to attend Carnaval itself, these **rehearsals**—which usually start in mid-September or early October—are an absolute must, the closest thing you'll experience to the event itself. (See below for a list of rehearsals.)

In the 2 weeks leading up to the big event, you'll begin to see the **blocos.** These are community groups—usually associated with a particular neighborhood or sometimes with a bar—who go around the neighborhood playing music, singing, and dancing through the streets. Some draw throngs of followers in the tens of thousands. (See "Blocos," later in this chapter for a list of the popular ones.)

Carnaval finally kicks off on the Friday before Ash Wednesday with an explosion of lavish **balls** (*bailes*). Originally the bailes were reserved for the elite, while the unwashed masses partied it up in vulgar splendor on the streets. Nowadays, the distinctions haven't gotten more than a bit blurred. The **Copacabana Palace ball** remains *the* society event in Rio. Attire is black-tie and expensive evening frock—either a designer dress or a fancy costume. Other balls are gay or just notoriously raunchy. (See "Bailes," later in this chapter, for a list.)

Then there is the pièce de résistance, the **Samba School Parade,** the event that the samba schools work and plan and sweat over for an entire year. Starting Sunday and continuing Monday night, the 14 top-ranked samba schools (seven each night) show their stuff in the **Sambodromo,** a mile-long (1.5km) concrete parade ground built especially in the center of Rio for this once-a-year event. Each night over 60,000 spectators watch live, while millions more tune in on TV to catch this feast for the senses.

WATCHING THE SAMBA PARADE

One of Carnaval's unique events, the **Samba School Parade** is an all-night feast of color and sound. Tens of thousands of costumed

The Samba Parade Grounds (Sambodrome)

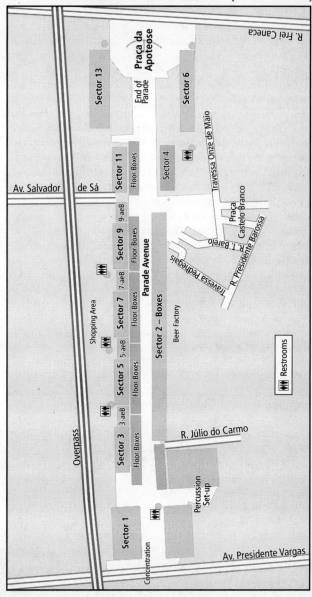

dancers, thousands of percussionists, and hundreds of gorgeous performers atop dozens of floats all move in choreographed harmony to the non-stop rhythm of samba. Over the course of two nights, 14 teams compete for the honor of putting on the best show ever. You will never look at a parade the same way.

Even before the parade starts, the streets surrounding the **Sambodromo** are closed to car traffic, while the grounds around this purpose-built samba stadium are transformed into Carnaval central. A main stage hosts a variety of acts and performances and hundreds of vendors set up shop with food and drinks. This *terreirão do samba* (samba land) as Riotur calls it, is open the weekend prior to Carnaval, from Friday through Tuesday during Carnaval, and then again for the Saturday afterwards for the Parade of Champions. Contact **Riotur** (© **021/2217-7563**) for more detailed programming information.

Tip: On the day of each parade the schools arrive outside the parade ground to assemble their floats and gear. The streets around the Sambodromo, including Avenida Presidente Vargas, are closed for traffic and pedestrians can stroll at leisure, watching the schools put the finishing touches on a year's worth of work. A great opportunity to take a close-up look at the floats, take pictures, and meet some of the people who put it all together.

For information on tickets, contact the **Liga das Escolas de Samba** (© **021/2253-7676** or check www.liesa.com.br). You can also purchase through a designated travel agency such as **Blumar** (© **021/2511-3636**). Tickets for the best bleacher sections cost R$350 ($175); chairs start at R$580 ($290) in sectors 9 and 11. As a last case resort, try your hotel but expect to pay a fair premium for this service. If you have tickets, you can head directly to the Sambodromo. The parade grounds are divided into sections (see map): Even-numbered sections can be accessed from the Central Station side (metrô: Central); odd-numbered sections can be accessed from the Praça XI side (metrô: Praça XI). Don't worry, there are lots of police and staff around to point you in the right direction. Unless you snag some fancy front-row seats or box seats (very pricey, starting at R$580/$290!) you will be sitting on concrete bleachers. There are pillows for sale or you can bring your own.

The best sections are 5, 7, 9, and 11. These place you more or less in the middle of the parade avenue, allowing you to see up and down as the school comes through. Sections 9 and 11 are exclusively reserved for tourists, and tickets are sold through agencies. The advantage is your spot on the concrete bleacher bears a number so

---

Tips **Carnaval Redux**

If you miss the parade during Carnaval or only want to see the best of the best, attend the Parade of Champions on the Saturday after Carnaval. The top five schools (in ascending order) restage their performances in all their glory. Tickets go on sale the Thursday after Carnaval. At R$80 ($40) and up for a good spot, they're considerably less expensive than the original event. Contact the **Liga das Escolas de Samba** (*©* **021/2253- 7676**), **Alô Rio** (*©* **021/2542-8080**), or **Blumar** (*©* **021/2511- 3636**) for ticket sales.

---

you don't have to fight to squeeze in. Avoid sitting at the start or the end of the Avenida (sections 1, 3, 4, 6, and 13).

The parade starts at 9pm, but unless you want to stake out a particular spot, you may as well take your time arriving as the event will continue nonstop until about 6am. We recommend leaving a bit early as well to avoid the big crunch at the end when the entire crowd tries to squeeze through a narrow set of revolving gates.

A FEW HELPFUL HINTS

Whether you are attending a rehearsal, following a bloco, or watching the parade, here are a few helpful hints to ensure you have a good time.

- Dress casually and comfortably. The weather is usually hot and humid, so a tank top or bikini top and shorts are fine. Comfortable shoes are a must as you will be on your feet for hours, dancing and jumping to the music.
- Pack light. A purse or any extra accessories are not recommended, especially at the rehearsals and the blocos, as you will be dancing and moving around. Make sure you bring enough cash for the evening and some form of ID (driver's license or some other picture ID that is not your passport) and maybe a small camera you can tuck into your pocket. Leave valuables, including an expensive watch and jewelry, at home.
- The events are very safe, just be aware of pickpockets in large crowds and make sure that at the end of the event you take a taxi or walk with the crowds, avoiding any deserted streets or unfamiliar neighborhoods.
- Keep in mind that prices of food and drinks will be slightly higher than what you are used to in Brazil.

- Plan to have enough cash for the entire Carnaval period. All financial institutions close for the duration, and it's not unusual for bank machines to run out of money.

PARTICIPATING IN THE PARADE

If you think watching the parade from up close sounds pretty amazing, imagine being in it. Dressed in an outlandish and colorful costume, you dance and sing your way down the Avenida, surrounded by thousands of other paraders and floats and engulfed in samba music so loud it makes your innards tremble. Looking up you see the 60,000 spectators in the grandstands dancing and singing in tune to the same beat, all of them cheering you on. Now, that sounds pretty amazing.

Every year, the samba schools open up positions for outsiders to participate in the parade. Why? Mostly because they need the money. Putting on this extravaganza is expensive and by selling the costumes and the right to parade, the schools are able to recuperate some of their costs. But outside paraders are also needed for artistic and competitive reasons. To score high points, the school needs to have enough people to fill the Avenida and make the parade look full and colorful. A low turn out can make the school lose critical points.

To parade (*desfilar* in Portuguese), you need to commit to a school and buy a costume. Many schools now have websites with pictures of their costumes. Some even allow you to choose one and pay for it online. The logistics of pickup can be a bit more complicated. Depending on the school, they may courier the costume or arrange for a pickup downtown just before the parade or you may have to make the trek out to wherever they are.

To get an idea of what the costumes look like, have a look at some of the websites. Some sites are in English as well as Portuguese; if not, look under *fantasia* (costume). To contact a school directly, see the websites and phone numbers below under "Rehearsals." Prices range from R$150 to R$500 ($75–$250) for a costume bought directly from a school.

For those who want to take the easy way out, a number of agencies in Rio will organize it all for you, getting you in with a school and arranging the costume. You will pay a bit more for this service but it saves you the hassle of chasing after schools and leaving messages—an important consideration if you want to spend your time on the beach getting all tanned for the big event. **Blumar** (✆ 021/2511-3636) can organize the whole event for you for

R$600 ($300). For other organizations, contact **Alô Rio** at ✆ **021/2542-8080.**

Note: As a participant in the parade, you do not automatically get a ticket to watch the rest of the event. If you want to see the other schools, you need to purchase a separate ticket.

REHEARSALS

Every Saturday from September (or even as early as August) until Carnaval, each samba school holds a general samba rehearsal (*ensaio*) at their home base. The band and key people come out and practice their theme songs over and over to perfection. While that may sound a tad repetitious, you'd be amazed how a good band playing the same song over and over can generate a really great party. People dance for hours, taking a break now and then for snacks and beer. The income generated goes towards the group's floats and costumes. The general rehearsals usually don't involve costumes or practicing dance routines. There are also dress rehearsals, but these are much less frequent. Inquire with the schools if you're interested in attending one of these.

Most of the samba schools are based in the poorer and quite distant suburbs, but both Mangueira and Salgueiro are located no more than an R$25 ($12.50) cab ride from Copacabana. Nor should you worry overly much about safety. Rehearsals take place in the warehouse or open-air space where the school builds its floats and sews its costumes. There is always security and the rehearsals are very well attended. Plan to arrive anytime after 11pm. When you are ready to leave, there'll be lots of taxis around. Just don't go wandering off into the neighborhood unless you're familiar with the area. Many hotels will organize tours to the samba school rehearsals, but unless you prefer to go with a group, it's not really necessary and it's certainly a lot cheaper to go on your own. To find out more about rehearsals or participating in the parade, contact the **Liga das Escolas de Samba** at ✆ **021/2253-7676** or check www.liesa.com. br. You can also contact the schools directly: **Imperatriz** (the recent champion), Professor Lacê 235, Ramos (✆ **021/2560-8037;** www. imperatrizleopoldinense.com.br); **Império,** Av. M. Edgard Romero 114, Madureira (✆ **021/3359-4944;** www.imperioserrano.art.br); **Mangueira,** Rua Visconde de Niterói 1072, Mangueira (✆ **021/2567-4637;** www.mangueira.com.br); **Salgueiro,** Rua Silva Telles 104, Andaraí (✆ **021/2238-5564;** www.salgueiro.com.br). If you can't find anyone who speaks English, contact **Alô Rio** for assistance at ✆ **021/2542-8080.**

BLOCOS

To experience the real street Carnaval, don't miss the blocos: neighborhood groups of musicians and merrymakers who parade through the streets in the days and nights before and during Carnaval. These blocos often have strong neighborhood links. The key to the blocos' popularity is their informality: Everyone is welcome and you don't need a costume, just comfortable clothes and shoes. Different blocos do have certain styles or attract certain groups (see below) so pick one that suits you and have fun. Note also that while traditionally Rio blocos have been free of charge, in recent years a few blocos have picked up on the Salvador practice of charging a small fee and issuing participants a T-shirt to serve as a very visible proof of purchase.

Riotur publishes an excellent brochure called *Bandas, Blocos and Ensaios,* available through **Alô Rio** (© **021/2542-8080**). Also available from Riotur is the *Rio Incomparavel* brochure, which has a full listing of all the events.

Below is a list of worthwhile blocos by neighborhood. The days of the week refer specifically to the days of Carnaval unless otherwise stated.

IN CENTRO **Bloco Cacique de Ramos** parades on Sunday, Monday, and Tuesday at 6pm. Easily identified by their Indian costumes, the participants meet in Centro on the corner of Avenida Presidente Vargas and Avenida Rio Branco and parade down along Avenida Rio Branco to Cinelândia. For early risers, the Saturday morning **Cordão do Bola Preta** meets in front of the Bola Preta Club on the corner of Rua Treze de Maio and Rua Evaristo da Veiga just across from the Theatro Municipal in Cinelândia. This group is serious about having fun and the men often dress in drag.

IN COPACABANA Leave it to a good bar to put on a great Carnaval event. Lots of musicians join in the **Bloco do Bip Bip** and they specialize in playing more traditional Carnaval tunes. Bip Bip is the first and last bloco to parade, the first time beginning at the stroke of midnight on Friday when Carnaval officially begins and the last time starting at 9:30pm on Tuesday evening, with Ash Wednesday looming just a few hours away. Where do they meet? At the bar, of course, at Rua Almirante Gonçalves 50 (close to the Luxor Regente Hotel).

Why parade if you can just hang out, have fun, make music, and drink? That's certainly the **Banda Santa Clara**'s idea. Meeting at

3pm on Sunday at the corner of Rua Santa Clara and Avenida Atlântica, this group remains on that very spot and parties at length.

IN IPANEMA For some of the bigger blocos, head over to Ipanema. The biggest of them all is the **Banda de Ipanema,** counting up to 10,000 followers in its throng. This group has been around since 1965 when it was founded to protest and make fun of the military regime. Nowadays, the members still make noise, if only to declare the "state of Carnaval." The group meets on the two Saturdays preceding Carnaval as well as on Saturday during Carnaval at 3pm starting at the Praça General Osorio. You'll see quite a few costumes at this parade, although not as many as at the **Banda da Carmen Miranda,** the prime gay parade. This bloco is an absolute blast, with outlandish costumes, extravagant drag queens, great music, and even some floats. Unlike most, it takes place before Carnaval—on the prior Sunday in fact—gathering at 4pm on the corner of Avenida Visconde de Pirajá and Rua Joana Angelica.

The only bloco so far with a website, **Simpatia é quase amor** ("affection is almost love"), has close to 10,000 followers who all dress in the group's lilac and yellow shirts. The shirts are for sale at the meeting place, Praça General Osorio, starting at 3pm on the Saturday before Carnaval and the Sunday during Carnaval. Check the site **www.sitesbrasil.com/simpatia** to see some wonderful pictures of the crowds having a ball.

IN CATETE A relative newcomer to the bloco scene, **Concentra mas Não Sai** (meeting without parading) doesn't hide its intentions. Why waste all that energy walking up and down to end up where you started? Join this gregarious group after 7pm at the Rua Ipiranga 57 (close to the Largo do Machado metrô station) on Saturday. Don't worry if you're late; they'll be right there for the rest of the night.

BAILES
More formal than the blocos, the samba balls (*bailes*) are where you go to see and be seen. Traditionally reserved for Rio's elite, some—such as the Copacabana Palace ball—remain the height of elegance, while others have become raunchy and risqué bacchanals. Numerous clubs around town host Carnaval balls. The listings below are simply the most famous.

The notorious ***Baile Vermelho e Preto*** (Red and Black Costume Ball) is held every year on Carnaval Friday in honor of Rio's most popular soccer club, Flamengo. A great spot to rub shoulders with soccer players and their groupies, in 2000 this event last year outgrew the Flamengo clubhouse and moved to the ATL Hall in Barra da Tijuca. Known for both the beauty of the female attendees and the skimpiness of their costumes, the Red and Black Ball can get downright raunchy by evening's end. The *Baile do Preto Branco* (Black and White Ball) also takes place on Carnaval Friday, at the Clube Botafogo (Av. Venceslau Brás 72, Botafogo). For both events contact **Âlo Rio** (© **021/2542-8080**) for details and ticket information.

The popular Copacabana nightclub **Le Boy** (see p. 145) organizes a differently themed ball every night during Carnaval, Friday through Tuesday included. These balls are gay-friendly but by no means gay only. Call © **021/2240-3338** for details and ticket information.

The prime gay event—and one of Rio's most famous balls—is the Tuesday-night *Gala Gay* at the Scala nightclub, Av. Afranio de Melo Franco 296, Leblon (© **021/2239-4448**). TV stations vie for position by the red carpet a la Oscar night to interview illustrious or notorious arrivals while the crowds greet the exotically or extravagantly dressed with cheers and applause.

The grand slam of all Carnaval balls is the Saturday-night extravaganza at the Copacabana Palace Hotel, the *Baile do Copa.* Lavishly decorated, the Palace plays host to the crème-de-la-crème of Rio's and Brazil's high society. Politicians, diplomats, models, business tycoons, and local and international movie stars arrive in tuxedos and elegant costumes. Tickets start at R$500 ($250) per person and sell out quickly. Call © **021/2548-7070** for more details.

9

Side Trips from Rio

On weekends and holidays, many Cariocas direct their tires north-ward to the beach resorts dotting the warm Atlantic coast. First and most famous of these is the town on **Búzios,** "discovered" in the 1960s by a bikini-clad Brigitte Bardot. Now a haven for Rio society, visiting Argentineans, and anyone else who loves their beaches Brazilian style—civilized, that is to say, with a beachside table always in sight, and a caipirinha often in hand.

Heading up and inland, one finds the summer refuge of an earlier, pre–beach generation, the mountain resort **Petrópolis,** the former summer capital of Emperor Pedro II. Just an hour or so from Rio, this green and graceful refuge offers good strolling, some great museums, and mountain hiking in the Atlantic rain forest.

1 Búzios

It's anyone's guess how small or sleepy the fishing town of Búzios truly was when French starlet Brigitte Bardot stumbled onto its sandy beaches in 1964, but it's certain that in the years since, the little town used the publicity to turn itself into Rio's premier beach resort. So phenomenal was the growth that at the height of the 1999 season, Búzios's mayor appeared live on Rio TV and begged people to stop coming. No one paid him any mind: In the summer, the town is packed with Brazilians on vacation, many Carioca celebrities own places here, and Argentineans continue to invade with a gusto not seen since the Falklands. And despite the influx, the town has managed to retain a good deal of the charm of its fishing village past.

Much of that charm is due to the sheer beauty of the surroundings. The town sits on the tip of a long and beach-rich peninsula jutting out into the clear blue Atlantic. The sheer number of beaches close to town make it easy to experience all the wonderful combinations and permutations of Brazilian beach culture.

Finally, on top of serious inquisitions into beach culture, there are more trivial pursuits such as diving, sailing, and windsurfing, fine cuisine, and endless opportunities to shop.

ESSENTIALS
GETTING THERE

BY VAN/TAXI   Búzios Radio Taxi (℃ **022/2623-1911;** buzios radiotaxi@uol.com.br) offers transfer to and from Rio by van and taxi. Cost in a 15-person air-conditioned minibus is R$35 ($17.50) per person. A four-person private taxi costs R$180 ($90) total.

BY BUS   The bus company **Auto Viação 1001** (℃ **0800/25-1001**) has departures for Búzios seven times a day from Rio's main bus station at Novo Rio Rodoviaria, Av. Francisco Bicalho 1, Santo Cristo (℃ **022/2291-5151**). The cost of the 2½-hour trip is approximately R$15 ($7.50). In Búzios, buses arrive and depart from the Búzios bus station (℃ **022/2623-2050**) on Estrada da Usina at the corner of Rua Manoel de Carvalho, a 10-minute walk from the center of town.

GETTING AROUND

BY WATER TAXI   Water taxis are an efficient and fun way to get around, but note that they run only during daylight hours and only on the protected side of bay, from João Fernandes to Tartaruga. To catch a water taxi, you can hail one from the beach or the pier in town or phone ℃ **022/2620-8018.** When being dropped off by water taxi, you can set a time for pickup. From Centro to Azeda beach costs R$3 ($1.50) per person and from Centro to João Fernandes beach R$5 ($2.50) per person. Water taxis carry up to seven people.

BY TAXI   Taxis in Búzios can be hailed at the ponto in Praça Santos Dumont (℃ **022/2623-2160**) or by calling **Búzios Rádio Táxi** (℃ **022/2623-1911**).

BY RENTAL CAR   Cars and beach buggies can be rented from **Búzios Car Turismo,** Rua das Pedras 275, loja 1, Centro (℃ **022/2623-2863;** buzioscar@mar.com.br). Prices range from R$48 ($24) per day for a buggy to R$71 ($35.50) per day for a VW Golf. Prices include 62 miles (100km) free. Additional miles cost approximately R$0.35 (18¢) per half mile (1km). **Buggy Car Turismo,** Av. José Bento R. Dantas 1279 (℃ **022/2623-2610**), has similar products and prices.

VISITOR INFORMATION

The **Búzios Tourism Secretariat** operates an information kiosk on the downtown Praça Santos Dumont 111 (℃ **0800/2-4999** or 022/2623-2099), open daily from 9am to 10pm. Two

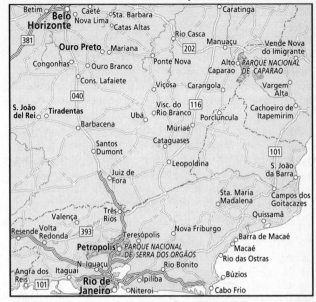

good websites on Búzios are **www.buziosonline.com.br** and **www.buziosturismo.com**.

FAST FACTS   There's a branch of **Banco do Brasil** at Rua Manuel de Carvalho 73 (about 4 blocks from Rua das Pedras). It's open Monday through Friday from 11am to 6pm (the ATMs are available 24 hours).

For Internet access, go to **Búzios Cybar,** Shopping de Búzios, loja 4, at the corner of Rua Turibe (© **022/2623-2969**). This cafe has 12 computers, plus coffee. Connections cost R$5 ($2.50) per half hour.

EXPLORING BUZIOS
HITTING THE BEACHES

The charm of Búzios lies largely in its beaches, the 20 stretches of sand large and small within a few miles of the old town. Thanks to the irregular topography of this rugged little peninsula, each beach is set off from the other and has developed its own beach personality. Furthest from the old town is **Manguinhos** beach. Sheltered from the heavy surf, this gentle beach is where many learn to sail and windsurf. A short hop over the neck of the peninsula lies **Geribá** beach, a wonderful long stretch of sand facing out toward the open ocean. This is the beach for surfing, boogie boarding, and windsurfing. Closer to town is **Ferradura** or **Horseshoe** beach. Nestled between rocky headlands in a beautiful horseshoe bay, this beach offers calm crystal-clear waters, making it the perfect place for a long lazy afternoon's snorkel. Tiny and beautiful, **Olho de Boi** (Bull's Eye) beach is tucked away on its own at the far end of a small ecological reserve. It can only be reached by a 20-minute walk from surfers' favorite, **Brava** beach. Thanks to this isolation, Bull's Eye beach has been adopted by Búzios's clothing-optional crowd. Back on the calm inland side of the peninsula, **João Fernandes** and the pocket-sized **João Fernandinho** beaches are busy, happening places lined with beachside cafes and full of people intent on getting and showing off their tans.

OUTDOOR ACTIVITIES & WATERSPORTS

There's little in the way of watersports equipment that can't be rented in Búzios, generally right on the beach.

On Ferradura beach, **Happy Surf** (✆ **022/2623-2016**) rents sailboards, lasers, Hobie Cats, and kayaks. Happy Surf also conducts courses. A 6-hour beginner's sailboard course costs R$150 ($75). For more advanced students, there are 1- and 2-hour courses costing from R$35 to R$60 ($17.50–$30). Lasers rent for R$35 ($17.50) per half hour, R$45 ($22.50) with instructor. Hobie Cats rent for R$25 ($12.50) per half hour, R$40 ($20) with instructor. Kayaks rent for R$5 ($2.50) per half hour, R$8 ($4) per hour. Paddleboats can be rented for R$6 ($3) per half hour, R$12 ($6) per hour.

The following equipment is available at João Fernandes beach: kayak rental, R$5 ($2.50) for 30 minutes; mask and snorkel package, R$10 ($5) per hour; and sailboard, R$30 ($15) per hour.

On Manguinhos beach, two clubs rent lasers and sailboards: **Búzios Vela Club,** Rua Maurício Dutra 303 (✆ **022/2623-6206**), and **Yucas Beach Club,** Rua Maurício Dutra 356 (✆ **022/2623-2001**). Prices are comparable to those listed above.

BOATING   Schooner trips are a great way to spend a day in Búzios. A small fleet of converted fishing schooners make a circuit of about eight of Búzios's beaches plus three offshore islands. Onboard you trundle along in the sunshine, eating complementary fresh fruit and drinking free caipirinhas (or mineral water). At any of the beaches, you're free to get off, hang out, and swim for a bit and then hop back on. One company is **Escuna Buziana** (✆ 022/ 9972-7030), but there's really no need to seek them out. Just walk along Rua das Pedras anywhere near the pier and you're guaranteed to be approached by a schooner tout. The exact price depends on how many of you there are and how hard you negotiate, but competition between various schooner operators keeps things fairly competitive. Expect to pay from R$12 to R$25 ($6–$12.50) for a half day's cruise.

DIVING   The islands just off Búzios are—along with Angra dos Reis and Arraial do Cabo—some of the best diving spots within a 1-day drive of Rio. Diving takes place at a number of islands about a 45-minute trip off the coast. Water temperature is normally around 22°C. Visibility ranges from 33 to 49 feet (10–15m). Coral formations are fairly basic—mostly soft coral—but there's always lots of parrotfish and often sea turtles (green and hawksbill) and sting rays of considerable size.

The two dive shops in town are **True Blue,** Av. Bento Ribeiro Dantas 21, loga 13, at the beginning of Rua das Pedras (✆ 022/ 2623-2357), and **Ponto Mar,** Rua das Pedras 212 (✆ 022/2623-2173). Both offer a full range of services including cylinder refill and courses all the way from basic to nitrox. The companies' equipment, dive boats, and prices are nearly identical. For a certified diver, a two-dive excursion costs R$60 ($30). Regulator, BCD, wet suit, and mask/fins/snorkel each cost R$10 ($5) to rent, so if you've brought no equipment with you, a two-dive excursion will cost R$100 ($50) all told.

GOLF   The **Búzios Golf Club & Resort** (✆ 022/2629-1240; buziosgolf@openlink.com.br) is located just in from Manguinhos beach. Greens fees for this 18-hole course are: Monday through Friday R$60 ($30) per day for unlimited golf; Saturday, Sunday, and holidays R$70 ($35) per day for unlimited golf. No carts allowed but caddies are available.

SURFING   Geribá and Tocuns beaches are the best surfing options. They're located on the way in to Búzios, about 3 miles (5km) from downtown. Closer to town is the smaller Brava beach, which also often has good waves. Note that board rentals are currently unavailable in Búzios.

ADVENTURE SPORTS   **Canoar,** Travessa Oscar Lopez 63, loja 02, Búzios (✆ 022/2623-2551), runs nature treks, rappelling trips, and rafting expeditions in the Serramar region, about 30 minutes inland from Búzios. A 2-hour trek to a waterfall along the Pai João Trail costs R$25 ($12.50), transfer and light lunch included. A 3-hour rappelling trip, including a descent down an 83-foot (25m) cliff-face, costs R$49 ($24.50), transfer and light lunch included. Rafting trips leave twice daily, once at 9am and once at 2pm. Participants descend 3 miles (5km) down a Class III river in either six-person or two-person inflatable rafts. Cost is R$56 ($28). Minimum age is 12.

SHOPPING

With so many of Brazil's rich and famous visiting Búzios, the shopping is excellent if somewhat on the pricey side. Shops are concentrated around the Rua das Pedras in Centro and sell everything to let you enjoy Búzios in style. Very popular items for women are bikinis and beachwear such as kangas and colorful slippers. Men can outfit themselves at the various surf shops that sell board shorts, sunglasses, and fashionable Bermudas and shirts. Both men and women can get all dolled up for the evening in the many boutiques that specialize in casual evening wear such as designer jeans, slinky dresses, fancy tops, and sandals. Note that most boutiques and shops in Búzios have adapted themselves to the somewhat nocturnal biorhythm of visiting tourists: Shops are closed during the day when everybody is on the beach and open up at 5 or 6pm, staying open until at least 11pm in summer.

WHERE TO STAY

Búzios is well known for its pousadas, similar to a North American bed-and-breakfast. These small, often owner-operated hotels provide excellent personalized service. However, Búzios is generally a quite expensive destination. By avoiding high season (Dec–Mar and July) and weekends throughout the year, you should be able to get a discount, although you will still end up paying more than you would anywhere else in Brazil.

VERY EXPENSIVE

Colonna Park Hotel 🐠🐠   Colonna Park Hotel offers a superb setting, straddling the hill between the beaches of João Fernando and João Fernandinho. To venture out to the João Fernando, the most happening beach in town, just go down the stairs and out the gate. Rooms in this sprawling Mediterranean-style mansion are spacious and simply yet elegantly furnished in cool tones of white and blue. Each features a pleasant sitting area. Forty-eight of the 63 rooms provide an ocean view. If you're in the mood for a splurge, try suite 20: It comes with a Jacuzzi tub and a large deck with a view of both beaches.

Praia de João Fernandes, Armação dos Búzios, RJ 28950-000. ℂ **022/2623-2245.** Fax 022/2623-2923. www.colonna.com.br. 63 units (shower only). High season R$325 ($162.50) double no view, R$460 ($230) double with view, R$485 ($242.50) suite; low season R$180–R$220 ($90–$110) double no view, R$220–R$250 ($110–$125) double with view, R$250–R$300 ($125–$150) suite. AE, DC, MC, V. Street parking. Children 9 and under stay free in parents' room. Extra person 30%. **Amenities:** 2 restaurants, bar; outdoor pool; sauna; game room; 24-hr. room service; massage; laundry service. *In room:* A/C, TV, minibar, fridge, hair dryer, safe.

La Bohème 🐸 *Kids*   At the beginning of João Fernandes beach, La Bohème overlooks the beach and the ocean from its hillside vantage point. The apartments all offer beautiful views and are within walking distance of the main village and the beaches. All the apartments have kitchenettes and are very spacious, perfect for families traveling with children or a group. A few of the town houses are split-level suites and sleep up to seven people; the remainder of the apartments is on one level only, accommodating up to four people comfortably. The pool area includes a great children's pool, and the beach just 330 feet (100m) below the hotel is safe enough even for the little ones, with almost no waves and perfect bathtub temperature.

Praia de João Fernandes, lote 1, Armação dos Búzios, RJ 28950-000. ℂ **022/2623-1744.** www.labohemehotel.com. 32 units (shower only). High season R$320 ($160) double; low season R$180 ($90) double. Children 4 and under stay free in parents' room, 5 and over R$40 ($20) extra. AE, DC, MC, V. Free parking. **Amenities:** Restaurant; 2 pools; tour desk; car-rental desk; limited room service; laundry service. *In room:* A/C, TV, kitchen, minibar, safe.

Pousada Byblos 🐸🐸   Tucked away on Orla Bardot, Byblos is in a very quiet spot, yet just a 5-minute walk from the nightlife and restaurants of the busy Rua das Pedras. The rooms are spacious, with comfortable beds, and offer either an ocean or garden view. The best rooms are the oceanview rooms with balconies (the top two floors). The top floor of the pousada boasts a fabulous rooftop deck with a small swimming pool and a lounge. This pousada is not recommended for young children or people who have difficulty with stairs, as access is on narrow spiral stairways and the facilities are spread out over several floors.

Morro do Humaitá 8, Praia da Armação, Armação dos Búzios, RJ 28950-000. ℂ **022/2623-1162.** Fax 022/2623-2828. 23 units (shower only). Standard room (garden view) Dec–Mar R$220 ($110), Apr–Nov R$195 ($97.50); Deluxe room (ocean view) Dec–Mar R$290 ($145), Apr–Nov R$220 ($110). AE, DC, MC, V. Street parking. **Amenities:** Restaurant, bar; pool; tour desk; 24-hr. room service; laundry service. *In room:* A/C, TV, minibar, fridge, safe.

MODERATE

Búzios Internacional Apart Hotel   One of the few relatively inexpensive options in town is this modern apart-hotel located just a few blocks from Rua das Pedras. Each unit is a self-contained flat (as with all apart-hotels) equipped with a living room with foldout couch, a kitchen, and either one or two bedrooms. All units are pleasantly if simply furnished, and come with a balconies and hammocks looking out over a central garden. In the high season, rental goes by the week, while the rest of the year, daily rentals are available. The price is the same whether you're one person or four (or six in the two-bedroom units).

Estrada da Usina Velha 99 (2 blocks from Rua das Pedras), Armação dos Búzios, RJ 28950-000. ✆ and fax **022/2537-3876**. apart@buziosbeach.com.br. 44 units. High season Dec 22–Mar 9 R$1,400–R$2,000 ($700–$1,000) per week; low season (rest of year excluding holidays) R$700–R$960 ($350–$480) per week or R$140–R$200 ($70–$100) per day. AE, V. Free parking. **Amenities:** Pool; laundry. *In room:* A/C, TV, kitchen, minibar, fridge, hair dryer, safe.

Hotel-Pousada La Coloniale 🦋   Smack in the middle of Búzios, on the sought-after Rua das Pedras, La Coloniale leaves you within steps of all the shops and restaurants. The colonial-style pousada is built around a central courtyard with 20 apartments; eight of those are duplexes providing a spacious and comfortable suite. The furniture is quite basic but nonetheless clean and pleasant. The four large duplexes overlooking the Rua das Pedras are great for families or a group of friends traveling together, but tend to be very noisy during high season, especially on weekends. Of course, if you're out having fun, too, it really doesn't matter.

Rua das Pedras 52, Armação dos Búzios, RJ 28950-000. ✆ **022/2623-1434**. lacoloniale@uol.com.br. 20 units (shower only). High season R$190 ($95) double, R$220 ($110) double duplex; low season R$130 ($65) double, R$145 ($72.50) double duplex. Children 4 and under stay free in parents' room, ages 5 to 10 20% of room rate, children 10 and older 30% of room rate. AE, DC, MC, V. **Amenities:** Restaurant, bar; Jacuzzi; laundry service, tour desk. *In room:* A/C, TV, minibar, fridge, safe.

WHERE TO DINE

You couldn't be any closer to the beach than at **Recanto do Sol,** Praia João Fernandes s/n, Armação de Búzios (✆ **022/2623-2293**). Just steps above João Fernandes beach, the tables are set up in the sand. The menu offers seafood and seafood: grilled fish, moqueca stews, shrimp, or squid. In the evening there is live music after 8pm, usually MPB or Bahian-style dance music. Curious for its architecture, **Guapo Loco,** Rua das Pedras 233 (✆ **022/2623-2657**), lives in a kind of topsy-turvy Frank Gehry hacienda. The menu includes tacos, quesadillas, and burritos as well as house specialties such as the Drunken Chicken—chicken breast sautéed in tequila, peppers, oregano, onions, and lemon juice. **Boom,** Rua Manoel Turibe de Farias 110 (© **022/2623-6254**), with its rustic-looking decor with old wood beams, iron window frames, and dark-red tile, is an excellent kilo restaurant. The price is R$19 ($9.50) per kilo, which puts it at the upper end of kilo fare, but the quality is very high and the selection is good: salads, stewed meats, bean dishes, and chicken, sausage, and fresh picanha right off the grill. **Estancia Don Juan,** Rua das Pedras 178 (© **022/2623-2169**), is the place in town for fine steak. You can mix and match between Brazilian and Argentinean beef. Side dishes such as broccoli, baked potatoes, or carrots must be ordered separately.

BUZIOS AFTER DARK

If you're on a mission for a night out, Rua das Pedras is the place to crawl. This 3,960-foot (1,200m) street boasts pubs, bars, discos, and restaurants open on weekends until 3 or 4 in the morning.

One of the most popular spots is the Mexican bar and disco **Zapata,** very busy during vacations and weekends. Next to it, **Skipper** serves pizzas and has a nightclub, which is normally open on Fridays and Saturdays. To simply sit, sip a drink, and check out the action, the place to be is **Ponto Bar,** which serves Japanese food with a musical background of Rolling Stones, Eric Clapton, and others. If you'd prefer your entertainment live, there's **Pátio Havana,** which features a nightly selection of jazz, blues, and MPB. The other advantage of the Havana is that should you get bored of the band, you can wander out to the oceanside patio, light up a cigar, and enjoy the nighttime view. Smack in the middle of Rua das Pedras is **Takatakataka,** a bar run by Kaiser, an expatriate Dutchman who personally serves up a variety of pink and fruity and heavily alcoholic cocktails.

2 Petrópolis

Known as the Imperial City, *Cidade Imperial,* Petropólis is one of Rio de Janeiro's premier mountain resorts, located 2,805 feet (850m) above sea level. Only an hour from Rio, it seems light years away from the traffic-jammed streets, concrete high-rises, and beaches. The lovely tree-lined streets, palaces, mansions, and museums can be comfortably explored on foot or by horse and buggy and the mountain air ensures a pleasant climate all year-round. Once just a stopover on the gold route between Minas Gerais and Rio de

Janeiro, its fine location and cool climate drew the attention of Dom Pedro I who purchased a piece of land in the area. He passed away before doing anything much, but his son D. Pedro II developed an urban plan and in 1843 founded the city of Petrópolis—named after Pedro himself—and built the summer palace (now the Museu Imperial) on the piece of land acquired by his father. Construction of the first railway in 1854 from Porto de Mauá to Raiz da Serra opened up easy access to the new city. In addition to the royal family, the Baron of Mauá (builder of the railway), the Baron of Rio Negro, and a number of industrialists, coffee moguls and politicians built their summer residences here, turning Petrópolis into the de facto capital of Brazil during the hot summer months.

Nowadays Petrópolis is a favorite weekend getaway for Cariocas; in the summer to escape from the hot and humid climate in Rio, in the fall and winter for a chance to experience "really cold" weather, wear winter clothes, eat fondue, and sit by the fireplace. The historic part of the city, centered around the Museu Imperial and the cathedral and more or less bounded by Avenida Barão Rio Branco and Rua Imperador, contains the majority of the monuments and museums. The tree-lined canals and large squares make for a pleasant atmosphere and many of the side streets are worth exploring just to have a peek at the many mansions and villas.

In addition to the Cariocas' noble pursuit of culture and nature, they also flock here to visit the Rua Teresa, the best shopping street in Brazil. The area around Petrópolis has many textile factories and the Rua Teresa has become the prime retail and wholesale outlet for cotton and knitwear at unbelievably low prices.

Exploring Petrópolis can easily be done as a day trip from Rio using public transit, but to experience the atmosphere of the city and take in some of the mountain air, it's worthwhile to spend the night.

ESSENTIALS
GETTING THERE

BY BUS **Unica/Facil** (© **0800/24-0900**) offers daily service from Rio to Petrópolis. The trip takes a little over an hour. Buses leave Monday through Friday between 5:15am and midnight every 15 minutes. On Saturday and Sunday, buses leave at 5:30am, 6:15am, and 7am and then every 15 minutes until approximately 10pm. Tickets cost R$8 ($4). Buses depart from the main bus

> ## ⟨Tips⟩ Time Your Visit
>
> The absolute worst day to visit Petrópolis is Monday, as most attractions are closed and the shops at the Rua Teresa only open at 2pm. Some attractions are also closed on Tuesday and many restaurants are closed Monday through Wednesday. The best days to visit are Wednesday through Friday. Weekends can be busy; book accommodations ahead of time. Avoid holidays, as the lineups for museums and traffic can be very bad.

station in Rio, **Novo Rio Rodoviaria,** Av. Francisco Bicalho 1, Santo Cristo (✆ **021/2291-5151**). Buses arrive at Petrópolis's main bus station, which is within walking distance of all the attractions.

GETTING AROUND

All the sites in the historic center are within walking distance of the bus station and each other. There is no need to drive or take a taxi.

BY RENTAL CAR   Useful only if you're thinking of checking out some of the nearby national parks. In Petrópolis, cars can be rented from **Imperial Coop,** Rua do Imperador 288, Centro (✆ **024/2246-0066**).

BY TAXI   For trips outside the city center to pousadas or restaurants, call ✆ **0800/24-1516** for taxi service or just hail one of the many circulating taxis.

BY HORSE & BUGGY   A great way to see the majority of the attractions without doing all of the walking is by horse and buggy. The buggies depart only from the main entrance of the Museu Imperial. (Buggies in front of other attractions are waiting for their clients to come back from the visit and are not available). You have two options for sightseeing: The first tour, R$50 ($25) per buggy for up to six people, stops at the Cathedral, Palacio de Crystal, Casa de Santos Dumont, Palacio Rio Negro, and Palacio Barão de Mauá, allowing you to get off and visit each site while the buggy waits. It takes about an hour and a half. On the second, cheaper option, you cover the same route but the buggy never stops, so you see the sights only from the outside. Cost is R$40 ($20) for up to six people and it takes about 30 minutes. Tours run year-round, Tuesday through Sunday. Please note that the tour does not include admission charges to the sights.

VISITOR INFORMATION

Petrotur has a number of offices around town. The main office is at Av. Koeler 245 Centro, Petrópolis (℃ **024/2243-3561**). Kiosks are located at Rua do Imperador (by the Obelisk) and Casa do Barão de Mauá; both are open Monday through Sunday from 9am to 5pm. Ask for the English-language version of the excellent *Petrópolis Imperial Sightseeing* brochure. It comes with a map, visitor information, and open hours for each of the attractions.

The **Banco do Brasil** branch is located on the Rua do Imperador 940 (corner of Rua Alencar Lima).

EXPLORING PETROPOLIS

The historic heart of Petrópolis can easily be explored on foot: The city is fairly flat and extremely safe; even traffic is less hectic than in Rio. Following the directions below will take you to most points of interest. A more detailed description is included below for those sights that merit more information.

Starting on the corners of Avenida Ipiranga and Tiradentes, the first thing you see is the **Cathedral São Pedro de Alcantara,** a neo-gothic church named for both the patron saint of the empire and—not coincidentally—the Emperor Dom Pedro II himself. Construction began in 1876 but the celebratory first Mass wasn't held until 1925. Just inside the main doors to the right is the Imperial Chapel containing the remains of the emperor Dom Pedro II, the empress Dona Teresa, their daughter Princess Isabel, and her husband, whose name no one remembers. The princess lived in the beautiful mansion immediately across the street, now known as the **Casa da Princesa Isabel.** (Currently not open to visitors, but with renovations underway, the house should soon open to the public.) Continuing along the Avenida Koeler as it follows the tree-lined canal, it's a 5-minute walk to the beautiful **Praça da Liberdade.** The bridge in front of this square offers the best view of the Cathedral and the canal. Just behind the Praça da Liberdade is the **Casa de Santos Dumont,** Rua do Encanto 22 (℃ **024/2231-3011**). Dumont was Brazil's most famous aviator and the first in the world in 1906 to take off and land under his own power (unlike the Wright brothers who were catapulted on their first flight at Kitty Hawk).

From here, follow Avenida Roberto Silveira, then turn right on Rua Alfredo Pachá to the **Palacio de Cristal,** Rua Alfredo Pachá s/n (℃ **024/2237-7953**). Ordered by Princesa Isabel and built in France, the structure was inaugurated in 1894 as an agricultural exhibition hall. Nowadays, the palace is used for cultural events and exhibits. Crossing the bridge to Avenida Piabanha you come to the **Casa Barão de Mauá,** Praça da Confluencia s/n (℗ **024/2231-2121**). Built in 1854 in neoclassic style by the industrial baron who constructed Brazil's first railway, the house is open for guided visits Monday through Saturday from 9am to 6pm, Sunday and holidays from 9am to 5pm. Only a few rooms are open for visitors and just a small number of personal belongings have been preserved, as the high-flying baron was forced to sell off his possessions just prior to his death to pay off his many debts. The columns surrounding the winter garden are solid iron, made by the baron himself. Admission is free.

Continue by taking Rua 13 de Maio—right across the street from the Casa Barão de Mauá—towards the Cathedral and then turning left on Avenida Ipiranga at the intersection just before the Cathedral. Along this street are a number of interesting buildings as well as some gorgeous mansions and villas. Standing on the right side of the street at No. 346 is the 1816 **Igreja Luterana,** the oldest church in Petrópolis (open for visitation only during Sun morning service at 10am). A bit further along the Avenida Ipiranga at No. 716 is the lovely **Casa de Petrópolis,** a museum, cultural center, restaurant, and garden, Rua Ipiranga 716 (℗ **024/2246-0996**). Guided tours of this beautifully preserved house will take you through numerous salons lavishly decorated with satin curtains and wallpaper, gold-leaf chandeliers, and ornate and beautiful furniture. The banquet room is a marvel of jacaranda wood; the floors, walls, windows, and ceiling are all made of this now-rare tropical hardwood. Weekly concerts take place on Saturday night at 8pm; tickets cost R$10 ($5). From here, it's a simple matter to retrace your steps to the Cathedral.

Museu Imperial ✸✸   Built by Dom Pedro II in 1845 as his summer palace, the much loved Museu Imperial is now Petrópolis's premier museum. (Sunday and holidays the lineups can be fierce.) The self-guided visits take you through numerous ground-floor salons decorated with period furniture, household items, and lovely paintings and drawings depicting life and landscapes of 19th-century Rio. Best of all is Brazil's equivalent of the crown jewels: Dom Pedro II's crown, weighing almost 4 pounds, encrusted with 639 diamonds and 77 pearls. Upstairs, visitors can see the bedrooms, including lovely baby cribs made out of jacaranda wood and decorated with bronze and ivory—fit for a pair of princesses. In the garden, the palace's coach house has a beautiful collection of 18th-and-19th century carriages and coaches. The highlight is the royal carriage, painted in gold and pulled by eight horses. Expect to spend 1½ hours.

Rua da Imperatriz 220. ℂ 024/2237-8000. Gardens can be visited for free. R$4 ($2) adults, R$2 ($1) children 7–14, free for children under 7. Tues–Sun 11am–5pm.

OUTDOOR ACTIVITIES

HIKING Petrópolis has great hiking in the hills surrounding the town. For information on day hikes, contact **Petrotur** at ℂ **0800/24-1516. Açu Expedições** offers guided hikes as well as rafting, rappelling, and rock climbing. Contact the agency at ℂ **024/2221-3832.**

HORSEBACK RIDING To book a horseback ride, contact the **Haras Analu** at ℂ **024/2222-1261.** Their rides vary from gentle 2-hour beginner rides to bum-busting full-day treks covering up to 25 miles (40km).

WHERE TO STAY

Though Petrópolis has a number of hotels and pousadas in the historic part of town, the majority take advantage of the spectacular scenery and the lush green forest and secrete themselves in hills and valleys close to town. It's always a good idea to contact your pousadas for instructions on how to get there; some can arrange for pickup or send a taxi. Petrópolis does not have a pronounced low or high season and rates don't fluctuate very much.

Casablanca Hotel ℛ *Value* More central would be almost impossible. Located next door to the Museu Imperial on one of Petrópolis's fine canals, Casablanca is within easy walking distance of all the city's historic sights. The hotel consists of two buildings, the original mansion and a modern annex. The nicest rooms are the deluxe ones on the second floor of the original building. These rooms have sky-high ceilings, air-conditioning, bathtubs, and antique dark-wood furniture. On the same floor, there is also a lovely fireplace reading lounge looking out over the canal. The standard rooms with showers only—in the annex and on the ground floor of the main house—are still pleasant but lack the character of the prime ones on the first floor. The only drawback to this hotel's central location is the neighboring school; it gets very noisy during recess, but by then you should be out exploring Petrópolis anyway, right?

Rua da Imperatriz 286, Petrópolis, RJ 25610-320. ℰ 024/2242-6662. www. casa blancahotel.com.br. 39 units (7 units with bathtub, 32 units shower only). R$99 ($48) standard; R$110 ($55) deluxe. Extra bed R$33 ($15). AE, DC, MC, V. Free parking. **Amenities:** Pool; sauna; game room; limited room service; laundry service. *In room:* A/C (in luxo rooms only, standard rooms have fans), TV, minibar, fridge.

Colonial Inn   Just past the Casa Santos Dumont, the Colonial Inn is located on a very busy street. As nice as the original house is, the better rooms are in the modern annex located in the back away from the traffic. The Colonial Inn offers reasonably priced accommodations within walking distance of all the sights. The rooms are simply furnished and the lowest-priced rooms are quite small. The two corner rooms are the more spacious and suitable for a family traveling together, as these can more easily accommodate an extra bed.

Rua Monsenhor Bacelar 125. ℰ 024/2224-1590. www.colonialinn.com.br. 20 units (shower only). R$90 ($45) small room facing the street; R$120–R$150 ($60–$75) large room in annex. Extra person R$30 ($15). Children's rate negotiable. AE, DC, MC, V. Free parking. **Amenities:** Pool; sauna; small game room; laundry service. *In room:* TV, minibar, fridge.

Pousada Tankamana ⟨⟨⟨   Nestled in the picturesque Cuiabá valley, 3,400 feet (1,100m) above sea level, Pousada Tankamana is less an inn than a destination in itself. Eleven spacious log cabins and five suites (town house style) are spread out over the lush green hillside, thus ensuring each a fabulous mountain view. Each chalet is fully self-contained; all are uniquely decorated and come with a fireplace, king-size bed, sitting area, TV/VCR, and CD player. As a member of the Roteiros de Charme group of exclusive pousadas and inns, the service is top-notch and staff are very friendly and helpful. The little extras such as a towel warmer, teakettle, and the best chocolate truffles you have ever had are just icing on the cake. The pousada offers daily horse rides, short ones for free on the trails around the hotel and longer ones booked through a stable nearby. Walking trails lead through the beautiful forest surrounding the pousada where you'll spot numerous birds, some lizards, and with luck maybe a sloth, *mico leão* monkey, or *jaguatirica* (a small cousin of the jaguar).

Estrada Aldo Gelli km.37, Vale do Cuiabá. ℰ 024/2222-2706. www.tanka-mana.com.br or www.roteirosdecharme.com.br. 16 units. R$200–R$240 ($100–$120) double suite; R$240–R$340 ($120–$170) double (price depends on size of cabin). DC, MC, V. Free parking. To reach the pousada on public transit, take bus 700 from the Petrópolis Rodoviaria to the final stop at terminal Itaipava. Inside

The Historical Cities of Minas Gerais

The inland state of Minas Gerais struck it rich on gold just about the time the baroque was reaching its elaborate architectural heights. The newly wealthy citizens needed something to blow their money on, and having exhausted the joys of women and booze, they turned instead to architecture. The result is several small cities boasting cobblestone streets, soaring palaces, and elaborate churches that rival St. Petersburg or Prague. Largest of the these is the hilltop town of **Ouro Prêto;** its cobblestone streets wander up and down hills crowned with more than a dozen ornately carved and elaborately decorated baroque churches. Each corner turns on new surprises: mansions, fountains, ruins, beautiful terraced gardens, and towers glowing with colored tiles.

A little bit farther afield stand the twin cities of **São João del Rei** and **Tiradentes.** São João is the larger of the two, but Tiradentes is nearly perfectly preserved, like an 18th-century heirloom inherited intact. Set by a river surrounded by rocky bluffs, Tiradentes offers hiking opportunities in the surrounding area, but the best trail is within the town itself. Wander from the riverside up a steep cobbled colonial street, past the palatial town hall (veranda in the front, jail in the rear) to the hilltop where stands the Igreja Matriz de Santo Antônio. Push inside the elaborate jacaranda-wood doors and it's like you've entered radium-land. Everything glows because every available surface in chancel, nave, and

the transfer station, take bus 705 (Cuiabá) to its final stop, where the pousada staff will pick you up (call ahead to announce your approximate arrival time.) Expect to take 1 hr. and 15 min. in total. **Amenities:** Restaurant, bar; pool; sauna; game room; limited room service; laundry service. *In room:* TV/VCR, minibar, fridge, hair dryer, safe.

WHERE TO DINE

Petrópolis offers a range of dining opportunities, from schnitzel to sushi to churrasco. Check opening times carefully, though, as a number of restaurants are closed Monday through Wednesday or Monday through Thursday.

Never was the house specialty so clearly advertised as at **Tankamana Restaurant,** Estrada Aldo Gelli km. 37 (see "Pousada transepts has been slathered with a thick gilding. Hundreds of pounds were used in all. Catch it towards evening when the candles are lit for Mass, and you, the church, the town, and the surrounding hillsides all seem to gleam.

Ouro Prêto is a 7-hour bus ride from Rio de Janeiro. **Util** (℗ **021/2253-3884** in Rio) runs a nightly bus from Rio to Ouro Prêto, arriving in the morning. Ticket prices range from R$10 to R$30 ($5–$15). For tour guides, contact the **Ouro Prêto Tour Guide Association** at ℗ **031/3551-2655.** A tour of Ouro Prêto with an English-speaking tour guide costs R$63 ($31.50) for a 4-hour tour with up to 10 people.

As there are no direct long-distance buses to Tiradentes, visitors must first travel to São João del Rei (℗ **032/371-5617**) and from the rodoviaria connect with one of the 11 buses a day that cover the 8¾ miles (14km) to Tiradentes in 20 minutes for R$1.60 (80¢). Regular buses connect São João del Rei to São Paulo and Rio de Janeiro. The Paraibuna line (℗ **032/371-5437**) runs at least three buses a day from Rio. You can also take a taxi from the São João del Rei rodoviaria for about R$30 ($15); for taxi service, call ℗ **032/9965-0138.**

Tip: To arrive in style, take the 115-year-old narrow-gauge steam train (called *Maria Fumaça*) from São João del Rei to Tiradentes. Trains depart São João del Rei Friday through Sunday and holidays at 10am and 2:15pm. One-way tickets cost R$7 ($3.50) for adults, R$3 ($1.50) for children 10 and under.

Tankamana," above, for directions; ℗ **024/2222-2706**). Look through the glass that forms the floor of this restaurant and you'll see a lake teeming with hundreds of trout. The chef serves up these little swimmers in at least a dozen ways: there's truta oriental, grilled in garlic butter and flambéed in sake, and the truta tropical combines delicate herbs with a maracujá (passion fruit) sauce. Yes, there are other dishes, too. Popular in the fall and winter are the fondues for two, made with cheese, meat, or Chinese ingredients (broth and seafood).

Hidden in the former coach house of the Casa de Petrópolis is **Arte Temperada,** Rua Ipiranga 716 (℗ **024/2246-0996**). Rustic decorations, a wood-burning stove, and long tables give the place a barnlike feel, but the food is far from unsophisticated. The main courses include a number of excellent trout dishes, and duck dishes are the other specialty: duck breast with blackberry sauce or the winter favorite, duck breast with red cabbage and applesauce. Located in the Praça da Liberdade, the **Rink Marowil,** Praça Rui Barbosa 27 (© 024/2243-0743), is a great place to stop for lunch while strolling through Petrópolis's historic center. At lunchtime, the excellent kilo buffet serves up at least 12 different salads and some excellent black-bean dishes as well as freshly grilled chicken, steak, and sausage. The lovely wood structure allows for excellent views of the main square. Tucked away in the left corner of the gardens surrounding the museum, the **Museu Imperial Tearoom,** Rua da Imperatriz 220 (© 024/2237-8000), is lovely and the perfect place for lunch. Full tea service is available, including cakes, pies, croissants, Madeleines, toast, jam, cold cuts, and pâté. For a smaller lunch or snack, the restaurant also serves a variety of quiches and sandwiches, as well as pastas. A traditional-looking steakhouse with wood panels and booths, **Churrascaria Majoricá,** Rua do Imperador 754 (© 024/2242-2498), is a local favorite for a good steak. Make your choice: T-bone, picanha, entrecôte, half and half (tenderloin pork and beef), or grilled chicken.

Index

See also Accommodations and Restaurant indexes below.

ACCOMMODATIONS

FROMMER'S® COMPLETE TRAVEL GUIDES

Alaska
Alaska Cruises & Ports of Call
Amsterdam
Argentina & Chile
Arizona
Atlanta
Australia
Austria
Bahamas
Barcelona, Madrid & Seville
Beijing
Belgium, Holland & Luxembourg
Bermuda
Boston
British Columbia & the Canadian Rockies
Budapest & the Best of Hungary
California
Canada
Cancún, Cozumel & the Yucatán
Cape Cod, Nantucket & Martha's Vineyard
Caribbean
Caribbean Cruises & Ports of Call
Caribbean Ports of Call
Carolinas & Georgia
Chicago
China
Colorado
Costa Rica
Denmark
Denver, Boulder & Colorado Springs
England
Europe
European Cruises & Ports of Call
Florida
France

Germany
Great Britain
Greece
Greek Islands
Hawaii
Hong Kong
Honolulu, Waikiki & Oahu
Ireland
Israel
Italy
Jamaica
Japan
Las Vegas
London
Los Angeles
Maryland & Delaware
Maui
Mexico
Montana & Wyoming
Montréal & Québec City
Munich & the Bavarian Alps
Nashville & Memphis
Nepal
New England
New Mexico
New Orleans
New York City
New Zealand
Nova Scotia, New Brunswick & Prince Edward Island
Oregon
Paris
Philadelphia & the Amish Country
Portugal
Prague & the Best of the Czech Republic
Provence & the Riviera

Puerto Rico
Rome
San Antonio & Austin
San Diego
San Francisco
Santa Fe, Taos & Albuquerque
Scandinavia
Scotland
Seattle & Portland
Shanghai
Singapore & Malaysia
South Africa
South America
Southeast Asia
South Florida
South Pacific
Spain
Sweden
Switzerland
Texas
Thailand
Tokyo
Toronto
Tuscany & Umbria
USA
Utah
Vancouver & Victoria
Vermont, New Hampshire & Maine
Vienna & the Danube Valley
Virgin Islands
Virginia
Walt Disney World & Orlando
Washington, D.C.
Washington State

FROMMER'S® DOLLAR-A-DAY GUIDES

Australia from $50 a Day
California from $70 a Day
Caribbean from $70 a Day
England from $75 a Day
Europe from $70 a Day

Florida from $70 a Day
Hawaii from $80 a Day
Ireland from $60 a Day
Italy from $70 a Day
London from $85 a Day

New York from $90 a Day
Paris from $80 a Day
San Francisco from $70 a Day
Washington, D.C., from $80 a Day

FROMMER'S® PORTABLE GUIDES

Acapulco, Ixtapa & Zihuatanejo
Amsterdam
Aruba
Australia's Great Barrier Reef
Bahamas
Baja & Los Cabos
Berlin
Big Island of Hawaii
Boston
California Wine Country
Cancún
Charleston & Savannah
Chicago
Disneyland

Dublin
Florence
Frankfurt
Hong Kong
Houston
Las Vegas
London
Los Angeles
Maine Coast
Maui
Miami
New Orleans
New York City
Paris

Phoenix & Scottsdale
Portland
Puerto Rico
Puerto Vallarta, Manzanillo & Guadalajara
San Diego
San Francisco
Seattle
Sydney
Tampa & St. Petersburg
Vancouver
Venice
Virgin Islands
Washington, D.C.

FROMMER'S® NATIONAL PARK GUIDES

Family Vacations in the National Parks
Grand Canyon

National Parks of the American West
Rocky Mountain
Yellowstone & Grand Teton

Yosemite & Sequoia/ Kings Canyon
Zion & Bryce Canyon

FROMMER'S® MEMORABLE WALKS

Chicago	New York	San Francisco
London	Paris	

FROMMER'S® GREAT OUTDOOR GUIDES

Arizona & New Mexico	Northern California	Vermont & New Hampshire
New England	Southern New England	

SUZY GERSHMAN'S BORN TO SHOP GUIDES

Born to Shop: France	Born to Shop: Italy	Born to Shop: New York
Born to Shop: Hong Kong, Shanghai & Beijing	Born to Shop: London	Born to Shop: Paris

FROMMER'S® IRREVERENT GUIDES

Amsterdam	Los Angeles	San Francisco
Boston	Manhattan	Seattle & Portland
Chicago	New Orleans	Vancouver
Las Vegas	Paris	Walt Disney World
London	Rome	Washington, D.C.

FROMMER'S® BEST-LOVED DRIVING TOURS

Britain	Germany	New England
California	Ireland	Scotland
Florida	Italy	Spain
France		

HANGING OUT™ GUIDES

Hanging Out in England	Hanging Out in France	Hanging Out in Italy
Hanging Out in Europe	Hanging Out in Ireland	Hanging Out in Spain

THE UNOFFICIAL GUIDES®

Bed & Breakfasts and Country Inns in:	Florida with Kids	New Orleans
California	Golf Vacations in the Eastern U.S.	New York City
New England	The Great Smoky & Blue Ridge Mountains	Paris
Northwest		San Francisco
Rockies	Hawaii	Skiing in the West
Southeast	Inside Disney	Southeast with Kids
Beyond Disney	Las Vegas	Walt Disney World
Branson, Missouri	London	Walt Disney World for Grown-ups
California with Kids	Mid-Atlantic with Kids	
Chicago	Mini Las Vegas	Walt Disney World for Kids
Cruises	Mini-Mickey	Washington, D.C.
Disneyland	New England & New York with Kids	World's Best Diving Vacations

SPECIAL-INTEREST TITLES

Frommer's Adventure Guide to Australia & New Zealand
Frommer's Adventure Guide to Central America
Frommer's Adventure Guide to India & Pakistan
Frommer's Adventure Guide to South America
Frommer's Adventure Guide to Southeast Asia
Frommer's Adventure Guide to Southern Africa
Frommer's Britain's Best Bed & Breakfasts and Country Inns
Frommer's France's Best Bed & Breakfasts and Country Inns
Frommer's Italy's Best Bed & Breakfasts and Country Inns
Frommer's Caribbean Hideaways

Frommer's Exploring America by RV
Frommer's Gay & Lesbian Europe
Frommer's The Moon
Frommer's New York City with Kids
Frommer's Road Atlas Britain
Frommer's Road Atlas Europe
Frommer's Washington, D.C., with Kids
Frommer's What the Airlines Never Tell You
Israel Past & Present
The New York Times' Guide to Unforgettable Weekends
Places Rated Almanac
Retirement Places Rated